Mastering AWS

Learn how to build and deploy serverless applications

Yohan Wadia
Udita Gupta

BIRMINGHAM - MUMBAI

Mastering AWS Lambda

First published: August 2017

Production reference: 1100817

Published by Packt Publishing Ltd.
Livery Place
35 Livery Street
Birmingham
B3 2PB, UK.

ISBN 978-1-78646-769-0

www.packtpub.com

Credits

Authors
Yohan Wadia
Udita Gupta

Copy Editors
Juliana Nair
Stuti Srivastava

Reviewer
Legorie Rajan

Project Coordinator
Virginia Dias

Commissioning Editor
Kartikey Pandey

Proofreader
Safis Editing

Acquisition Editor
Heramb Bhavsar

Indexer
Tejal Daruwale Soni

Content Development Editor
Sharon Raj

Graphics
Kirk D'Penha

Technical Editor
Khushbu Sutar

Production Coordinator
Aparna Bhagat

About the Authors

Yohan Wadia is a client-focused evangelist and technologist with more than 7 years' experience in the cloud industry, primarily focused on helping customers succeed with the cloud.
As a technical consultant for one of the world's leading IT companies, Yohan provides guidance and implementation services to customers looking to leverage cloud computing through either Amazon Web Services, Windows Azure, or Google Cloud Platform, helping them come up with pragmatic solutions that make practical as well as business sense.
Yohan is also an avid blogger and the author of two successful books:

- *Learning VMware vCloud Air--2015*
- *Administering AWS: The Definitive Guide--2016*

He loves speaking about, blogging about, and training people on cloud platforms and technologies.

I wish to start off by dedicating yet another book to my small and crazy family...Ma, Pa, Sister, and Fred! Thank you for all your love, support, and encouragement.

I would also like to thank the entire Packt Publishing team for giving me yet another wonderful opportunity, especially Sharon Raj (for the constant follow-ups and pushes to complete the chapters on time...I know I gave him a really tough time on this) and Heramb Bhavsar (for all the help and support with my book's payments! Yeah, can't forget that now, can I?).
Not to forget my bestie and biggest competitor, Mitesh Soni. Thank you for being a role model whom I can look up to! PS: I think it's high time we wrote a book together as well.

And finally, special thanks and shout out goes to Udita as well. This book would have been a lot emptier if it weren't for your code! Really appreciate all the effort and work you put into this.

All we have to decide is what to do with the time that is given to us.
- J. R. R. Tolkien

Udita Gupta is an experienced cloud engineer with a passion for developing customized solutions, especially on the Amazon Web Services Cloud platform. She loves developing and exploring new technologies and designing reusable components and solutions around them. She particularly likes using the serverless paradigm, along with other upcoming technologies such as IoT and AI.

A highly animated creature and an avid reader, Udita likes to spend her time reading all kinds of books, with a particular interest in Sheryl Sandberg and Khaled Hosseini. She is also an AWS Certified Solutions Architect.

First and foremost, I would like to dedicate this book to my family; my parents and my dear sister. I wouldn't have taken up writing this book without their love and support.

I would also like to thank the entire team at Packt for giving me this opportunity and guiding me through the entire authoring process.

I also wish to thank the technical reviewers for their effort, time, and keen suggestions and recommendations. It is your effort that makes this book complete! We couldn't have done it without you!

Last but definitely not least, I'd like to thank the entire AWS community for their help, support, and insights, that were invaluable to us when writing this book.

About the Reviewer

Legorie Rajan is a cloud consultant working with enterprise customers in the banking and insurance domains. His love for computers drove him to pursue a degree in CS, and he has not looked back since. He started his career as a mainframe developer and is currently migrating and architecting solutions on the cloud. His love for new technologies has never ceased, and he uses his spare time to hack around Node.js, Mongo, and Kubernetes. He has a BTech(CS) degree from Pondicherry University and an MS in management from Grenoble School of Business.

I would like to thank my wife, Anitha Sophie, for being my rock, and the team at Packt for the opportunity.

www.PacktPub.com

For support files and downloads related to your book, please visit www.PacktPub.com.

Did you know that Packt offers eBook versions of every book published, with PDF and ePub files available? You can upgrade to the eBook version at www.PacktPub.com and as a print book customer, you are entitled to a discount on the eBook copy. Get in touch with us at service@packtpub.com for more details.

At www.PacktPub.com, you can also read a collection of free technical articles, sign up for a range of free newsletters and receive exclusive discounts and offers on Packt books and eBooks.

https://www.packtpub.com/mapt

Get the most in-demand software skills with Mapt. Mapt gives you full access to all Packt books and video courses, as well as industry-leading tools to help you plan your personal development and advance your career.

Why subscribe?

- Fully searchable across every book published by Packt
- Copy and paste, print, and bookmark content
- On demand and accessible via a web browser

Customer Feedback

Thanks for purchasing this Packt book. At Packt, quality is at the heart of our editorial process. To help us improve, please leave us an honest review on this book's Amazon page at https://www.amazon.com/dp/1786467690.

If you'd like to join our team of regular reviewers, you can e-mail us at customerreviews@packtpub.com. We award our regular reviewers with free eBooks and videos in exchange for their valuable feedback. Help us be relentless in improving our products!

Table of Contents

Preface
1

Chapter 1: Introducing AWS Lambda
7

What is serverless computing?
8

Pros and cons of serverless computing
9

Introducing AWS Lambda
11

How it works
12

Getting started with AWS Lambda
13

Using the AWS Management Console
14

Using the CLI
23

Pricing and limitations
29

Planning your next steps
32

Summary
33

Chapter 2: Writing Lambda Functions
35

The Lambda programming model
35

Handler
36

The context object
39

Logging
43

Exceptions and error handling
46

Versioning and aliases
49

Environment variables
56

Packaging and deploying
59

APEX
60

Claudia.js
63

Recommendations and best practices
64

Planning your next steps
65

Summary
66

Chapter 3: Testing Lambda Functions
67

The need for testing Lambda function
67

Manually testing your functions with the AWS Management Console
69

Testing functions with Mocha and Chai
70

Testing functions using the npm modules
77

Testing with a simple serverless test harness
81

Recommendations and best practices
85

Planning your next steps	86
Summary	87

Chapter 4: Event-Driven Model — 89

Introducing event-driven architectures	90
Understanding events and AWS Lambda	91
Lambda architecture patterns	92
Exploring Lambda and event mapping	94
Mapping Lambda with S3	95
Mapping Lambda with DynamoDB	103
Mapping Lambda with SNS	108
Mapping Lambda with CloudWatch events	112
Mapping Lambda with Kinesis	117
Creating the Kinesis Stream	118
Setting up the log streaming	118
Packaging and uploading the function	120
Planning your next steps	123
Summary	124

Chapter 5: Extending AWS Lambda with External Services — 125

Introducing Webhooks	125
Integrating GitHub with AWS Lambda	127
Integrating Slack with AWS Lambda	136
Invoking Lambda using an external application	144
Planning your next steps	151
Recommendations and best practices	151
Summary	152

Chapter 6: Build and Deploy Serverless Applications with AWS Lambda — 153

Introducing SAM	153
Writing SAM templates	154
AWS::Serverless::Function	155
AWS::Serverless::Api	156
AWS::Serverless::SimpleTable	157
Building serverless applications with SAM	157
Introducing AWS step functions	166
Under the hood	167
Getting started with step functions	169
Building distributed applications with step functions	174
Planning your next steps	181
Summary	182

Chapter 7: Monitoring and Troubleshooting AWS Lambda — 183
Monitoring Lambda functions using CloudWatch — 184
Introducing AWS X-Ray — 187
Monitoring Lambda functions using Datadog — 193
Logging your functions with Loggly — 201
Recommendations and best practices — 208
Summary — 209

Chapter 8: Introducing the Serverless Application Framework — 211
What is the Serverless Framework? — 211
Getting started with the Serverless Framework — 212
Working with the Serverless Framework — 214
Recommendations and best practices — 229
Summary — 230

Chapter 9: AWS Lambda - Use Cases — 231
Infrastructure management — 232
Scheduled startup and shutdown of instances — 232
Periodic snapshots of EBS volumes using Lambda — 235
Enabling governance using EC2 tags and Lambda — 242
Data transformation — 253
Summary — 258

Chapter 10: Next Steps with AWS Lambda — 259
Processing content at the edge with Lambda@Edge — 260
Building next generation chatbots with Lambda and Lex — 265
Processing data at the edge with Greengrass and Lambda — 274
Introducing Snowball Edge — 280
Summary — 282

Index — 283

Preface

AWS is recognized as one of the market leaders for cloud computing, and why not? It has evolved a lot since it started out providing basic services such as EC2 and S3. Compare that to today: they go all the way from IoT to machine learning, image recognition, chatbot frameworks, and much more! One of these recent services that is also gaining a lot of traction is AWS Lambda. Although seemingly simple and easy to use, Lambda is a highly effective and scalable compute service that provides developers with a powerful platform to design and develop serverless event-driven systems and applications.

The book begins with a high-level introduction to the world of serverless computing and its advantages and use cases, followed by a deep dive into AWS Lambda. You'll learn what services AWS Lambda provides to developers; how to design, write, and test Lambda functions; as well as how to monitor and troubleshoot them. The book is accompanied by a vast variety of real-world examples, use cases, and code samples that will enable you to quickly get started on your journey toward serverless applications.

By the end of the book, you will have gained all the skills required to work with and master AWS Lambda services!

What this book covers

Chapter 1, *Introducing AWS Lambda*, covers the introductory concepts and general benefits of serverless computing, along with an in-depth look at AWS Lambda. The chapter also walks you through your first steps with AWS Lambda, including deploying your first functions using the AWS Management Console and the AWS CLI.

Chapter 2, *Writing Lambda Functions*, covers the fundamentals of writing and composing your Lambda functions. The chapter introduces you to concepts such as versioning, aliases, and variables, along with an easy-to-follow code sample.

Chapter 3, *Testing Lambda Functions*, discusses the overall importance of testing your function for code defects and bugs. It also introduces you to some out-of-the-box testing frameworks in the form of Mocha and Chai, and summarizes it all by demonstrating how you can test your functions locally before actual deployments to Lambda.

Chapter 4, *Event-Driven Model*, introduces the concept of the event-based system and how it actually works. The chapter also provides a deep dive into how Lambda's event-based model works with the help of event mappings and a few easy-to-replicate, real-world use cases.

Chapter 5, *Extending AWS Lambda with External Services*, discusses the concept and importance of Webhooks and how they can be leveraged to connect your serverless functions with any third-party services. The chapter also provides a few real-world use cases, where Lambda functions are integrated with other services such as Teamwork, GitHub, and Slack.

Chapter 6, *Build and Deploy Serverless Applications with AWS Lambda*, provides you with a hands-on approach to building scalable serverless applications using AWS services such as SAM and Step Functions with a few handy deployment examples.

Chapter 7, *Monitoring and Troubleshooting AWS Lambda*, covers how you can leverage AWS CloudWatch and X-ray to monitor your serverless applications. The chapter also introduces other third-party tools, such as Datadog and Loggly, for effectively logging and monitoring your functions.

Chapter 8, *Introducing the Serverless Application Framework*, provides a brief introduction and outlines the benefits provided by the Serverless Framework, followed by some hands-on implementation and deployment of functions using it.

Chapter 9, *AWS Lambda - Use Cases*, provides a comprehensive set of real-world serverless use cases with some easy-to-follow code examples and snippets.

Chapter 10, *Next Steps with AWS Lambda*, summarizes the next phase in the evolution of serverless applications and discusses how new and improved enhancements in Lambda are expected to come about in the near future.

What you need for this book

To start using this book, you will need the following set of software installed on your local desktop:

- An SSH client such as PuTTY, a key generator such as PuTTYgen, and a file transferring tool such as WinSCP
- You can alternatively even set up your own development/sandbox server on Linux using VirtualBox
- Any modern web browser, preferably Mozilla Firefox

Who this book is for

This book is intended for any and all IT professionals and developers who wish to learn and implement the ins and outs of serverless computing using AWS Lambda. Although no prior experience or knowledge is required, it will be beneficial for you to have at least a basic development background--preferably with Java or Node.js--hands-on Linux knowledge, as well as some understanding of AWS's core services, such as IAM, EC2, and VPCs.

Conventions

In this book, you will find a number of text styles that distinguish between different kinds of information. Here are some examples of these styles and an explanation of their meaning. Code words in text, database table names, folder names, filenames, file extensions, pathnames, dummy URLs, user input, and Twitter handles are shown as follows: "The `describe-log-groups` command will list all the log groups that are prefixed with `/aws/lambda`."

A block of code is set as follows:

```
exports.myHandler = function(event, context, callback) {
  console.log("value = " + event.key);
  console.log("functionName = ", context.functionName);
  callback(null, "Yippee! Something worked!");
};
```

When we wish to draw your attention to a particular part of a code block, the relevant lines or items are set in bold:

```
exports.myHandler = (event, context, callback) => {
  console.log('remaining time =', context.getRemainingTimeInMillis());
  console.log('functionName =', context.functionName);
  console.log('AWSrequestID =', context.awsRequestId);
  console.log('logGroupName =', context.logGroupName);
  console.log('logStreamName =', context.logStreamName);
```

Any command-line input or output is written as follows:

```
# aws lambda list-functions
```

New terms and **important words** are shown in bold. Words that you see on the screen, for example, in menus or dialog boxes, appear in the text like this: "In the **Review** page, select the **Create function** option."

Warnings or important notes appear like this.

 Tips and tricks appear like this.

Reader feedback

Feedback from our readers is always welcome. Let us know what you think about this book-what you liked or disliked. Reader feedback is important for us as it helps us develop titles that you will really get the most out of. To send us general feedback, simply e-mail feedback@packtpub.com, and mention the book's title in the subject of your message. If there is a topic that you have expertise in and you are interested in either writing or contributing to a book, see our author guide at www.packtpub.com/authors.

Customer support

Now that you are the proud owner of a Packt book, we have a number of things to help you to get the most from your purchase.

Downloading the example code

You can download the example code files for this book from your account at http://www.packtpub.com. If you purchased this book elsewhere, you can visit http://www.packtpub.com/support, and register to have the files e-mailed directly to you. You can download the code files by following these steps:

1. Log in or register to our website using your e-mail address and password.
2. Hover the mouse pointer on the **SUPPORT** tab at the top.
3. Click on **Code Downloads & Errata**.
4. Enter the name of the book in the **Search** box.
5. Select the book for which you're looking to download the code files.
6. Choose from the drop-down menu where you purchased this book from.
7. Click on **Code Download**.

Once the file is downloaded, please make sure that you unzip or extract the folder using the latest version of:

- WinRAR / 7-Zip for Windows
- Zipeg / iZip / UnRarX for Mac
- 7-Zip / PeaZip for Linux

The code bundle for the book is also hosted on GitHub at `https://github.com/PacktPubl ishing/Mastering-AWS-Lambda`. We also have other code bundles from our rich catalog of books and videos available at `https://github.com/PacktPublishing/`. Check them out!

Downloading the color images of this book

We also provide you with a PDF file that has color images of the screenshots/diagrams used in this book. The color images will help you better understand the changes in the output. You can download this file from `https://www.packtpub.com/sites/default/files/down loads/MasteringAWSLambda_ColorImages.pdf`.

Errata

Although we have taken every care to ensure the accuracy of our content, mistakes do happen. If you find a mistake in one of our books--maybe a mistake in the text or the code--we would be grateful if you could report this to us. By doing so, you can save other readers from frustration and help us improve subsequent versions of this book. If you find any errata, please report them by visiting `http://www.packtpub.com/submit-errata`, selecting your book, clicking on the **Errata Submission Form** link, and entering the details of your errata. Once your errata are verified, your submission will be accepted and the errata will be uploaded to our website or added to any list of existing errata under the Errata section of that title. To view the previously submitted errata, go to `https://www.packtpub.com/book s/content/support`, and enter the name of the book in the search field. The required information will appear under the **Errata** section.

Piracy

Piracy of copyrighted material on the Internet is an ongoing problem across all media. At Packt, we take the protection of our copyright and licenses very seriously. If you come across any illegal copies of our works in any form on the Internet, please provide us with the location address or website name immediately so that we can pursue a remedy. Please contact us at copyright@packtpub.com with a link to the suspected pirated material. We appreciate your help in protecting our authors and our ability to bring you valuable content.

Questions

If you have a problem with any aspect of this book, you can contact us at questions@packtpub.com, and we will do our best to address the problem.

1
Introducing AWS Lambda

I still remember the days when there was a clear demarcation between IT developers and system administrators; so much so that, each time a developer wanted a simple software platform or environment to be set up on their workstations, they would have to log one or more change requests, then dubiously wait for an IT admin to come along, who would more often than not provide you with an incorrect version of the software that you requested. Basically, you would end up wasting a week's effort just to get some simple software like Java or Tomcat to be setup, right? Many of us have sometime or the other been through this so called **vicious cycle** in IT and some still do, even today. But what if I told you that there is some ray of light around the corner! What if you, as a developer had the flexibility to simply write your code and put it up for execution; without having to worry about the underlying software platform, the OS or the hardware on which your code will run? Sounds too good to be true? Well fret no more, because that is what this book is all about! How you, as a developer start leveraging certain cloud-based services to develop, test, and host applications without having to even manage anything! Welcome to the amazing world of serverless computing!

In this chapter, we are going to get an understanding of the following topics:

- What serverless computing is, along with its pros and cons
- Introduction of AWS Lambda as a service and how it works
- Getting started with AWS Lambda using the AWS Management Console, as well as the CLI
- Pricing and a few of Lambda's limitations

So, without further ado, let's get started!

What is serverless computing?

To understand what serverless computing is all about and how it came to be, we first need to travel back in time to the era of mainframes and traditional data centers! Sounds like a long-lost time, right? Don't worry, we are not going that far back. This is probably in the time when most IT organizations had massive in-house data centers for hosting almost all enterprise applications and services. First, these applications were hosted directly on physical servers, and then eventually migrated onto the virtualized environments that provided a better utilization of resources as well as helped to slash down the overall costs and time for deployments from months to days. With the advent of the virtualization era, we also started to develop and use more convenient deployment tools that helped to deploy our applications with more ease, but it still meant managing the application's underlying operating system, software platform, and so on:

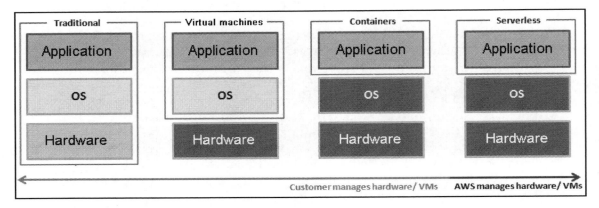

With virtualization clearly not having all the answers, we started looking for a much simpler application deployment model and, in return, found **Containers**. Unlike their earlier counterparts, **Virtual Machines**, **Containers** don't require a lot of resources or overhead to run. They are far easier and quicker to deploy, hence, reduce the overall application deployment time from days to minutes! You could now easily roll out a new patch for your application, scale your application dynamically based on incoming requests, and even orchestrate various other functions using a vast variety of container management products. However, the question of managing the **Containers** still remains, and trust me, managing a fleet of thousands of **Containers** and their underlying physical servers is no easy task. A better, more efficient, deployment model was needed; something that provided us with the agility and flexibility of containers, but without all the hassle and trouble of managing them. Enter serverless computing!

Serverless computing is all about running your application code on small ingots of some CPU and memory without having to worry about the OS type, the software platform, or any of the underlying hardware either. Just take your code and run it! Yes! It's that simple! Serverless computing today is offered by most public cloud providers, such as Amazon Web Services, Google Cloud Platform, Microsoft Azure, and even by IBM as a managed service. This essentially means that all you need to do is write your code or functions that perform a very specific task, select the quantity of resources (in this case RAM) required to run your code and submit it to the serverless cloud computing service to execute on. The service makes sure that your code gets the required amount of memory and CPU cycles it needs to execute. Hence, the collective term **Function as a Service (FaaS)**.

Pros and cons of serverless computing

Here is a quick look at some of the key benefits that you, as a developer, can attain with the help of serverless computing:

- **No ware to manage**: Perhaps one of the biggest reasons for the hype about serverless computing is the fact there is absolutely no hardware or software to manage. The management of the serverless computing environment all the way from the underlying hardware to the OS, to even the application's platform layer, is managed by the cloud provider itself.

- **Faster execution time**: Unlike your standard cloud instances, which generally take a good minute or two to boot up, functions, on the other hand, spin up very quickly, mostly in a matter of seconds. This could be due to the fact that the functions are made to run on top of a containerized platform.

- **Really low costs**: Since there is virtually no opex involved with serverless computing, it is fairly cheap, even when compared to hosting and managing instances in the cloud. Also, the pricing model for serverless computing is a little different from that of your traditional cloud pricing model. Here, you are generally billed on the duration of your function's execution and the amount of memory it consumed during its execution period. The duration is calculated from the time your code begins executing until it returns or otherwise terminates and is rounded up to the nearest 100 ms.

- **Support of popular programming languages**: Most cloud providers that provide serverless computing frameworks today, support a variety of programming languages, such as Java, Node.js, Python, and even C#. Azure functions allows the use of F#, PHP, Bash, Batch and PowerShell scripts in addition to the few mentioned.

- **Microservices compatible**: Since serverless computing functions are small, independent chunks of code that are designed to perform a very specific set of roles or activities, they can be used as a delivery medium for microservices as well. This comes as a huge advantage as compared to hosting your monolithic applications on the cloud, which do not scale that effectively.
- **Event-driven applications**: Serverless functions are an ideal choice for designing and running event-driven applications that react to certain events and take some action against them. For example, an image upload operation to a cloud storage triggers a function that creates associated thumbnail images for the same.

Feeling excited already about giving serverless computing a try? Hold on! There are a few cons to serverless computing as well that you should be aware of before we proceed further:

- **Execution duration**: Serverless functions are designed to run for short durations of time, ideally somewhere under 300 seconds only. This is a hard limit set by most cloud providers, however, there are a few workarounds to this as well.
- **Stateless**: Serverless functions are purely stateless, which means that once the function completes its execution or is terminated for some reason, it won't store any data locally on its disk.
- **Complexity**: The smaller you make things, the more complex it's going to become. Although writing functions that perform very particular tasks is a good idea, it can cause complexity issues when you view your application as a whole system. A simple example can break one large application into some ten different functions such that each perform a specific task. Now you need to manage ten different entities rather than just one. Imagine if you had a thousand functions instead.
- **Lack of tools**: Although serverless computing is all at its hype, it still doesn't provide a lot of out-of-the-box tools for management, deployment, and even monitoring. Most of your monitoring tools that you use today were designed for long-running, complex applications; not for simple functions that execute in a mere seconds.
- **Vendor lock-in**: With each cloud provider providing its own unique tool sets and services around serverless computing, you often tend to get tied down to a particular vendor. This means that you cannot change your cloud provider without making some changes to your functions as well.

With these key points in mind, let us get to understanding and learning a bit more about the core serverless computing service that this book is all about--AWS Lambda.

Introducing AWS Lambda

So, here we are, finally to the fun part! In this section, we will learn what Lambda is actually all about, what some of its salient features are, how it works and some steps on getting started with your very first Lambda invocation.

AWS Lambda was first introduced way back in 2014, at the yearly *AWS re:Invent* conference in Las Vegas. The idea back then, and which pretty much holds true even today, is that Lambda is a simple compute service that runs your code in response to certain events. These events can be anything, from an upload operation of an object to an S3 bucket, a record insertion in a DynamoDB table, or even some form of event triggered from your mobile app. The idea here is simple--you simply provide your code to AWS Lambda. Lambda will internally take care of provisioning and managing the underlying infrastructure resources, making sure your code gets deployed successfully; even things like your code's scalability and high availability are taken care of by Lambda itself! Now, that's neat!

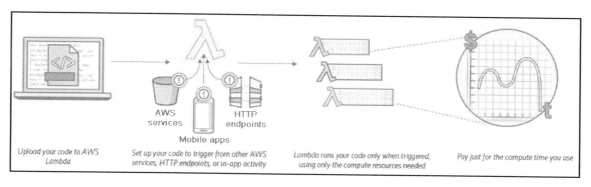

Source: https://aws.amazon.com/lambda/

Lambda was specially introduced by AWS to answer a very particular issue with EC2. Although EC2 still remains one of the most widely used core AWS services, it's still not designed to handle or respond to events; something that is required more often than not in today's applications. For example, a simple image upload activity to an S3 bucket triggers some form of operation, such as checking whether the object is actually a valid image, or whether it contains any viruses or unwanted malware. You can even have a requirement to create thumbnails of the uploaded image and put that up on your website. Now, imagine an EC2 instance doing all these activities for you. Firstly, you would have to program some mechanism for S3 to notify your EC2 instances to periodically perform checks on your S3 bucket, as EC2 has no way of telling when a new object has been uploaded.

Then again, you would have to manage the EC2 instance and handle all failovers, such as what happens if the EC2 instance fails to poll the S3 bucket, or what happens if the EC2 instance gets terminated for some reason. There's also the issue of scalability, right? Today you may be uploading just about 30-40 odd images, enough for a single EC2 instance to work on; but what happens when there is a large surge of upload operations? Will your EC2 instances scale effectively? And most important of all and by far the biggest issue for most enterprises--cost. Your EC2 instance will be running even on those days when there are no upload operations occurring in your S3 bucket. Sure there are many ways in which we can create workarounds for this, such as by creating a separate instance that polls continuously and by leveraging SQS or SNS as well, but isn't all that really overkill for something so simple? That's exactly the reason why Lambda is so popular and so widely used today. It just makes things simple!

How it works

Well, we do know for sure that Lambda powers your code on some form of container technology which explains how AWS is able to get it to spin up so quickly as compared to running your code on standard EC2 instances. These containers are spun up on underlying EC2 instances that are all created from a common image (Amazon Linux AMI: `amzn-ami-hvm-2016.03.3.x86_64-gp2`). Once again, we cannot control or see these containers or EC2 instances; they are managed by AWS itself.

 There is a short latency between the time a Lambda function is invoked. This is primarily because AWS has to bootstrap the container that runs your code and provides the necessary resources for it to run as well. This latency is generally observed when the function is either invoked for the first time or when it is updated.

At the heart of the container is your code, which, as a rule of thumb, has to be written specifically to perform a single task or a few simple processes; similar to how you would write functions in your normal code. Each Lambda project that you deploy can thus be termed as a **Lambda function**, or just a **function**. At the time of writing this book, AWS supports Java, Python, Node.js, and even C# as programming languages for your functions. Each function can be invoked either on demand or invoked dynamically based on certain types of supported events. A few event examples are listed out as follows:

- **Amazon S3**: Lambda functions can be triggered when an object is created, updated, or deleted in an S3 bucket
- **Amazon DynamoDB**: Lambda functions are triggered when any updates are made to a particular DynamoDB table, such as row insertion, deletion, and so on

- **Amazon Simple Notification Service (SNS)**: Trigger a Lambda function when a message is published on a, SNS topic
- **Amazon CloudWatch Logs**: Use Lambda functions to process CloudWatch Logs as feeds
- **Scheduled events**: Run Lambda functions as scheduled events, just like a `cron` job
- **AWS CodeCommit**: Execute Lambda functions whenever new code is pushed to an existing branch, and so on

 For a complete list of the latest AWS services that are supported as Lambda invokers, refer to `http://docs.aws.amazon.com/lambda/latest /dg/invoking-lambda-function.html`.

When creating Lambda functions, you have to specify the amount of memory resource your function will require, as well as the approximate time it will take to execute before timing out. The memory can be set from 128 MB to 1.5 GB of RAM and the timeouts anywhere from one second to a max of 300 seconds. Both the memory and duration values are upper limits to your Lambda function, which means that if you have allocated 512 MB of RAM to your function, it doesn't mean the function will have to use all 512 MB, of it. It can work at any value up to 512 MB post which Lambda will simply throw you an error message stating that your function ran out of memory. The same applies for the duration of your function as well. You may set your function to timeout after 60 seconds and the function may only run for, say, 10 seconds. However, if your function fails to complete its processing by the 60th second, Lambda once again will time it out and pop you up an error message.

It is important to note, however, that varying the amount of memory for your function or the duration of the timeout also impacts the cost of your Lambda function. We will have a look at Lambda's pricing and limitations a bit later on in this chapter. For now, let us learn a bit more on how to actually get started with deploying Lambda functions using the AWS Management Console, as well as the AWS CLI.

Getting started with AWS Lambda

In this section, we will look at how easy and effortless it is to execute a simple Lambda function using both the AWS Management Console, as well as the AWS CLI, and in the process learn a few necessary components and configurable items along the way.

Using the AWS Management Console

The AWS Management Console is by far the simplest way to getting started with AWS Lambda. Now I'm going to assume that you already have a valid AWS account and some basic hands-on knowledge with the core AWS services and products such as EC2, IAM, S3, and so on. If not, then you can always create a new account with AWS and leverage the awesome one-year Free Tier scheme as well.

 To read more about Free Tier usage, check out this link here `https://aws.`
`amazon.com/free/`.

The following are the steps to create a new Lambda function:

1. Log in to your AWS Management Console using your IAM credentials and from the **AWS Services** filter, type in `Lambda` to get started. You should see the AWS Lambda dashboard, as shown in the following screenshot.
2. Click on the **Get Started Now** option to create a new Lambda function:

Creating a Lambda function is a straightforward four-step process and it begins with the selection of a *function blueprint*. Just the way we have AMIs for easy and fast deployments of EC2 instances, the same applies for a Lambda function as well. Blueprints are nothing more than sample code that you can use as starting points to writing your very own functions. AWS provides a cool 70-odd blueprints that you can select from, this can help you integrate S3, DynamoDB, and Kinesis with Lambda for to perform specific tasks. For this section, we are going to be using a very simple `hello-world` Lambda function blueprint from the catalog. We can do so by following the given steps:

1. First, simply type in the keyword `hello` in the filter provided. You can optionally even select the runtime for your function as Node.js from the **Select runtime** drop-down list provided to narrow your search.
2. Select the **hello-world** blueprint, as shown here:

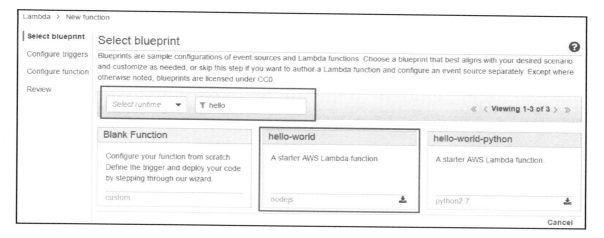

The second stage of creating your own Lambda function involves the configuration of the function's trigger mechanism. This is an optional page, however, it's worth paying attention to. Here, you can select a particular service that will trigger the Lambda function's invocation by selecting the highlighted box adjoining the Lambda function icon, as shown. To select a particular service, you will be required to populate some necessary fields pertaining to that service.

For example, if you happen to select S3 as the service, then you will be prompted with fields where you will need to provide the particular bucket name, the event type (whether to trigger the function based on an object's creation or deletion), and so on:

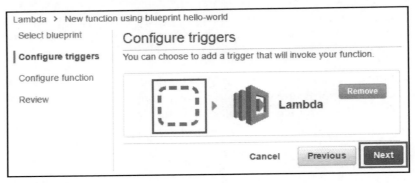

3. Select **Next** to continue with the wizard. The next page that shows up is the function's configuration page. Using this page, you can provide your function's basic configurable items, such as **Name**, **Description**, and **Runtime**.

4. Provide a suitable **Name** for your Lambda function. The **Description** field is optional, however, it is always a good practice to provide one. The **Runtime** for this scenario is already auto populated to **Node.js 4.3**. At the time of writing this book, the following runtimes are supported:
    *   **Node.js 4.3**
    *   **Edge Node.js 4.3**
    *   **Java 8**
    *   **Python 2.7**
    *   **C# (.NET Core 1.0)**

Edge Node.js is nothing but a new extension of the Lambda service called **Lambda@Edge**. This service basically allows you to run Lambda functions at various AWS Edge locations in response to CloudFront events. You can read more about it here at http://docs.aws.amazon.com/lambda/latest /dg/lambda-edge.html.

5. Post the runtime. You will also notice your Lambda code prewritten and ready for execution, shown as follows:

```
'use strict';
console.log('Loading function');
exports.handler = (event, context, callback) => {
  //console.log('Received event:',JSON.stringify(event, null,
  2));
  console.log('value1 =', event.key1);
  console.log('value2 =', event.key2);
  console.log('value3 =', event.key3);
  callback(null, event.key1);
  // Echo back the first key value
  //callback('Something went wrong');
};
```

The code itself can be broken up into three distinctive parts: the first is the invocation of the *function*. The function, in this case, is called **handler**, which gets exported from your Node.js code. This handler is then invoked by calling the function's file name (which in this case is *index*), followed by the function's name in this format: index.handler. The rest of the parameters go as follows: event is the variable where you get your function's event-related data; context is used to get some contextual information about your Lambda function, such as the function's name, how much memory it consumed, the duration it took to execute, and so on, callback is used to send back some value to your caller, such as an error or result parameter: callback(error,result).

Callbacks are optional however they are really useful when it comes to debugging errors in your function's code.

You can either edit your code inline using the code editor provided in the console or even upload a packaged code in the form of a ZIP file either from your local workstation or even from S3. We will be exploring these options later in the next chapter, for now let us continue moving forward.

The next section on the function configuration page is the **Lambda function handler and role** as shown in the following screenshot. Here you provide the **Handler*** for your code along with the necessary permissions it needs to run in the form of IAM roles. You have three options to select from the **Role*** drop-down list. The first in the list is, **Choose an existing role** that basically allows you to select an IAM role from a list of predefined one. For this scenario, I've gone ahead and selected the role `lambda_basic_execution` which as the name suggests, provides basic execution rights to your Lambda function:

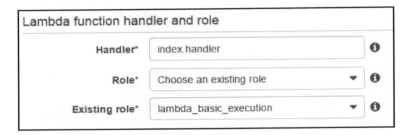

The other two options are **Create a custom role** or **Create a role from a template**. You can use either of these options to create new roles based on your requirements.

Make sure your role has the necessary permissions to view CloudWatch Logs as that's where your function's execution logs are displayed.

The final section on the function configuration page is the **Advanced settings** section. Here you can configure your function's resource requirements along with a few necessary items as well. Let us have a quick look at each one:

- **Memory (MB)**: Select the appropriate amount of memory for your function to run. There is no provision for selecting the CPU resources for your function however the more RAM that you provide to your instance, the better CPU cycle it will get as well. For instance, a 256 MB function will generally have twice the CPU than that of a 128 MB function.

- **Timeout**: The **Timeout** field is used to specify your function's maximum execution time. Once the timeout is breached, AWS will automatically terminate your function's execution. You can specify any value between 1 second and 300 seconds.
- **DLQ Resource**: This feature is quite new, but a very useful feature when it comes to building fault tolerant asynchronous applications. By default, AWS automatically queues the various asynchronous events that the function has to invoke on. It can automatically retry the invocation twice before that particular event is discarded. If you do not wish the event to be discarded, you can now leverage either AWS **SQS** or **SNS** to push those stranded events to the dead letter queue. Selecting **SNS** prompts for a valid **SNS Topic** name and selecting **SQS** prompts you to enter a valid **SQS Queue** name:

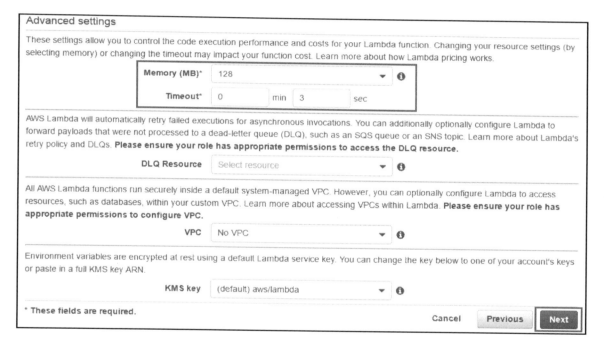

- **VPC**: By default, your Lambda functions are created and deployed in an AWS managed VPC. You can optionally toggle this setting and provide your own VPCs for the functions to run out of.

- **KMS key**: Lambda provides you to develop functions by passing environment variables as well. By default, when you create environment variables, AWS encrypts them using the KMS service. You can use this default service key or even create your own custom key using the IAM console.

6. With the **Advanced settings** out of the way, click **Next** to proceed. On the **Review** page, make sure you go through the items that you have configured during this section.

7. Once done, click on **Create function** to launch your first Lambda function. You should see your Lambda function successfully deployed as shown in the following screenshot. You can use this dashboard to edit your function's code inline, as well as change a few necessary parameters and even test it. Let's take a quick look at the tabs for a better understanding:

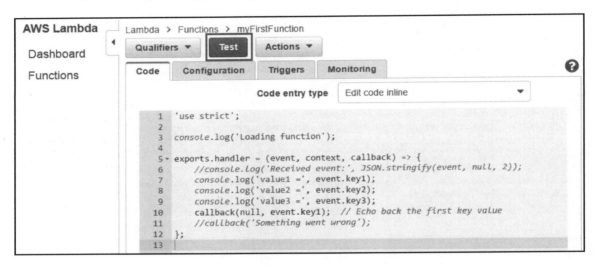

The tabs in the screenshot above are explained as follows:

- **Code**: Using this particular tab, you can edit the deployed code inline as well as upload a newer version of your code using either your local workstation or from S3. Once you have made changes to your code you will be prompted to **Save and test** the same.
- **Configuration**: This tab provides you with the same configurable items as described earlier in this very section. You mostly will use this tab to reconfigure your function's resources or change its execution duration.

- **Triggers**: Use this tab to configure your function's triggering mechanism. For this section, this would be blank anyways.
- **Monitoring**: This tab will display the function's invocation count, its duration, and whether any errors or throttling events occurred.

For now, let us run a quick and simple test to verify whether our function is working or not:

1. To do so, select the **Test** option. Here, you can select from a list of few a predefined test sample events using **Sample event template**, as shown in the following screenshot.
2. Select the template **Hello World**:

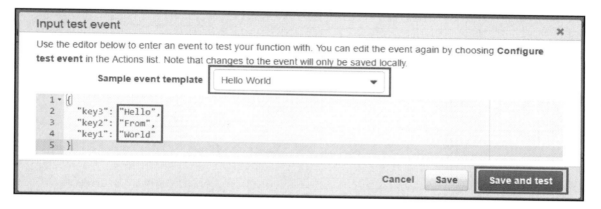

3. The function processes incoming events in the following format. Replace the `value` field with your own string values and click on **Save and test** to view the results of your function's execution:

```
{
  "key3": "value3",
  "key2": "value2",
  "key1": "value1"
}
```

4. If the execution goes well, you should see the following displayed on your dashboard. The first thing you need to notice here is the result of your code's execution, followed by the **Summary** of your function's execution. The **Summary** section displays the **Duration** the function took to execute, **Billed duration**, along with other important details such as the function's **Resources configured** and **Max memory used**.

You can always use these details to fine-tune the amount of resources you provide to your function to execute the next time:

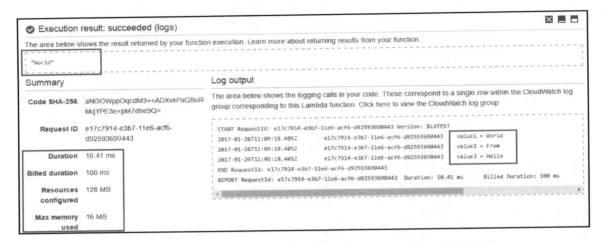

AWS Lambda rounds the function's execution duration to the nearest 100 ms.

The second important part is **Log output**, which displays a part of the function's execution logs. You can use these logs to rectify code errors and make performance improvements as well.

Here's a handy tip! You may notice your function might have taken some 10 ms to execute on an average. That's not too, bad but still it is way too long for something as simple as this function, especially when there is no computation involved. So rerun the test again and verify the duration now. It should be significantly less, right? This is the same latency issue that we talked about earlier, and this is just a way to demonstrate the same.

So, with just a few simple clicks we were able to create, run, and test our first Lambda function, and all the while we did not bother about setting up the development platform nor managing the underlying infrastructure! That's exactly what serverless architecture is all about! There are still quite a few options available from the dashboard that we can use, however, we will keep them aside for the next chapter. For now, let us explore how the AWS CLI can be leveraged to spin up and manage Lambda functions as well.

Using the CLI

As you may be well aware of, AWS provides a rich and easy to use CLI as well for managing your cloud resources. In this section, we will be using the AWS CLI to create, package, and invoke a simple Lambda function:

1. To begin with, make sure your AWS CLI is set up and ready for use. You can install the CLI on most major Linux OSes, as well as macOS, and Windows. You can go through the following guide for the installation, as well as the configuration steps:

   http://docs.aws.amazon.com/cli/latest/userguide/installing.html.

2. Next, create a new folder (in this case, I created a folder named lambda) and copy the following contents into a new file:

```
console.log('Loading function');
exports.handler = function(event, context) {
  var date = new Date().toDateString();

  context.succeed("Hello " + event.username +
  "! Today's date is " + date);
};
```

The following screenshot shows the output of the preceding file:

```
[root@YoYoNUX ~]#
[root@YoYoNUX ~]# cd lambda/
[root@YoYoNUX lambda]#
[root@YoYoNUX lambda]# cat index.js
console.log('Loading function');

exports.handler = function(event, context) {
var date = new Date().toDateString();
console.log("Function Name: " + context.functionName);
console.log("Request ID: " + context.awsRequestId);
console.log('Remaining Time =', context.getRemainingTimeInMillis());
console.log("Log Group Name: " + context.logGroupName);
console.log("Log Stream Name: " + context.logStreamName);
context.succeed("Hello " + event.username + "! Today's date is " + date);
};
[root@YoYoNUX lambda]#
[root@YoYoNUX lambda]#
```

3. Name the file `index.js` and save it. This particular code is fairly straightforward. It logs the current date and prints a user-friendly message with the user's name passed as the event.

4. Now, in order for the Lambda function to execute, we need to create a minimalistic IAM role that Lambda can assume for executing the function on our behalf. Create a file named `policy.json` and paste the following content into it:

```
{
  "Version": "2012-10-17",
  "Statement": [
    {
      "Effect": "Allow",
      "Principal": {
        "Service": "lambda.amazonaws.com"
      },
      "Action": "sts:AssumeRole"
    }
  ]
}
```

5. To create an IAM Role, we need to make use of the `create-role` command, as shown:

```
# aws iam create-role
--role-name basic-lambda-role
--assume-role-policy-document file://policy.json
```

From the output of the preceding command, copy the ARN that and keep it handy. We will be requiring the same in the coming steps.

```
[root@YoYoNUX ~]#
[root@YoYoNUX ~]# cd lambda/
[root@YoYoNUX lambda]#
[root@YoYoNUX lambda]# cat index.js
console.log('Loading function');

exports.handler = function(event, context) {
var date = new Date().toDateString();
context.succeed("Hello " + event.username + "! Today's date is " + date);
};
[root@YoYoNUX lambda]#
[root@YoYoNUX lambda]#
```

6. With the role created, we can now go ahead and create our function. First, zip the `index.js` file using the following `zip` command. This is going to be our deployment package that will be uploaded to an S3 bucket and executed as a function by Lambda itself:

```
# zip -r mySecondFunction.zip index.js
```

Make sure you only zip the file and the folder it was created in.

7. Next, we use the `create-function` command to create our Lambda function. Type in the following command:

```
# aws lambda create-function
--region us-west-2
--function-name mySecondFunction
--zip-file fileb://mySecondFunction.zip
--role arn:aws:iam::00123456789:role/basic-lambda-role
--handler index.handler
--runtime nodejs4.3
--memory-size 128
```

Let us explore a few of the options that we just passed with the `create-function` command:

- `--function-name`: The name of the function that you will be uploading. You can optionally even provide a description for you function by passing the `--description` option.
- `--zip-file`: This is the path of the deployment package that we are uploading.
- `--role`: The ARN of the IAM role that Lambda will assume when it has to execute the function.
- `--handler`: The function name that Lambda will call to begin the execution of your code.

- `--runtime`: You can provide the runtime environment for the code that you will be executing. There are a few pre-defined values here that you can use, namely: `nodejs`, `nodejs4.3`, `nodejs4.3-edge`, `java8`, `python2.7`, and `dotnetcore1.0`.
- `--memory-size`: The amount of RAM you wish to allocate to your Lambda function. You can optionally set the timeout value as well by using the `--timeout` option.

The full list of options can be found here `https://docs.aws.amazon.com/cli/latest/reference/lambda/create-function.html`.

 By default, your functions will timeout after 3 seconds if no value is provided.

Once you have created the function, you should get a response similar to the one shown in the following screenshot. This means we are now ready to invoke our function:

```
"RoleId": "AROAJOIFGVHSL2JDV6NSE",
"CreateDate": "2017-01-28T05:44:37.204Z",
"RoleName": "basic-lambda-role",
"Path": "/",
"Arn": "arn:aws:iam::8            7:role/basic-lambda-role"
```

8. To invoke the function from the command line, we need to call the `invoke` command, as shown:

```
# aws lambda invoke
--invocation-type RequestResponse
--function-name mySecondFunction
--region us-west-2
--log-type Tail
--payload '{"username":"YoYo"}'
output.txt
```

Let us explore a few of the options from the `invoke` command:

- `--invocation-type`: The type of invocation your Lambda will undertake. By default, the `RequestResponse` invocation is invoked. You can also choose between `event` meant for asynchronous executions or the `dryrun` invocation if you want to verify your function without running it.
- `--log-type`: Used to display the log of your function's execution. Do note, however, that the `Tail` parameter only works when the `--invocation-type` is set to `RequestResponse`.
- `--payload`: The data you wish to send to your Lambda function in JSON format.
- `output`: The file where you want to log the output of your function's execution.

The full specification can be found here `https://docs.aws.amazon.com/cli/latest/reference/lambda/invoke.html`.

9. Once you have successfully invoked the function, check the output of the execution in the `output.txt` file:

```
{
    "FunctionName": "mySecondFunction",
    "CodeSize": 412,
    "MemorySize": 128,
    "FunctionArn": "arn:aws:lambda:us-west-2:8        7:function:mySecondFunction",
    "Handler": "index.handler",
    "Role": "arn:aws:iam::8        7:role/basic-lambda-role",
    "Timeout": 3,
    "LastModified": "2017-01-28T05:47:48.049+0000",
    "Runtime": "nodejs4.3",
    "Description": ""
}
```

There you have it! You have now successfully created and launched a Lambda function using the AWS CLI. There are a few other important commands that you should also keep in mind when working with the CLI, here's a quick look at some of them:

- `list-functions`: A simple command to list your published Lambda functions. You can invoke it by using the following command:

```
# aws lambda list-functions
```

You can optionally use other parameters, such as `--max-items`, to return a mentioned number of functions at a time:

```
[root@YoYoNUX lambda]#
[root@YoYoNUX lambda]# cat output.txt
"Hello YoYo! Today's date is Sat Jan 28 2017"[root@YoYoNUX lambda]# 
```

- `get-function` and `get-function-configuration`: As the name suggests, both commands return the configuration information of the Lambda function that was created using the `create-function` command. The difference being that the `get-function` command also provides a unique URL to download your code's deployment package (ZIP file). The URL is pre-signed and is valid for up to 10 minutes from the time you issue the `get-function` command:

```
# aws lambda get-function <FUNCTION_NAME>
(or)
# aws lambda get-function-configuration
<FUNCTION_NAME>
```

The following screenshot shows the output for the preceding command:

```
[root@YoYoNUX lambda]#
[root@YoYoNUX lambda]# aws lambda list-functions
{
    "Functions": [
        {
            "FunctionName": "myFirstFunction",
            "MemorySize": 128,
            "CodeSize": 333,
            "FunctionArn": "arn:aws:lambda:us-west-2:            7:function:myFirstFunction",
            "Handler": "index.handler"
        },
        {
            "FunctionName": "mySecondFunction",
            "MemorySize": 128,
            "CodeSize": 412,
            "FunctionArn": "arn:aws:lambda:us-west-2:8          7:function:mySecondFunction",
            "Handler": "index.handler"
        }
    ]
}
```

To get a complete list of the CLI supported commands, click here
`http://docs.aws.amazon.com/cli/latest/reference/lambda/`.

Pricing and limitations

As discussed sometime earlier in this chapter, a Lambda function's cost depends on the amount of compute resources (RAM) supplied to it, as well as the duration of the function's execution. But that's not all! A Lambda function is even billed based on the total number of requests collectively across all your functions. The cost is calculated each time Lambda responds to a request generated either by an event or by a manual invocation. This also includes responses triggered during testing of your Lambda function using the Amazon Management Console. At the time of writing, AWS charges $0.20 per 1 million requests ($0.0000002 per request). The best part is that, each month, you get one million requests and 400,000 GB of compute time for free. This feature does not expire, even after your Free Tier validity is over.

Let's take a simple example to understand this better. Consider your Lambda function has been allocated the minimal 128 MB of RAM and it will execute a good 5 million times in one month for one second each. In that case, the cost is calculated as follows:

1. First, we calculate the monthly compute charge. The monthly compute price is $0.00001667 per GB and the Free Tier provides 400,000 GB for free each month:

$$Total\ Compute\ (Second) = 5\ Million\ executions\ ^{*}1\ Sec = 5,000,000\ seconds$$

$$Total\ Compute\ (GBs) = 5,000,000\ ^{*}128MB\ /\ 1024 = 625,000\ GBs$$

$$Monthly\ Billable\ Compute = Total\ Compute - Free\ Tier\ Compute$$

$$625,000\ Total\ Compute\ (GBs) - 400,000\ Free\ Tier\ GBs = 225,000\ GBs$$

$$Monthly\ Compute\ Charges\ (a) = 225,000\ ^{*}\$0.00001667 = \$3.75$$

2. Similarly, we now calculate the monthly request charge. The monthly request price is $0.20 per 1 million requests and the Free Tier provides 1 million requests per month:

> *Monthly Billable Compute = Total Compute − Free Tier Compute*
>
> *5 Million request − 1 Million Free Tier Requests = 4 Million Monthly Billable Requests*
>
> *Monthly request charges (b) = 4*$0.2 / M = $0.8*

3. So, your total cost for running a Lambda function with 128 MB of RAM for a duration of 1 second a million times is >> *Monthly Compute Charges (a) + Monthly Request Charge (b) = $3.75 + $0.8 = $4.55.*

4. Not impressed? Let's take a look at how a Lambda function fares with an EC2 instance when it comes to pricing with a simple example.

5. Consider a really simple Lambda function that will execute roughly 300,000 requests in one month with 3 seconds for each. We will give our function a good 512 MB of RAM for execution. The monthly compute charge is calculated as follows:

> *Total Compute (seconds) = 300,000* (3 Sec) = 900,000 seconds*
>
> *Total Compute (GBs) = 900,000* 512MB / 1024 = 450,000 GBs*
>
> *Monthly billable compute GBs = Total compute − Free tier compute*
>
> *450,000 GBs − 400,000 free tier GBs = 50,000 GBs*
>
> *Monthly compute charges (a) = 50,000*$0.00001667 = $0.8335*

6. Similarly, we calculate the monthly request charge as follows:
   - The monthly request price is $0.20 per 1 million requests and the Free Tier provides 1 million requests per month:

> *Monthly billable requests = Total requests − Free tier requests*

- Since the number of requests is less than that given in Free Tier, the *monthly request charge (b)* evaluates to *$0*:

$$Total\ charges = Compute\ charges + Request\ charges = \$0.8335 + \$0 = \$0.8335\ per\ month$$

Compare that with an EC2 t2.nano (512 MB) instance, running 24/7 for a full month, amounts to $4.32! Now that's really cheap!

Let's also check out some common Lambda limitations as well. For starters, Lambda is not designed for applications that have a long execution time. The maximum execution time supported for a Lambda function is 300 seconds. There are also some hard limits on the amount of RAM you can assign to your Lambda functions. The minimum is 128 MB and it goes all the way up to 1536 MB in increments of 128. Each Lambda function also receives 500 MB of non-persistent scratch space that is generally mounted to /tmp.

If you are looking for persistent storage options, you may want to leverage S3, RDS, or DynamoDB for the same.

There are also some limitations set on the size of the code that you can upload to Lambda. Each Lambda function supports a max upload of 50 MB of code, bundled either as a .zip or .jar file. You can read more about the various limits set on Lambda code deployments, as well as executions here: http://docs.aws.amazon.com/lambda/latest/dg/limits.html.

Besides these limits, you should also know that, at the time of writing this book, AWS Lambda only supports Java, Node.js, Python, and C# as programming languages. There are ways in which you can even execute other non-supported languages and codes, such a, PHP, Go, and Ruby, but that is out of the scope of this book, as we will be primarily concentrating on development using Node.js itself. You can still get a good hands-on feel for the other non-supported scripting languages on Lambda by looking at https://aws.amazon.com/blogs/compute/scripting-languages-for-aws-lambda-running-php-ruby-and-go/.

Planning your next steps

With the basics out of the way, it is equally important to understand a few additional concepts about serverless computing and Lambda functions in general. Firstly, when to use what? Here is a simple breakdown of a few AWS services that offer compute capabilities, and when you should ideally use them:

Requirement	Management	Deployed as	AWS Service
Run simple workloads or websites continuously at predictable rates. Less control required.	You control the server, its OS, and software.	Virtual private servers	Amazon Lightsail
Run almost any workloads at any scale. More control and flexibility required.	You control the instance, the OS and software. You can scale and manage your instances.	Instances	Amazon EC2
Run microservices-based application on Dockerized containers.	You control the provisioning and scaling. AWS manages cluster state and deployment of your application.	Containers	Amazon EC2 Container Service
Run applications that are event driven and stateless.	You provide the application code. AWS manages the deployment and scaling of the infrastructure.	Code	AWS Lambda

Secondly, the code that we are going to be using and developing in this book is predominantly going to be around Node.js, but that shouldn't stop you from using either Java or Python, or even C# for that matter. Do keep in mind however, that each of these programming languages offers a different level of performance. Dynamic languages like Python and Node.js will naturally provide slightly better performances as compared to static languages such as Java and C#. But as I always say, when in doubt, do it yourself, so write a few simple lines of code in each of the supported languages and benchmark the same.

Summary

Let's quickly recap the things we have learned in this chapter. For starters, we got to learn a bit about the birth of serverless computing along with few of its features, pros and cons. With the basics out of the way, we started our journey into the amazing world of AWS Lambda by understanding its nuances and how it works. We then explored the rich AWS Management Console and saw how easy and effortless it is to deploy a simple function. We even learnt how to package and invoke our functions using the AWS CLI as well. Towards the end of the chapter we learnt about how Lambda is priced along with few examples and what some of its limits are as well. Finally, we ended the chapter by exploring a quick comparison between the AWS compute services and learnt which service to use and when.

In the next chapter, we will be turning things up a notch by actually learning the anatomy of writing a Lambda function; its basic building blocks, how to log, and handle few common exceptions, as well as working with versioning and environment variables. So stick around, we are just getting started!

2
Writing Lambda Functions

In the previous chapter, we understood serverless computing and took a quick look at how easy it is to get started with AWS Lambda functions using the AWS Management Console, as well as with the AWS CLI.

In this chapter, we are going to take things a step further by learning the anatomy of a typical Lambda function, and also how to actually write your own functions. The following topics are covered in this chapter:

- Understanding the programming model for a Lambda function using simple functions as examples
- Working with environment variables and versioning
- Leveraging third-party tools for a quick and effortless code deployment to Lambda

So no more talking, let's get coding!

The Lambda programming model

So far we have seen that certain applications can be broken down into one or more simple nuggets of code called as **functions** and uploaded to AWS Lambda for execution. Lambda then takes care of provisioning the necessary resources to run your function along with other management activities such as auto-scaling of your functions, their availability, and so on. So what exactly are we supposed to do in all this? A developer basically has three tasks to perform when it comes to working with Lambda--writing the code, packaging it for deployment, and finally monitoring its execution and fine-tuning.

In this section, we are going to explore the different components that actually make up a Lambda function by understanding what AWS calls as a **programming model** or a **programming pattern**. Currently, AWS officially supports Node.js, Java, Python, and C# as the programming languages for writing Lambda functions, with each language following a generic programming pattern that comprises of the following concepts.

Handler

As discussed briefly in the earlier chapter, the handler is basically a function that Lambda calls first for execution. A handler function is capable of processing incoming event data that is passed to it as well as invoking other functions or methods from your code.

 In this book, we will be concentrating a lot of our code and development on Node.js; however, the programming model remains more or less the same for the other supported languages as well.

A skeleton structure of a handler function is shown as follows:

```
exports.myHandler = function(event, context, callback) {
  // Your code goes here.
  callback();
}
```

Here, `myHandler` is the name of your handler function. By exporting it, we make sure that Lambda knows which function it has to invoke first. The other parameters that are passed with the handler function are:

- `event`: Lambda uses this parameter to pass any event related data back to the handler.
- `context`: Lambda again uses this parameter to provide the handler with the function's runtime information such as the name of the function, the time it took to execute, and so on.
- `callback`: This parameter is used to return any data back to its caller. The `callback` parameter is the only optional parameter that gets passed when writing handlers. If not specified, AWS Lambda will call it implicitly and return the value as `null`. The `callback` parameter also supports two optional parameters in the form of `error` and `result`; `error` will return any of the function's error information back to the caller, while `result` will return any result of your function's successful execution.

Here are a few simple examples of invoking callbacks in your handler:

- `callback()`
- `callback(null, 'Hello from Lambda')`
- `callback(error)`

> Callback is supported only in Node.js runtime v4.3. You will have to use the `context` methods in case your code supports earlier Node.js runtime (v0.10.42)

Let us try out a simple handler example with a code:

```
exports.myHandler = function(event, context, callback) {
  console.log("value = " + event.key);
  console.log("functionName = ", context.functionName);
  callback(null, "Yippee! Something worked!");
};
```

The preceding code snippet will print the value of an event (key) that we will pass to the function, print the function's name as part of the `context` object, and finally print the success message `Yippee! Something worked!` if all goes well!

Follow the given steps to create a Lambda function:

1. Login to the AWS Management Console and select **AWS Lambda** from the dashboard.
2. Select the **Create a Lambda function** option as we did in our earlier chapter.
3. From the **Select blueprint** page, select the **Blank Function** blueprint.
4. Since we are not configuring any triggers for now, simply click on **Next** at the **Configure triggers** page.

5. Provide a suitable **Name** and **Description** for your Lambda function and paste the preceding code into the inline code editor as shown:

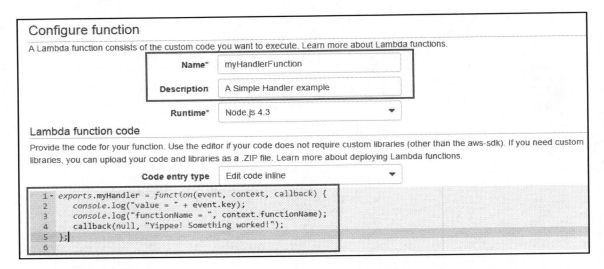

6. Next, in the **Lambda function handler and role** section on the same page, type in the correct name of your **Handler*** as shown. The handler name should match with the handler name in your function to work. Remember also to select the **basic-lambda-role** for your function's execution before selecting the **Next** button:

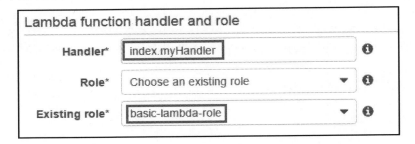

7. In the **Review** page, select the **Create function** option.
8. With your function now created, select the **Test** option to pass the sample event to our function.

9. In the **Sample event** section, pass the following event, and select the **Save and test** option:

```
{
  "key": "My Printed Value!!"
}
```

With your code execution completed, you should get a similar execution result as shown as follows. The important things to note here are the values for the `event`, `context`, and `callback` parameters. You can note the `callback` message being returned back to the caller as the function executed successfully. The other `event` and `context` object values are printed in the **Log output** section as highlighted:

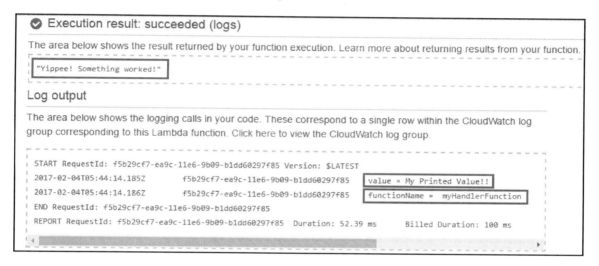

 In case you end up with any errors, make sure the handler function name matches the handler name that you passed during the function's configuration.

The context object

As discussed earlier, the `context` object is a really useful utility when it comes to obtaining runtime information about your function. The `context` object can provide information such as the executing function's name, the time remaining before Lambda terminates your function's execution, the log name, and the stream associated with your function and much more.

The `context` object also comes with its own methods that you can call to correctly terminate your function's executions such as, `context.succed()`, `context.fail()`, and `context.done()`. However, post April 2016, Lambda has transitioned the Node.js runtime from v0.10.42 to v4.3 which does support these methods. However, it encourages the use of `callback()` function for performing the same actions.

Here are some of the commonly used `context` object methods and properties described as follows:

- `getRemainingTimeInMillis()`: It returns the number of milliseconds left for execution before Lambda terminates your function. This comes in really handy when you want to perform some corrective actions before your function exits or times out.
- `callbackWaitsForEmptyEventLoop`: This property is used to override the default behavior of a `callback()` function, that is, to wait till the entire event loop is processed, and only then return back to the caller. If set to `false`, this property causes the `callback()` function to stop any further processing in the event loop even if there are any other tasks to be performed. The default value is set to `true`.
- `functionName`: It returns the name of the executing Lambda function.
- `functionVersion`: The current version of the executing Lambda function.
- `memoryLimitInMB`: The amount of resource in terms of memory that is set for your Lambda function.
- `logGroupName`: It returns the name of the CloudWatch Log group that stores the function's execution logs.
- `logStreamName`: It returns the name of the CloudWatch Log stream that stores the function's execution logs.
- `awsRequestID`: It returns the request ID associated with that particular function's execution.

 If you are using Lambda functions as mobile backend processing services, you can then extract additional information about your mobile application using the context of the `identity` and `clientContext` objects. These are invoked using the AWS Mobile SDK. To learn more, visit `http://docs.aws.amazon.com/lambda/latest/dg/nodejs-prog-model-context.html`.

Let us look at a simple example to understand the `context` object a bit better. In this example, we are using the `context` object `callbackWaitsForEmptyEventLoop` and demonstrating its working by setting the object's value to either `yes` or `no` on invocation:

1. Login to the AWS Management Console and select **AWS Lambda** from the dashboard.
2. Select the **Create a Lambda function** option as done in the earlier chapter.
3. From the **Select blueprint** page, select the **Blank Function** blueprint.
4. Since we are not configuring any triggers for now, simply click on **Next** at the **Configure triggers** page.
5. Provide a suitable **Name** and **Description** for your Lambda function and paste the following code in the inline code editor:

```
exports.myHandler = (event, context, callback) => {
  console.log("Hello, Starting Lambda Function");
  console.log("We are going to learn about context object
   and its usage");
  console.log('value1 =', event.key1);
  console.log('value2 =', event.key2);
  console.log('value3 =', event.key3);
  console.log('remaining time =',
   context.getRemainingTimeInMillis());
  console.log('functionName =', context.functionName);
  console.log('AWSrequestID =', context.awsRequestId);
  console.log('logGroupName =', context.logGroupName);
  console.log('logStreamName =', context.logStreamName);
  switch (event.contextCallbackOption) {
    case "no":
      setTimeout(function(){
        console.log("I am back from my timeout of 30
        seconds!!");
      },30000); // 30 seconds break
      break;
    case "yes":
      console.log("The callback won't wait for the setTimeout()
      n if the callbackWaitsForEmptyEventLoop is set to
      false");
      setTimeout(function(){
        console.log("I am back from my timeout of 30
        seconds!!");
      },30000); // 30 seconds break
      context.callbackWaitsForEmptyEventLoop = false;
      break;
    default:
      console.log("The Default code block");
  }
  callback(null, 'Hello from Lambda');
};
```

6. Next, in the **Lambda function handler and role** section on the same page, type in the correct name of your **Handler*** as shown. The handler name should match with the handler name in your function to work. Remember also to select the **basic-lambda-role** for your function's execution.

7. The final change that we will do is, to change the **Timeout** value of our function from the default 3 seconds to 1 minute specifically for this example. Click **Next** to continue:

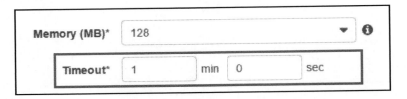

8. In the **Review** page, select the **Create function** option.

9. With your function now created, select the **Test** option to pass the sample event to our function.

10. In the **Sample event** section, pass the following event and select the **Save and test** option:

```
{
    "contextCallbackOption": "yes"
}
```

You should see a similar output in the **Log output** window shown as follows:

Log output

The area below shows the logging calls in your code. These correspond to a single row within the CloudWatch log group corresponding to this Lambda function. Click here to view the CloudWatch log group.

```
11e6-8c90-31ed440615d9 Version: $LATEST
32872986-ebb7-11e6-8c90-31ed440615d9      remaining time = 59998
32872986-ebb7-11e6-8c90-31ed440615d9      functionName = myContextExample
32872986-ebb7-11e6-8c90-31ed440615d9      AWSrequestID = 32872986-ebb7-11e6-8c90-31ed440615d9
32872986-ebb7-11e6-8c90-31ed440615d9      logGroupName = /aws/lambda/myContextExample
32872986-ebb7-11e6-8c90-31ed440615d9      logStreamName = 2017/02/05/[$LATEST]8ac71ac7c3564acc8f1a9cbbbd99156t
32872986-ebb7-11e6-8c90-31ed440615d9      The callback won't wait for the setTimeout()
                                          if the callbackWaitsForEmptyEventLoop is set to false
```

With the `contextCallbackOption` set to `yes`, the function does not wait for the 30 seconds `setTimeout()` function but it will exit, however, it prints the function's runtime information such as the remaining execution time, the function name, and so on. Now set the `contextCallbackOption` to `no`, and re-run the test and verify the output. This time, you can see the `setTimeout()` function, and verify the same by comparing the remaining time left for execution with the output of the earlier test run:

```
11e6-b491-6191bf96cdfb Version: $LATEST
32872986-ebb7-11e6-8c90-31ed440615d9    I am back from my timeout of 30 seconds!!
8c2e0785-ebba-11e6-b491-6191bf96cdfb    remaining time = 59992
8c2e0785-ebba-11e6-b491-6191bf96cdfb    functionName = myContextExample
8c2e0785-ebba-11e6-b491-6191bf96cdfb    AWSrequestID = 8c2e0785-ebba-11e6-b491-6191bf96cdfb
8c2e0785-ebba-11e6-b491-6191bf96cdfb    logGroupName = /aws/lambda/myContextExample
8c2e0785-ebba-11e6-b491-6191bf96cdfb    logStreamName = 2017/02/05/[$LATEST]8ac71ac7c3564acc8f1a9cbbbd99156b
8c2e0785-ebba-11e6-b491-6191bf96cdfb    I am back from my timeout of 30 seconds!!
```

Logging

You can always log your code's execution and activities using simple log statements. The following statements are supported for logging with Node.js runtime:

- `console.log()`
- `console.error()`
- `console.warn()`
- `console.info()`

The logs can be viewed using both the AWS Management Console as well as the CLI. Let us quickly explore both these options:

- **Using the AWS Management Console**: We have already been using Lambda's dashboard to view the function's execution logs, however, the logs are only for the current execution. To view your function's logs from the past, you need to view them using the CloudWatch Logs section.
  To do so, search, and select **CloudWatch** option from the AWS Management Console. Next, select the **Logs** option to display the function's logs as shown in the following screenshot:

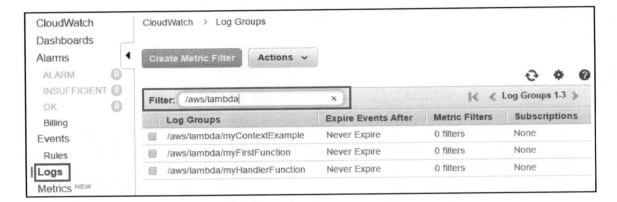

You can use the **Filter** option to filter out your Lambda logs by typing in the `Log Group Name Prefix` as `/aws/lambda`.

Select any of the present **Log Groups** and its corresponding log stream name to view the complete and detailed execution logs of your function.

If you do not see any Lambda logs listed out here it is mostly due to your Lambda execution role. Make sure your role has the necessary access rights to create the log group and log stream along with the capability to put log events.

- **Using the CLI**: The CLI provides two ways using which you can view your function's execution logs. The first is using the Lambda function's `invoke` command itself which we tried a while back in `Chapter 1`, *Introducing AWS Lambda*. The `invoke` command when used with the `--log-type` parameter will print the latest 4 KB of log data that is written to CloudWatch Logs. To do so, first list out all the available functions in your current region using the following command:

  ```
  # aws lambda list-functions
  ```

  Next, pick a Lambda function that you wish to invoke and substitute that function's name and payload with the example snippet written as follows:

  ```
  # aws lambda invoke
  --invocation-type RequestResponse
  --function-name myFirstFunction
  --log-type Tail
  --payload '{"key1":"Lambda","key2":"is","key3":"awesome!"}'
  output.txt
  ```

  The second way, is by using a combination of the `context()` object and the CloudWatch CLI. You can obtain your function's `--log-group-name` and the `--log-stream-name` by using the `context.logGroupName` and the `context.logStreamName`. Next, substitute the data gathered from the output of these parameters in the following command:

  ```
  # aws logs get-log-events
  --log-group-name "/aws/lambda/myFirstFunction"
  --log-stream-name
      "2017/02/07/[$LATEST]1ae6ac9c77384794a3202802c683179a"
  ```

> If you run into the following error `The specified log stream does not exist` in spite of providing the correct values for the log group name and stream name; then make sure to add the \ escape character in the [$LATEST] as shown.

Let us look at a few options that you can additionally pass with the `get-log-events` command:

- `--start-time`: The start of the log's time range. All times are in UTC.
- `--end-time`: The end of the log's time range. All times are in UTC.
- `--next-token`: The token for the next set of items to return. (You received this token from a previous call.)

- `--limit`: Used to set the maximum number of log events returned. By default the limit is set to 10,000 log events.

Alternatively, if you don't wish to use the `context()` objects in your code, you can still filter out the log group name and log stream name by using a combination of the following commands:

```
# aws logs describe-log-groups
--log-group-name-prefix "/aws/lambda/"
```

The `describe-log-groups` command will list all the log groups that are prefixed with `/aws/lambda`. Make a note of your function's log group name from this output. Next, execute the following command to list your log group name's associated log stream name:

```
# aws logs describe-log-streams --log-group-name
"/aws/lambda/myFirstFunction"
```

Make a note of the log stream name and substitute the same in the next, and the final command to view your log events for that particular log stream name:

```
# aws logs get-log-events --log-group-name
"/aws/lambda/myFirstFunction"
--log-stream-name "2017/02/07/[$LATEST]1ae6ac9c77384794a3202802c683179a"
```

Once again, make sure to add the backslash \ in the `[$LATEST]` to avoid the `The specified log stream does not exist` error. With the logging done, let's move on to the next piece of the programming model called **exceptions**.

Exceptions and error handling

Functions have the ability to notify AWS Lambda in case it failed to execute correctly. This is primarily done by the function passing the error object to Lambda which converts the same to a string and returns it to the user as an error message.

The error messages that are returned also depend on the invocation type of the function; for example, if your function performs a synchronous execution (the `RequestResponse` invocation type), then the error is returned back to the user and displayed on the AWS Management Console as well as in the CloudWatch Logs. For any asynchronous executions (the `event` invocation type), Lambda will not return anything. Instead it logs the error messages to CloudWatch Logs.

Let us examine a function's error and exception handling capabilities with a simple example of a calculator function that accepts two numbers, and an operand as the test event during invocation:

1. Login to the AWS Management Console and select **AWS Lambda** from the dashboard.
2. Select the **Create a Lambda function** option as done in the earlier chapter.
3. From the **Select blueprint** page, select the **Blank Function** blueprint.
4. Since we are not configuring any triggers for now, simple click on **Next** at the **Configure triggers** page.
5. Provide a suitable **Name** and **Description** for your Lambda function and paste the following code in the inline code editor:

```
exports.myHandler = (event, context, callback) => {
  console.log("Hello, Starting the "+ context.functionName
  +" Lambda Function");
  console.log("The event we pass will have two numbers and
  an operand value");
  // operand can be +, -, /, *, add, sub, mul, div
  console.log('Received event:',
  JSON.stringify(event, null, 2));
  var error, result;
  if (isNaN(event.num1) || isNaN(event.num2)) {
    console.error("Invalid Numbers");
    // different logging
    error = new Error("Invalid Numbers!");
    // Exception Handling
    callback(error);
  }
  switch(event.operand)
  {
    case "+":
    case "add":
      result = event.num1 + event.num2;
      break;
    case "-":
    case "sub":
      result = event.num1 - event.num2;
      break;
    case "*":
    case "mul":
      result = event.num1 * event.num2;
      break;
    case "/":
    case "div":
      if(event.num2 === 0){
```

```
        console.error("The divisor cannot be 0");
        error = new Error("The divisor cannot be 0");
        callback(error, null);
      }
      else{
        result = event.num1/event.num2;
      }
      break;
    default:
      callback("Invalid Operand");
      break;
  }
  console.log("The Result is: " + result);
  callback(null, result);
};
```

6. Next, in the **Lambda function handler and role** section on the same page, type in the correct name of your **Handler***. The handler name should match the handler name in your function to work. Remember also to select the **basic-lambda-role** for your function's execution.

7. Leave the rest of the values to their defaults and click **Next** to continue.

8. In the **Review** page, select the **Create function** option.

9. With your function now created, select the **Test** option to pass the sample event to our function.

10. In the **Sample event**, pass the following event and select the **Save and test** option. You should see a similar output in the **Log output** window shown as follows:

```
{
  "num1": 3,
  "num2": 0,
  "operand": "div"
}
```

The following screenshot shows the execution result for the preceding code:

```
● Execution result: failed (logs)

{
  "errorMessage": "The divisor cannot be 0",
  "errorType": "Error",
  "stackTrace": [
    "exports.myHandler (/var/task/index.js:32:25)"
  ]
}
```

So what just happened there? Well first, we can print simple user friendly error messages with the help of the `console.error()` statement. Additionally, we can also print the `stackTrace` of the error by passing the error in the `callback()` as shown in the following snippet:

```
error = new Error("The divisor cannot be 0");
callback(error, null);
```

You can also view the custom error message and the `stackTrace` JSON array both from the Lambda dashboard as well as from the CloudWatch Logs section. Next, give this code a couple of tries with some different permutations and combinations of events and check out the results. You can even write your own custom error messages and error handlers that can perform some additional task when an error is returned by the function.

With this we come towards the end of a function's generic programming model and its components. In the next section, we will be taking up few advanced topics such as function versioning and aliases along with a look at how to configure your functions with environment variables.

Versioning and aliases

In the real world, we often have different environments to work out of, for example development, QA, staging, pre-production, production, and so on. Having to manage a single Lambda function across all these environments can be a real pain, and also tricky especially, when each of your environments provide different configuration options, such as different connection strings for databases hosted for development and production, different roles and resource settings.

Lambda thus provides few add-on services that help you better categorize, and manage functions in the form of versions and aliases.

Versioning is a simple way to create one or more versions of your working Lambda code. Each version that you create is basically a snapshot of your origin function. Versions are also immutable which means, that each version you create from the origin or [$LATEST] branch cannot be edited or its configuration parameters change as well. Lambda assigns simple incremental version numbers *(1, 2, 3, ..., n)* to your versions each time they are created.

Following is a simple example depicting a function and its associated versions. Note however, that the version numbers are never reused, even if your function gets deleted or re-created:

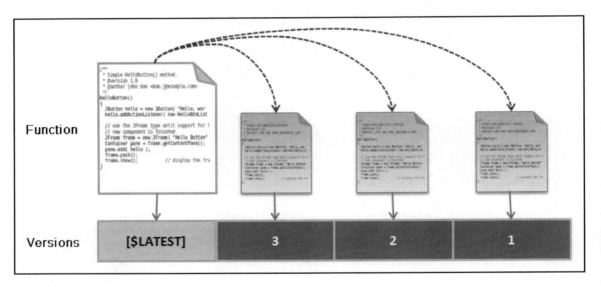

You can create and assign your function's versions using both, the AWS Management Console as well as the CLI.

In the following scenario, I'll be reusing the `calculator.js` code that we published and executed from our earlier steps however feel free to try these steps on any function of your own as well.

Let us look at the AWS Management Console first:

1. From the Lambda dashboard, select your function for which you wish to create the version.
2. Next, from the **Actions** tab, select the **Publish new version** option.
3. At this point, you will be publishing a new version of the code from the **$LATEST** version. Provide a suitable description for your new version in the **Version description** field and click **Publish** when done.
4. Note that the function is an exact copy of our $LATEST code with the same configurations as well, however we are not able to edit this code. To go back to the $LATEST version, simply select the **Version: 1** drop-down list and pick the **$LATEST** version as shown as follows:

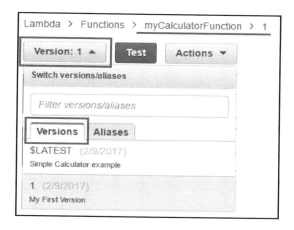

You can similarly create versions using the CLI as well. With the CLI, you get two options: The first is to create the version when you first create the function itself. This can be done by using either the create-function or the update-function-code command and pass the parameter --publish along with it as shown in the following snippet:

```
# aws lambda create-function
--function-name myNewFunction
--zip-file fileb://myNewFunction.zip
--role arn:aws:iam::001234567890:role/basic-lambda-role
--handler index.myHandler
--runtime nodejs4.3
--memory-size 128
--publish
```

Alternatively, you can also publish a function's version explicitly using the `publish-version` command. But first, let us list out the current versions associated with our function using the `list-versions-by-function` command as shown:

```
# aws lambda list-versions-by-function
--function-name myCalculatorFunction
```

The preceding command's output can be seen in the following screenshot:

```
{
    "Version": "$LATEST",
    "CodeSha256": "uqPrE+DeUan8/QvsXstvlVOhbMTNx131a875JwUua2c=",
    "FunctionName": "myCalculatorFunction",
    "FunctionArn": "arn:aws:lambda:us-east-1:8        7:function:myCalculatorFunction:$LATEST",
    "Handler": "index.myHandler",
    "Description": "Simple Calculator example"
},
{
    "Version": "1",
    "CodeSha256": "uqPrE+DeUan8/QvsXstvlVOhbMTNx131a875JwUua2c=",
    "FunctionName": "myCalculatorFunction",
    "FunctionArn": "arn:aws:lambda:us-east-1:8        7:function:myCalculatorFunction:1",
    "Handler": "index.myHandler",
    "Description": "My First Version"
}
```

From the output, we can see that our calculator example has two versions associated with it. Each version also has its own unique ARN that you can use to invoke that particular function.

Now to publish a new version, we first need to make some change in our [$LATEST] version as Lambda will not create a newer version of your function unless, there is actually some change in it. So go ahead and either tweak some resource parameter or change some text around in your code; you can use the AWS Management Console to do the same. Make sure to save the changes performed in the [$LATEST] version and once done, type in the following command as shown:

```
# aws lambda publish-version
--function-name myCalculatorFunction
--description "A second version created by CLI"
```

Once executed successfully, you should now see a new version (in this case: *2*) of your code along with a new ARN of the following format:

```
arn:aws:lambda:[REGION]:[ACCOUNT_ID]:function:[FUNCTION_NAME]:[VERSION_NUMB
ER]
```

However as time goes by, you would end up with a lot of different versions of a particular function. This can be problematic, especially if you are working with environments like development or production where you need to frequently change a function's versions to match the environment. That's where aliases help out. Aliases are nothing but simple pointers that point to a particular Lambda function at a given point in time. They are basically simple name-like values that get invoked by a caller and thus abstract the version value that the alias was pointing to.

For example, consider a scenario where a developer pushes some function code from the base [$LATEST] version to a new version **1**. Let us assign this version **1** an alias called as **DEV**. When invoked, the alias **DEV** that points to version **1** gets invoked by the caller:

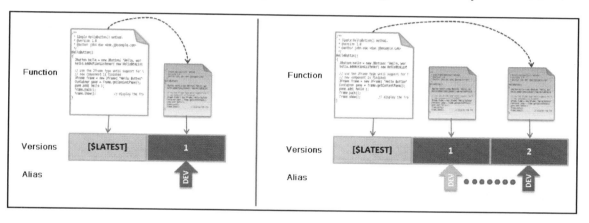

Now, the developer makes some modifications to the code from the base version again and pushes out a new version **2**. Rather than updating the invoker each time a new version is created, all the developer has to do now is, remap the alias **DEV** from version **1** to version **2**. In this way, the developer can map and unmap the alias to any current function version without changing the invoker.

Each alias that you create gets its own individual ARN as well.

Aliases can also help in simplifying event source mappings where instead of using your Lambda function's ARN, you substitute it with an alias ARN. This makes it easier for developers to work with event source mappings as now, they don't have to worry about changing the function's ARN each time they update to a newer version.

Here is an example format of an alias's ARN:

```
arn:aws:lambda:[REGION]:[ACCOUNT_ID]:function:[FUNCTION_NAME]:[ALIAS]
```

You can create, associate, and disassociate an alias with a version anytime you want. This makes them mutable unlike versions which cannot be changed once created. Let us look at a few essential examples of working with aliases using both the AWS Management Console, as well as the AWS CLI with a simple example:

1. First up, from the Lambda dashboard, select a particular function for which you wish to create the alias. In my case, I'll be using the same calculator code example that we used to create the two versions. From the **Actions** tab, select the **Create alias** option.
2. In the **Create a new alias** dialog box, provide a suitable **Name**, **Description**, and finally, select the **Version** for which you wish to associate the alias. In this case, I've associated it with the **$LATEST** version as shown in the following screenshot:

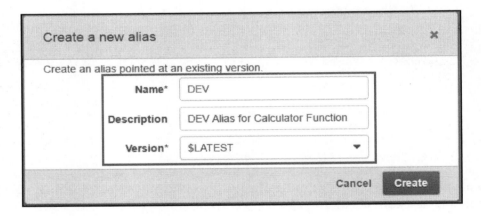

3. Click on **Create** to complete the process.

With this completed, your [$LATEST] version is now associated with the DEV alias. Let us quickly look at few commands from the CLI as well that can help us in creating and managing aliases.

First up, let us associate the version 1 of our calculator function with the alias PROD. To do so, we use the create-alias command as shown:

```
# aws lambda create-alias
--function-name myCalculatorFunction
--name PROD
--function-version 1
--description "PROD alias for my function"
```

With your new alias created, you can list out all associated aliases to your function using the list-aliases command as shown:

```
# aws lambda list-aliases
--function-name myCalculatorFunction
```

You should get a similar output as shown in the following screenshot. Note the individual alias ARNs, and the function versions to which they are mapped to:

```
"Aliases": [
    {
        "AliasArn": "arn:aws:lambda:us-east-1:8        7:function:myCalculatorFunction:DEV",
        "FunctionVersion": "$LATEST",
        "Name": "DEV",
        "Description": "DEV Alias for Calculator Function"
    },
    {
        "AliasArn": "arn:aws:lambda:us-east-1:8        7:function:myCalculatorFunction:PROD",
        "FunctionVersion": "1",
        "Name": "PROD",
        "Description": "PROD alias for my function"
    }
]
```

You can now substitute these ARNs for your event source mappings and go ahead with creating newer function versions as well. Let's assume you publish a new version of your code (in this case, version 2) and this new version has to be published to the PROD environment. All you need to do is update the alias PROD, and point it to the new version 2 using the update-alias command as shown:

```
# aws lambda update-alias
--function-name myCalculatorFunction
> --name PROD
> --function-version 2
```

Run the `list-aliases` command once again and verify the changes. Remember, all this time we have not touched the event source mapping for this function. We have only used aliases to point the new version of the function to the environment abstracting out. Simple isn't it!

With versioning and aliases done, let us quickly learn about environment variables and how you can use them with your Lambda functions.

Environment variables

Environment variables are special key value pairs that you can use to configure your function code or set some variable values dynamically. In simple terms, environment variables is an awesome mechanism to make your Lambda function reusable across different environments as now you don't have to make alterations to your application code each time a particular variable has to be changed.

For example, by declaring your database string as an environment variable, you can now use the exact same Lambda function for development, QA, or production environments by simply making the necessary connection string changes in the environment variable itself.

And to make things more interesting, environment variables can be leveraged with your Lambda function's versions and aliases as well. Once you have created a new copy of your function code in the [$LATEST] version along with the required resource settings, and the environment variables, you can create newer immutable snapshots or versions of the same and reuse them across your environments as needed. Let us look at how to work with environment variables using a simple code example:

```
exports.myHandler = (event, context, callback) => {
  console.log("Starting Version "+
   process.env.AWS_LAMBDA_FUNCTION_VERSION +" of "+
   context.functionName +" in "+process.env.AWS_REGION);
  // operand can be +, -, /, *, add, sub, mul, div
  console.log('Received event:', JSON.stringify(event, null, 2));
  var error;
  if (isNaN(process.env.NUM1) || isNaN(process.env.NUM2)) {
    console.error("Invalid Numbers");
    error = new Error("Invalid Numbers!");
    callback(error);
  }
  var res = {};
  res.a = Number(process.env.NUM1);
  res.b = Number(process.env.NUM2);
  var result;
  switch(process.env.OPERAND)
```

```
{
  case "+":
  case "add":
    result = res.a + res.b;
    break;
  case "-":
  case "sub":
    result = res.a - res.b;
    break;
  case "*":
  case "mul":
    result = res.a * res.b;
    break;
  case "/":
  case "div":
    if(res.b === 0){
      console.error("The divisor cannot be 0");
      error = new Error("The divisor cannot be 0");
      callback(error, null);
      //break;
    }
    else{
      result = res.a/res.b;
      //break;
    }
    break;
  default:
    callback("Invalid Operand");
    break;
}
console.log("The Result is: " + result);
callback(null, result);
};
```

There's a lot we are doing with this particular version of the calculator code example. First up, the code is going to print certain values in the form of process.env.AWS_LAMBDA_FUNCTION_VERSION and process.env.AWS_REGION. These are a certain form of environment variables that are internal to Lambda functions. For instance, AWS_LAMBDA_FUNCTION_VERSION prints the current executing function's version number while the AWS_REGION key prints the current AWS region executing the function. You can additionally obtain other useful information such as LAMBDA_RUNTIME_DIR that provides information on the runtime related artifacts and much more by reading the complete list provided here at http://docs.aws.amazon.com/lambda/latest/dg/current-supported-versions.html#lambda-environment-variables.

Next up, we can also see a few environment variables being read using the Node.js `process.env` property. This property returns an object containing the corresponding environment variable that was set. To set the environment variables, you can either use the AWS Management Console or the CLI as well. Let us look at the AWS Management Console first:

1. From the Lambda management dashboard, select the calculator function that we have been using throughout this chapter.
2. Copy and paste the preceding code into the inline code editor.
3. Next, in the **Environment variables** section, set the key and values for our function's execution:
   - NUM1: <NUMERIC_VALUE>
   - NUM2: <NUMERIC_VALUE>
   - OPERAND: <add>,<+>,<sub>,<->,<mul>,<*>,<div>,</>

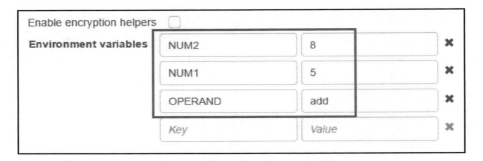

4. You can optionally select the **Enable encryption helpers** checkbox to enable Lambda to encrypt your environment variables using the AWS **Key Management Service (KMS)**. By default, AWS will create a default KMS key for encrypting and decrypting your environment variables however, you can always provide your own KMS keys here as well.
5. Next, from the **Actions** tab, select the **Publish new version** option. Provide a suitable **Description** for your new version and click **Publish** when done. Do remember that by doing so, your function version is now immutable, so you won't be able to change the environment variables as well. If you wish to change the values, you will need to create a new version out of it.

6. With the new version created (version 3 in this case), you can now simply select the **Test** option and validate the output as well:

```
  Execution result: succeeded (logs)                                    ☒ ■ ☐

   ┌──────┐
   │ 13   │
   └──────┘

  Log output

  f14 Version: 3
  -922c-65bb86e8ef14    Starting Version 3 of myCalculatorFunction in us-east-1
  -922c-65bb86e8ef14    Received event: {}
  -922c-65bb86e8ef14    The Result is: 13
  4
  ef14  Duration: 27.89 ms     Billed Duration: 100 ms     Memory Size: 128 MB     Max Memory Used: 13 MB
```

You can even use the CLI to pass environment variables during your function's creation using the `--environment` parameter in the `create-function` command as shown:

```
# aws lambda create-function
--function-name myCalculatorFunction
--zip-file fileb://myCalculator.zip
--role arn:aws:iam::001234567890:role/basic-lambda-role
--handler index.handler
--runtime nodejs4.3
--environment Variables="{NUM1=5,NUM2=6,OPERAND=add}"
--memory-size 128
```

With the core creation and writing concepts out of the way, let us move on to the final stage that covers how to package and deploy your functions to Lambda!

Packaging and deploying

We touched on the concept of packaging and deploying a simple Lambda function earlier in Chapter 1, *Introducing AWS Lambda* and parts of it in this chapter as well, however in this section, we will be doing things a bit differently! Rather than covering the steps all over again, we will be exploring a few simple and powerful open source Lambda deployment tools that are currently out there in the market today! Why tools you ask? Well, why not?

As a developer we always want to make the deployment and management of our codes simpler and hassle free, especially when it comes to working with a lot of Lambda projects at the same time. These tools accelerate time to development and also help us reduce any errors that may occur when working with the AWS Management Console or the AWS CLI. In this section we will be exploring two such tools that are gaining a lot of momentum in the market today: APEX and Claudia.js.

APEX

APEX is by far the most versatile and easy deployment and management tool that I've come across. It is extremely simple to install, and get started with. To install the tool on most major Linux distributions, you simply need to copy and paste the following command on your Terminal:

```
# curl https://raw.githubusercontent.com/apex/apex/master/install.sh | sudo
sh
```

 You can get APEX working on Windows as well. Check out the latest APEX releases from `https://github.com/apex/apex/releases`.

Before we go any further, make sure you have the AWS access and secret keys set in the `~/.aws/credentials` directory of your Linux workstation or alternatively if you are planning to perform these steps from an EC2 instance, then make sure the EC2 instance has at least the basic Lambda full access role attached to it in order to work.

With APEX installed, all you need to do now is initialize and create your first working Lambda project. The project is a high-level folder that contains all your functions and other resources required by Lambda to work. To do so, simply type in the following command:

```
# mkdir workdir && cd workdir
# apex init -r us-east-1
//Assuming you want to deploy the function in the us-east-1 region
```

This will bring up a wizard that simply requires you to provide a suitable **Project name** and **Project description**. Yes! That's all there is to it! The rest of the work is all done by Apex itself and that includes creating an IAM role for Lambda to execute your function, creation of a CloudWatch policy that will enable to function to log its output to CloudWatch, and finally the creation of a `project.json` and a directory to house all your Lambda functions called as functions.

The `project.json` file contains metadata about your functions such as the function name, description, the resources that the function will use (by default it is set to 128 MB and timeout to 5 seconds), and the IAM role required by the function to run. You can edit the `project.json` file to make changes as required by your functions:

```
   Project name: apex-helloworld
Enter an optional description of your project.
   Project description: My first function deployed using Apex

[+] creating IAM apex-helloworld_lambda_function role
[+] creating IAM apex-helloworld_lambda_logs policy
[+] attaching policy to lambda_function role.
[+] creating ./project.json
[+] creating ./functions

Setup complete, deploy those functions!
```

The project directory will resemble something similar to the one shown as follows with all your functions falling under the master directory:

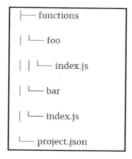

```
├── functions
│   └── foo
│   │   └── index.js
│   └── bar
│   └── index.js
└── project.json
```

Now by default, APEX will create a simple *hello world* node.js code and place it in the `index.js` file of your project. In this case we will use the same trusty example to demonstrate the ease of deploying your Lambda functions. To do so, simply type in the following command:

```
# apex deploy
```

Yes! That's it! With this command, APEX will automatically upload your function, assign it the IAM role for execution, and create a corresponding version for it as well! But that's not all, you can even invoke your function from the command line as well, and no prizes for guessing the command there:

```
# apex invoke hello
```

The name `hello` comes from the `functions/hello` folder name. This is created by default when we first initialized the directory using the `apex init` command:

```
[root@YoYoNUX workdir]#
[root@YoYoNUX workdir]# apex deploy
   • creating function            env= function=hello
   • created alias current        env= function=hello version=1
   • function created             env= function=hello name=apex-helloworld_hello version=1
[root@YoYoNUX workdir]#
[root@YoYoNUX workdir]# apex invoke hello
{"hello":"world"}
[root@YoYoNUX workdir]#
```

You can view your function's execution logs as well by using the following command:

```
# apex logs hello
```

Updating your functions is even more easier with APEX. Just make the required changes to your code and simply redeploy! APEX will automatically create a new version of your code and deploy it to Lambda. But the real power of APEX I guess, lies in its ability to even package and run functions that are written in other languages such as Java, Python, and even golang. This is made possible by a combination of a golang library and Node.js shim stdio interface. It also provides a variety of sub-tools using which you can perform rollbacks, view logs and metrics, and much more. To read more about APEX and its capabilities and features, read here at http://apex.run/.

Claudia.js

Unlike APEX, Claudia.js is designed to work only with Node.js. It simplifies the creation, deployment and management of your Node.js functions without having the need to make any alterations to your code. The prerequisites to get started with Claudia.js remain the same as APEX. Make sure your workstation has the AWS secret key and access key supplied in the `~/.aws/credentials` file or alternatively provide the basic IAM roles if you are working out off an EC2 instance itself.

Next, install Claudia.js using the following command:

```
# npm install claudia -g
```

 You will need Node 4.x installed on your local development workstation. You can download the correct Node.js version for your Linux distro from here at `https://nodejs.org/en/download/package-manager/`.

Next, create a separate work directory and create a simple *hello world* `index.js` file as shown as follows:

```
# vi index.js
console.log('starting function')
exports.handle = function(e, ctx, cb) {
  console.log('processing event: %j', e)
  cb(null, { hello: 'world' })
}
```

To deploy the function using Claudia.js, type in the following command:

```
# claudia create --region us-east-1 --handler index.handle
```

Remember to name the `--handler` parameter correctly to match the `module.method` format. In this case, the `module` is `index` and the `method` is called `handle`.

At this point, Claudia.js will validate the code, upload the same to Lambda and create the associated IAM roles as well for execution. Once your code is uploaded successfully, you can invoke the same using just a single command as shown as follows:

```
# claudia test-lambda
```

```
[root@YoYoNUX claudia]#
[root@YoYoNUX claudia]# claudia test-lambda
{
  "StatusCode": 200,
  "Payload": "{\"hello\":\"world\"}"
}
```

With the deployment and invocation done, you can further make changes to your code and upload newer versions of the same with relative ease. To know more about the various command-line arguments, as well as the packaging options provided by Claudia.js, visit ht tps://claudiajs.com/documentation.html.

With this we come towards the end of this chapter. Let us look at a few best practices and tips to keep in mind when writing Lambda functions.

Recommendations and best practices

Following is a list of some of the recommendations and best practices to follow:

- **Optimize your code**: Writing syntactically correct Lambda functions is one thing and writing optimized functions is totally another. For example, it's always a good practice to initialize any external services like DynamoDB, SNS outside your function code. The reason for this is simple, each time Lambda starts your code, the underlying container starts up. At this point, the code outside the handler runs first (initialization). When subsequent function calls are invoked, Lambda reuses the same container to run your functions and as a result you save resources and time by not instantiating the external services again.
- **Versioning and aliases**: As discussed before, versioning and aliases are a very important set of tools that you should leverage when creating and promoting Lambda functions from one environment to another. As a best practice, you should look at tools such as Claudia.js or APEX that help you automate versioning and thus reduce on errors during deployments.

- **Environment variables**: Leverage environment variables to create reusable Lambda functions. Additionally, you can also encrypt the environment variables for an added layer of security for your functions using either your own keys or the KMS service.
- **Security**: So far we haven't launched any of our Lambda functions in our own VPCs and have opted to use the defacto VPC that AWS uses to host the functions, however, in production environments it is highly advised you launch your functions in your own VPCs.
- **Incorrect/missing IAM permissions**: Always make sure you follow the least privileges approach when creating and assigning IAM permissions and roles to your functions. Also as a best practice, enable AWS CloudTrail on your prod accounts to audit your Lambda functions and look for any unauthorized calls to sensitive AWS resources.
- **Allocating correct amount of resources**: Remember that Lambda pricing varies based on the timeout as well as the amount of RAM that you provide to your functions. You should also note that the memory that you provide to your functions also impact the overall function performance; including CPU and network as well. So more the memory, the higher the cost as well.
- **Monitoring functions**: Although Lambda functions are designed around the concept of fire and forget, it is very important that you monitor your function's execution at all times using either third-party tools, services, or even with CloudWatch Logs. Monitoring your functions helps you to effectively optimize your code as well as strategize your function's resource requirements which have a direct impact on the costs of overall executions.

Planning your next steps

With the chapter almost at the end, here are few key next steps that I feel are worth trying out before we jump over to the next chapter. Firstly, create your own Lambda functions and deploy them either by using APEX or Claudia.js. This will help you in understanding versioning and aliases a bit better along with added simplicity to deploying functions as we move along this book. Additionally, there are other deployment tools and services present out there such as `lambda-tools`, `gordon`, and serverless which we will be covering in the later chapters.

Next, with the programming model in mind, try out developing the Lambda functions with Java and Python as well. In fact, you can use APEX to deploy your functions with golang as well. You can read more about the steps here at `https://www.wolfe.id.au/2016/08/13/bo otstrap-an-apex-golang-project/`. More importantly, check out the performance that you obtain by running the same type of code with different languages. You can accordingly use the correct language for developing your functions as suited by your needs.

Summary

It has been a long yet awesome chapter to learn. So let us summarize what we have learnt so far. First up, we deep dived into the Lambda programming model and understood each of its sub components (handlers, context objects, errors and exceptions) with easy to follow examples. Next, we covered how to effectively write and develop functions using the concepts of versioning and aliases. Finally, we concluded the chapter by understanding the use of environment variables and also looked at a few essentials recommendations and best practices to keep in mind when writing Lambda functions.

In the next chapter we will be learning about the importance of testing your code along with some really useful testing tools and frameworks. So stick around, we are just starting out!

3
Testing Lambda Functions

In the previous chapter, we explored the basics of writing simple Lambda functions as well as diving deep into Lambda's unique programming model that comprised of modules such as the context object, logging methods, and how to handle exceptions and errors. We also learned a bit about the concepts and benefits of versioning as well as how to create reusable functions with the help of environment variables.

The following chapter is a continuation of the previous chapter where we take a step further from writing the Lambda functions and look at the various ways and techniques used to test them. The following topics are covered in this chapter:

- Understanding the need for testing your Lambda functions
- Getting started with simple test cases using Mocha and Chai
- Exploring Lambda test harness
- Implementing third-party tools for testing your Lambda functions locally

The need for testing Lambda function

If you are new to the world of testing or don't write test cases, then you may be thinking "Hey, I am here to write and develop Lambda functions, why do I even need to read this chapter, right?" Well, not so right. Testing is a very crucial part of any code development and should be enforced at all times. The reason is that, tests are an effective way of documenting your codebase and they can also act as a safeguarding mechanism which ensures that only code that is working as expected, and nothing else, is pushed into a production environment.

There are a variety of different tests that you can run on your code, however, for simplicity we can always refer the following *test pyramid* as a reference:

To know more about the test pyramid, check out this link `https://martin fowler.com/bliki/TestPyramid.html`.

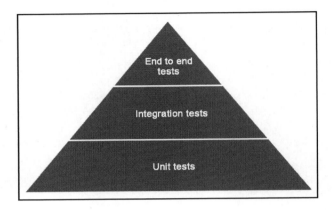

The following image depicts the three basic steps that you as a developer have to keep in mind when developing Lambda functions:

- **Unit Tests**: A unit test is a process in which you take the smallest piece of testable code from your application, isolate it from the remainder of the application, and subject it to a number of tests in order to verify it's proper operation. Each such piece of testable code is thus called as a **unit**.
- **Integration Tests**: As the name suggests, here many units effectively are combined and tested as a whole system. The main purpose of this testing is to expose any faults in the integration between multiple units.
- **End to End Tests**: These tests are conducted to ensure the flow of the application right from start to finish, check if they are behaving as expected and that data integrity is maintained between various systems and their components as well.

As a part of my experience, I have always gone ahead and created both unit tests as well as integration tests for my Lambda functions. The unit tests can be executed locally on the development system itself, as here we are simply testing the code's individual functionality and making sure each unit is working as expected. But, when it comes to integration testing, we generally have to deploy the function to AWS Lambda and then test its functionality as a whole.

Manually testing your functions with the AWS Management Console

We are definitely not new towards testing the functions manually using the AWS Management Console. Let us have a quick look at it once again before we go any further:

1. To test any of your functions manually, all you need to do is select the **Configure test event** option from the **Actions** drop-down list of your Lambda function. In this case, I'm using my trusty *Calculator* code example for this exercise (version: 2, alias: PROD).

2. In the **Input test event** dialog box, provide the test event as shown in the following screenshot. Remember, you can use either of these values as the operand **variable:** +, −, /, *, add, sub, mul, div.

3. Once you have provided the sample event, click on **Save and test**:

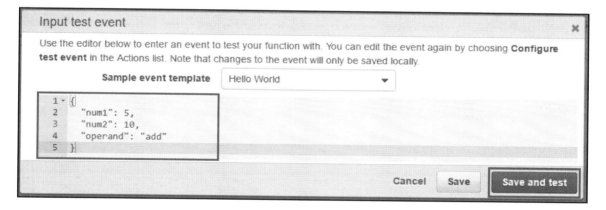

If all goes well, you should see the output of your function's execution in the **Execution result** area. Similarly, you can use the **Configure test event** option to simulate a variety of test events for your Lambda function ranging from simulated SNS messages to commits made to your repo in AWS CodeCommit and so on. This however, can become a very tedious and time consuming effort, especially when you have to develop various versions of the code, test it, run the code, and again repeat the entire cycle all over again. Fortunately for us, there are a few easier ways to test your functions even before you actually deploy them to Lambda. Let us take a look at how we can achieve this.

Testing functions with Mocha and Chai

The first step to creating a continuously deployable Lambda function is to write unit tests. One of the easiest and simplest ways to do so is by using a combination of two frameworks called **Mocha** and **Chai**.

First, a little bit about the two frameworks without going into too much information:

- **Mocha**: Mocha is a simple test framework for Node.js created to be easily extensible and fast for testing. It is used for unit and integration testing. You can read more about it at `https://mochajs.org/`.
  Mocha provides a unique ability to describe the features that we are implementing in our code by giving us a `describe` function that encapsulates our expectations:

  ```
  describe('myLambda',function(){
    //assertions about your code go here
  }
  ```

- **Chai**: Chai is a **Behaviour Driven Development (BDD)/ Test Driven Development (TDD)** assertion library for Node.js that works together with Mocha. You can read more about Chai here at `http://chaijs.com/guide/styles/`.
  Chai provides the following expressive assertion types that you can use to assert the behavior of the test result:
  - `assert`
  - `expect`
  - `should`
  - `difference`

For the purpose of this chapter, we will only concentrate on the `expect` interface. The `expect` interface uses simple chainable language to construct assertions, for example: `expect([1,2,3]).to.equal([1,2,3])`. Combining the `expect` assertion with the `describe` statement from Mocha looks something similar to the code snippet shown as follows:

```
describe('myLambda',function(){
    it('Check value returned from myLambda',function(){
    expect(retValue).to.equal('someValue');
}
```

Mocha has an assertion module of it's own, however I find Chai to be a little bit more flexible and extensible.

It is fairly simple and straightforward to setup Mocha and Chai on your development server. First up, create two folders; one to house the code that we are using and one to contain the test code:

```
# mkdir code
# mkdir test
```

Once this is done, install the Mocha framework and the Chai expectation library using the following commands:

```
# npm install mocha
# npm install chai
```

 You can optionally add the `--global` parameter to save the `npm` modules globally over your dev system.

With the necessary packages downloaded, we move on to the code part. Copy and paste the `calculator.js` file in the recently created `code` directory. Next, copy and paste the following code into the `test` directory:

```
# vi test/calculatorTest.js
var expect = require('chai').expect;
var myLambda = require('../lib/calculator');
var retError, retValue ;

describe('myLambda',function(){
  context('Positive Test Case', function(){
    before('Calling myLambda function', function(done){
      var event = {
        num1: 3,
        num2: 2,
        operand: "+"
      };
      var context= {
        functionName: "calculator"
      };
      myLambda.handler(event, context, function (err, value) {
        retError = err ;
        retValue = value ;
```

```
        done();
      });
    });
    it('Check that error is not returned from myLambda',function(){
      expect(retError).to.be.a('null');
    });
    it('Check value returned from myLambda',function(){
      expect(retValue).to.equal(5);
    });
  });
  context('Negative Test Case - Invalid Numbers', function(){
    before('Calling myLambda function', function(done){
      var event = {
        num1: "num",
        num2: 2,
        operand: "div"
      };
      var context= {
        functionName: "calculator"
      };
      myLambda.handler(event, context, function (err, value) {
        retError = err ;
        retValue = value ;
        done();
      });
    });
    it('Check that error is returned from myLambda',function(){
      //var retErrorString = retError.toString();
      expect(retError).to.equal("Invalid Numbers!");
    });
    it('Check value returned from myLambda is undefined',function(){
      expect(retValue).to.be.an('undefined');
    });
  });
  context('Negative Test Case - Zero Divisor', function(){
    before('Calling myLambda function', function(done){
      var event = {
        num1: 2,
        num2: 0,
        operand: "div"
      };
      var context= {
        functionName: "calculator"
      };
      myLambda.handler(event, context, function (err, value) {
        retError = err ;
        retValue = value ;
        done();
```

```
      });
    });
    it('Check that error is returned from myLambda',function(){
      //var retErrorString = retError.toString();
      expect(retError).to.equal("The divisor cannot be 0");
    });
    it('Check value returned from myLambda is undefined',function(){
      expect(retValue).to.be.an('undefined');
    });
  });
  context('Negative Test Case - Invalid Operand', function(){
    before('Calling myLambda function', function(done){
      var event = {
        num1: 2,
        num2: 0,
        operand: "="
      };
      var context= {
        functionName: "calculator"
      };
      myLambda.handler(event, context, function (err, value) {
        retError = err ;
        retValue = value ;
        done();
      });
    });
    it('Check that error is returned from myLambda',function(){
      //var retErrorString = retError.toString();
      expect(retError).to.equal("Invalid Operand");
    });
    it('Check value returned from myLambda is undefined',function(){
      expect(retValue).to.be.an('undefined');
    });
  });
});
```

Your final directory structure should resemble something like what is shown in the following screenshot:

```
ubuntu@ip-172-31-21-195:~/workdir$
ubuntu@ip-172-31-21-195:~/workdir$ tree -L 2
├── code
│   └── calculator.js
├── node_modules
│   ├── chai
│   └── mocha
└── test
    └── calculatorTest.js

5 directories, 2 files
ubuntu@ip-172-31-21-195:~/workdir$
```

With the setup all done, running your unit test on the calculator code is as easy as typing `mocha`!! Go ahead and execute the `mocha` command from your work directory. If all goes well, you should see a bunch of messages displayed on the screen, each taking about a particular test that was run against the `calculator.js` code. But where did all this come from? Let us look at it one step at a time.

First up, we wrote a bunch of unit test cases in the `calculatorTest.js` code using both Mocha and Chai.

The first couple of lines are to include the npm modules like Chai and the `calculator.js` code:

```
var expect = require('chai').expect;
var myLambda = require('../code/calculator');
var retError, retValue ;
```

Now, we will use the `describe` function of Mocha to describe the `myLambda` function. The `describe` function takes a simple string as its first argument and the second argument is a function while will represent the body of our expectations from the `myLambda` function:

```
describe('myLambda',function(){
```

Here we test the positive test case first. A *positive* test case is nothing more than providing the code with valid data to run.

Since `myLambda` is an asynchronous function and we need it to execute first before we can verify expect values, we use the `done` parameter with the before hook.

We define the `event` and `context` parameters and make a call to the `myLambda` function and calling done in its callback to let Mocha know that it can now move on to the expectations:

```
context('Positive Test Case', function(){
  before('Calling myLambda function', function(done){
    var event = {
      num1: 3,
      num2: 2,
      operand: "+"
    };
    var context= {
      functionName: "calculator"
    };
    myLambda.handler(event, context, function (err, value) {
      retError = err ;
      retValue = value ;
      done();
    });
  });
```

The output of this positive test block of unit test looks something like what is shown in the following screenshot:

```
myHandler
    Positive Test Case
Hello, Starting the Version 1 of testLambda Lambda Function
The event we pass will have two numbers and an operand value
Received event: {
  "num1": 3,
  "num2": 2,
  "operand": "+"
}
The Result is: 5
```

Here, we use the `expect` interface from the `chai` module and check our error and result values respectively:

```
    it('Check that error is not returned from myLambda',function(){
      expect(retError).to.be.a('null');
    });
    it('Check value returned from myLambda',function(){
      expect(retValue).to.equal(5);
    });
  });
```

Similarly, you can now add more assertions for positive and negative test cases as shown previously, changing the parameters with each test to ensure the `calculator.js` code works as expected.

Here is an example of a simple negative test case for our `calculator.js` code as well, we check how the code behaves if the values passed to it are non-numeric in nature (invalid data input):

```
context('Negative Test Case - Invalid Numbers', function(){
  before('Calling myLambda function', function(done){
    var event = {
      num1: "num",
      num2: 2,
      operand: "div"
    };
    var context= {
      functionName: "calculator"
    };
    myLambda.handler(event, context, function (err, value) {
      retError = err ;
      retValue = value ;
      done();
    });
  });
  it('Check that error is returned from myLambda',function(){
    //var retErrorString = retError.toString();
    expect(retError).to.equal("Invalid Numbers!");
  });
  it('Check value returned from myLambda is undefined',function(){
    expect(retValue).to.be.an('undefined');
  });
});
```

The following screenshot shows the output for the preceding code:

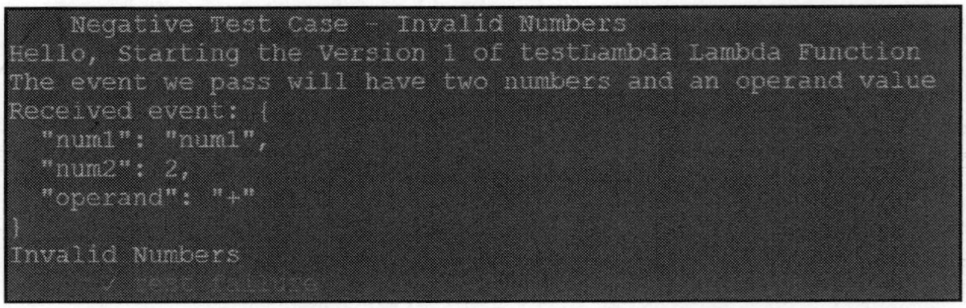

On similar lines, you can write and expand your own unit test cases to check and verify if the code is working as expected. Just do a few changes in the events and check the outcome!

Testing functions using the npm modules

There is a lot of testing that you can do with `mocha` and `chai`, however, with time, your test code becomes really long, complex, and difficult to manage. This can prove to be an issue, especially when it comes to adding newer functionality to your code and then requiring to retest it all over again.

That's one or more reasons why we now have a wide assortment of simpler, easier to use test frameworks that encapsulate a lot of the bulk validation code and help minimize the complexity of managing test cases. One such really interesting framework is provided as an npm module, so it makes it really easy to test Lambda functions that are written in Node.js and that module is called as `lambda-tester` created by Richard Hyatt.

The `lambda-tester` module is an open sourced, lightweight, and feature rich module that greatly simplifies writing and testing your Lambda functions. It is extremely easy to install and get started with.

I'll be comparing and demonstrating the `lambda-tester` module along with the `mocha` and `chai` example that we performed a while back so it's easier to see where `lambda-tester` brings it's uniqueness and flavor.

To install the `lambda-tester` npm module on your dev server, simply type the following command in your Terminal window:

```
# npm install lambda-tester
```

That's it! Simple, isn't it? Next, copy and paste the following code into a new file in your already existing `test` directory:

```
# vi test/calculatorLambdaTester.js

const LambdaTester = require( 'lambda-tester' );
var expect = require('chai').expect;
const myHandler = require( '../code/calculator' ).handler;

describe( 'myHandler', function() {
  context('Positive Test Case', function(){
    it( 'test success', function() {
      return LambdaTester( myHandler ).event( { num1: 3, num2: 2,
      operand: "+" } ).expectResult(function( result ) {
        expect( result ).to.equal( 5 );
```

```
              });
            });
          });
        context('Negative Test Case - Invalid Numbers', function(){
            it( 'test failure', function() {
              return LambdaTester( myHandler ).event( { num1: 'num1',
              num2: 2, operand: "+" } ).expectError(function( err ) {
                expect( err.message ).to.equal( 'Invalid Numbers!' );
              });
            });
          });
        context('Negative Test Case - Zero Divisor', function(){
            it( 'test failure', function() {
              return LambdaTester( myHandler ).event( { num1: 2, num2: 0,
              operand: "/" } ).expectError(function( err ) {
                expect( err.message ).to.equal( 'The divisor cannot be 0' );
              });
            });
          });
        context('Negative Test Case - Invalid Operand', function(){
            it( 'test failure', function() {
              return LambdaTester( myHandler ).event( { num1: 2, num2: 0,
              operand: "=" } ).expectError(function( err ) {
                expect( err.message ).to.equal( 'Invalid Operand' );
              });
            });
          });
        });
      });
```

If all goes well, your folder structure should look a bit like the following structure:

```
ubuntu@ip-172-31-21-195:~/workdir$ tree -L 2
├── code
│   └── calculator.js
├── node_modules
│   ├── chai
│   ├── lambda-tester
│   └── mocha
└── test
    ├── calculatorLambdaTester.js
    └── calculatorTest.js

6 directories, 3 files
```

To run the test, simply type in the following command as shown:

```
# mocha test
```

The output of this execution will be very similar to the one we got from our earlier mocha and chai test run, however, there's still a good amount of difference between the two approaches. Let us understand the code a bit better and compare it with the traditional approach of mocha and chai:

First up, is the declarative section which remains more or less same as the earlier test example:

```
const LambdaTester = require( 'lambda-tester' );
var expect = require('chai').expect;
const myHandler = require( '../code/calculator' ).handler;
```

Just like before, we describe myHandler function. Inside the it function we use lambda-tester module. This case simply verifies that the handler was called successfully that is, callback (null, result).

 I is important to return lambda-tester to the framework as lambda-tester is asynchronous in nature and it uses promises.

Notice that, while calling the myHandler function, we send the event we want to test it with and then use expectResult function where we use the expect from chai. The expectResult function is used when we are expecting a successful execution that is callback (null, result):

```
describe( 'myHandler', function() {
  context('Positive Test Case', function(){
    it( 'test success', function() {
      return LambdaTester( myHandler ).event( { num1: 3, num2: 2,
      operand: "+" } ).expectResult(function( result ) {
        expect( result ).to.equal( 5 );
      });
    });
  });
});
```

The following screenshot shows the output of the preceding code:

```
ubuntu@ip-172-31-21-135:~/workdir$ mocha test

  myHandler
    Positive Test Case
Hello, Starting the Version 1 of testLambda Lambda Function
The event we pass will have two numbers and an operand value
Received event: {
  "num1": 3,
  "num2": 2,
  "operand": "+"
}
The Result is: 5
```

Similarly, here is the case where we test our negative test case, where the handler calls the callback (err). In the event of a failure we use expectError in lambda-tester:

```
context('Negative Test Case - Invalid Numbers', function(){
  it( 'test failure', function() {
    return LambdaTester( myHandler ).event( { num1: 'num1', num2: 2,
    operand: "+" } ).expectError(function( err ) {
      expect( err.message ).to.equal( 'Invalid Numbers!' );
    });
  });
});
```

The following screenshot shows the output for the preceding code:

```
    Negative Test Case - Invalid Numbers
Hello, Starting the Version 1 of testLambda Lambda Function
The event we pass will have two numbers and an operand value
Received event: {
  "num1": "num1",
  "num2": 2,
  "operand": "+"
}
Invalid Numbers
    ✓ test failure
```

Similarly, we can go ahead and test the rest of the functionality as we did with mocha and chai. The main difference, however, is that the calculator test code with Mocha and Chai was 119 lines long whereas the same test cases code using lambda-tester is just 58 lines long! That's really impressive considering your code is now much cleaner and easier to test as well.

Testing with a simple serverless test harness

So far we have seen how simple and easy it becomes to test your Lambda functions out locally, right? But what happens once those Lambda functions are deployed on the cloud? How do you test those out? Don't worry, that's where Lambda can help out as well!

Our good folks at AWS have also provided us with a simple, customizable, and easy to use test harness function blueprint that in essence invokes unit test cases over other Lambda functions that are being tested, and stores the results of the tests in either DynamoDB, Kinesis or even S3 for that matter. The best part of this entire test harness is that you don't even bother about any of the underlying infrastructure, whether it's creating new resources for testing or shutting them down once the testing is over! It's all taken care by lambda itself!

Itching to give it a go? Let's get on with it then:

1. Login to the AWS Management Console and select **AWS Lambda** from the dashboard.
2. Select the **Create a Lambda function** option, as done in our earlier chapter.
3. From the **Select blueprint** page, select the `lambda-test-harness` blueprint. You can filter the blueprint using the **Filter** option as well.
4. The `lambda-test-harness` blueprint doesn't require any external triggers to be configured, so we will simply skip the **Configure triggers** page. Click **Next** to proceed.
5. Provide a suitable **Name** for your function.
6. Next, scroll down to the **Lambda function handler and role** section. Here, you will already have a predefined **Policy templates** already selected out for your function. Simply provide a suitable **Role name*** for the function as shown in the following screenshot:

7. Leave the rest of the values to their defaults and click on **Next** to proceed.
8. In the **Review** page, click the **Create function** once done.

With this step, the test harness is up and ready for use, but before we go ahead with the actual testing, we first need to create a really simple DynamoDB table that will store the results of the unit test cases.

The DynamoDB table will require just two attributes and a minimal of five read and write capacity for now:

- `testId` (string): Primary partition key
- `iteration` (number): Primary sort key

With the basics done, let us go ahead and test some functions with the test harness. The test harness comes in two execution modes, unit and load, which, as the names suggest, switch between unit testing and load testing of your Lambda functions. Let us examine the unit testing up first.

To unit test your Lambda function, you need to pass the following information to the test harness:

```
{
  "operation": "unit",
  "function": <Name/ ARN of the Lambda function under test>,
  "resultsTable": <DynamoDB table name that will store results>,
  "testId": <Some test identification>,
  "event": {<The event we want to pass to the function under test>}
}
```

Let us take a quick example to see how this works out. We had created our trusty `calculator.js` code and published it to Lambda back in `Chapter 2`, *Writing Lambda Functions* so I'm just going to reuse that itself and we will fire a few simple unit tests to make sure the code works as expected.

First up, from the test harness function's page, select the option **Configure test event** from the **Actions** drop-down list.

Next, in the **Input test event** section, provide the ARN of your calculator function as shown in the following code:

```
{
  "operation": "unit",
  "function": "arn:aws:lambda:us-east-1:01234567890:
    function:myCalculatorFunction:PROD",
  "resultsTable": "unit-test-results",
```

```
    "iteration": 1,
    "testId": "MyFirstRun1",
    "event": {
      "num1": 3,
      "num2": 7,
      "operand": "add"
    }
  }
```

Once done, click on the **Save and test** option. The test harness function invokes the calculator function and passes the test events to it. The output is then recorded to the DynamoDB table that we had created earlier:

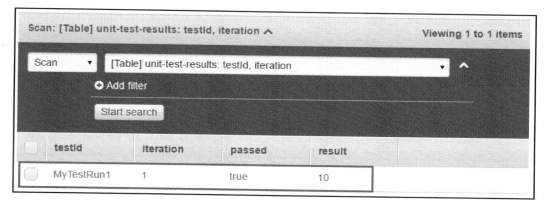

You can now play around with the test harness event and modify your test scenarios accordingly. For example, changing the iteration value to 5 or more to run the same test multiple number of times, or even changing the event values to make sure the calculator function is operating as expected, for example, passing the following event values will trigger the **Divisor cannot be zero** error, and so on.

```
    "event": {
      "num1": 8,
      "num2": 0,
      "operand": "div"
    }
```

You can alternatively run load tests as well using the same test harness function blueprint. The fundamentals stay the same once again with just a few minor exceptions. The first being the `operation` parameter now changes from `unit` to `load`; however, in the event section, we pass the same unit test case that we want to load test this time. What this will result in is a fleet of 10 functions executing the particular load test in parallel:

```
{
  "operation": "load",
  "iterations": 10,
  "function": "lambda_test_harness",
  "event": {
    "operation": "unit",
    "function": "arn:aws:lambda:us-east-1:01234567890:
      function:myCalculatorFunction:PROD",
    "resultsTable": "unit-test-results",
    "testId": "MyTestRun2",
    "event": {
      "num1": 8,
      "num2": 12,
      "operand": "+"
    }
  }
}
```

With the test completed, you can verify the load test output from the DynamoDB table as shown in the following screenshot:

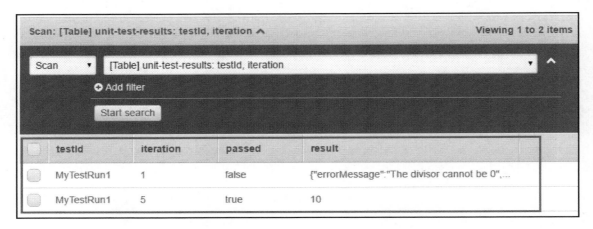

You can use this same functionality to load test your AWS API Gateways by simulating either POST or GET operations on the API Gateway endpoint. To learn more, visit `https ://aws.amazon.com/blogs/compute/serverless-testing-with-aws-lambda/`.

 Remember to clean up the DynamoDB table once your tests are all done.

Recommendations and best practices

Here a few common best practices and set of recommendations that you should always keep in mind when it comes to testing Lambda functions:

- **Don't take testing lightly**: Don't take testing your Lambda functions for granted. Make sure you start with unit testing of your functions and then even perform the integration tests to make sure all the components work together as expected. In some cases, you may even want to run.

- **Perform comprehensive unit testing**: Always ensure that each unit test should be able to run independent of other unit tests. Also remember to test each condition of the code one at a time, but test it individually multiple times to ensure that the same result comes up no matter how many times it is executed.

- **Maintaining logical separation**: It is always advised to keep the function's business logic separated from Lambda's own declarations. This makes the code much more reusable and even easier to test.

- **Testing functions locally**: There are a variety of tools and npm modules that you can use for testing your functions locally. It is always a good practice to test your code out first locally as much as possible to avoid any errors during deployment and actual runtime.

- **Log everything**: Make sure that, when you are developing or testing your Lambda functions, you log every action that is performed by the code. It is understood that logging has an impact over your code's performance, however, logging during development and QA stages is crucial.

Planning your next steps

Although we are predominantly talking and discussing about Node.js throughout this book, the concepts and terminologies still apply to the other supported languages as well. For example, running unit and integration tests on your Java function code using JUnit, running simulated load tests with Apache JMeter, and so on. Make sure you try it out.

There are also ways in which you can completely automate the build, test, and deployment of your functions using a **continuous integration and continuous deployment (CICD)** pipeline. This involves using tools such as subversion or Git with a continuous integration tool or an automation server such as Jenkins. The flow is pretty straightforward. Whenever a developer commits code into Git, it triggers a Jenkins job workflow that runs a bunch of predefined unit tests across the code. If the code passes the tests, then another Jenkins job can simply package the code and deploy it out to Lambda with a new version as well.

To learn more about how to integrate Jenkins and Lambda, you can visit the AWS Lambda plugin page provided here at `https://wiki.jenkins-ci.org/display/JENKINS/AWS+Lamb da+Plugin`. Additionally, AWS has a really cool blog that you can check out too to get some understanding on how you could setup a simple CICD for Lambda functions using Jenkins and Grunt: `https://aws.amazon.com/blogs/compute/continuous-integration-deploym ent-for-aws-lambda-functions-with-jenkins-and-grunt-part-2/`

Last, but not least; for all the IDE lovers out there, AWS provides a really good plugin/ toolkit for integrating AWS SDKs with Eclipse IDE. This comes in really handy when you are developing a lot of Java-based Lambda functions and you need to test and deploy them remotely. There is a really detailed guide provided by AWS themselves that you can give a try as well at `http://docs.aws.amazon.com/toolkit-for-eclipse/v1/user-guide//lam bda.html`.

Summary

So, once again, we come towards the end of yet another interesting chapter! In this chapter, we learnt a bit about the importance of testing and why you should fall into a habit of testing your functions regularly. We also learned about the various ways in which we can effectively test our functions, either by using a combination of testing frameworks such as Mocha and Chai or by leveraging some more recent and way simpler npm modules such as the `lambda-tester` module. We also saw how a Lambda function could potentially be used as a test harness and perform both unit as well as load tests on other Lambda functions with the help of the Lambda test harness blueprint. Towards the end, we topped it all off with a pinch of recommendations, best practices and few worthy next steps as well.

In the next chapter, we will be diving a bit further into the amazing world of Lambda and exploring one of it's biggest advantages over standard computing instances: the event driven model! So, don't go anywhere, we are just getting started!

4
Event-Driven Model

So far, we have learned a thing or two about serverless and AWS Lambda. We started off by understanding the entire concept behind serverless architecture and, later, dived into the amazing world of serverless computing with AWS Lambda. We learned how to effectively write, develop, package, and test Lambda functions and also picked up on a few best practices and recommendations along the way.

From this chapter onwards, we will be taking a slightly different approach to understand how few core functionalities of Lambda actually work. For example, how do you trigger Lambda functions to execute based on a trigger? That's exactly what this chapter is going to be all about. In this chapter, we will be covering the following topics:

- What event-driven model is all about
- Understanding the event-driven model of Lambda along with a few simple event-driven architectures for better understanding
- Getting started with simple event-driven use cases of Lambda that range from basic data manipulations to automated infrastructure management and so on

So, without any more delay, let's get started!

Introducing event-driven architectures

Till now we have been working and understanding Lambda using our trusty calculator example code, that simply accepts few parameters and values as inputs, and, when run, provides you with some desired output. What you may not have noticed is that the inputs that we were providing for the code to run were actually part of an event, that would trigger the code into running. Similarly, you can write Lambda functions that get activated or triggered when a particular message or event is generated. This is perhaps one of the biggest reasons why I love Lambda so much and why Lambda is so much better than your traditional EC2 instances! But, before we begin exploring the various triggers and events that Lambda can respond to, let us understand what Event Driven architectures are all about and how are they so useful.

Event-driven architecture (EDA) is basically a software architecture pattern that deals with the generation, detection, consumption, and reaction to one or more events. Events can be anything; from simple messages, notification calls, to state changes. In our AWS Lambda case, events can be something such as an object getting uploaded to an S3 bucket or a row getting deleted from a DynamoDB table and so on.

An event-driven architecture in general comprises of three essential pieces: an event emitter, an event channel, and an event consumer. In simpler terms, the entire process flow looks a bit like the following image:

The event emitters are responsible for gathering state changes or events that occur within the event-driven system. They simply get the event and send it to the next step of the process which is the event channel. Here, the channels serve two purposes; one is to simply channel or funnel the event to a particular waiting consumer where the event will be processed and acted upon. Alternatively, the channel itself can react to the event, and perform some level of pre-processing on the event and then send it down to the consumers for the final processing as represented earlier.

Now, keeping these basics in mind, let us look at how AWS Lambda enables event-driven architecture along with a few easy to understand use cases as well.

Understanding events and AWS Lambda

Lambda works in a very similar way, as explained in the previous section. For instance, the emitters and channels act as the Lambda event source while the functions that we have been creating all this time act as the event consumers.

All in all, when an event is triggered by a particular AWS service, or even from an external source such as an application, that event gets mapped to a particular Lambda function which in turn, executes an action based on the code that you have written for it. This one-to-one mapping of events with their corresponding Lambda functions is what we call as **Event Source Mapping** and it is responsible for the automatic invocation of your Lambda functions whenever an event is fired.

There are two main categories of event sources supported by Lambda:

- **AWS services:** Lambda supports a few of AWS's services as preconfigured event sources that you can use to develop easy event-driven systems with. Few of the services namely S3, SNS, SES, Cognito, CloudFromation, CloudWatch fall under a branch relatively termed as regular AWS services; whereas DynamoDB and Kinesis fall under something called as stream based services as in both these cases, Lambda polls the streams for any updates and when it does find one, it triggers the corresponding function to run. In this chapter, we will be looking at few of the commonly used AWS services used as event mappings and how you can leverage them to perform simple tasks for your cloud environment.
- **Custom applications**: Custom applications are your own home grown applications or external world entities that can generate their own events. This can be anything from a simple web based application or even mobile device.

Before we actually begin with the event mapping examples and use cases, let us quickly glance through some of the architecture patterns and use cases where Lambda's event mapping system comes into play.

Lambda architecture patterns

In this section, we will be looking at some of the commonly used Lambda architecture patterns that you can use as blueprints for building your own serverless and event based applications.

- **Serverless microservices**: Microservices are designed and developed to be independent and self-sufficient, which is exactly why they are an amazing candidate for running with the help of Lambda. A Lambda function too, in its own is an independent code that can execute for a finite time when triggered by an external source. The only downside here is that, because of the deep granularity, the sheer number of microservices and the corresponding Lambda functions that you will end up with will be really high. Managing that many functions can be a challenge especially when you need to do changes, new deployments and so on.

In the following depiction, we can see a number of Lambda functions hosting microservices frontended by an API Gateway and having one or more databases as backends.

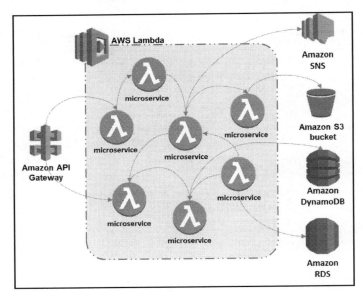

- **Serverless multi-tier applications**: Perhaps one of the most commonly used architecture patterns, Lambda is an ideal platform to host the business logic of your applications. With the presentation logic handled in S3 in the form of static website hosting, and the backend taken care of by a variety of database services ranging from DynamoDB, RDS to ElastiCache; Lambda is the perfect service to run the logic of your applications as shown in the image below:

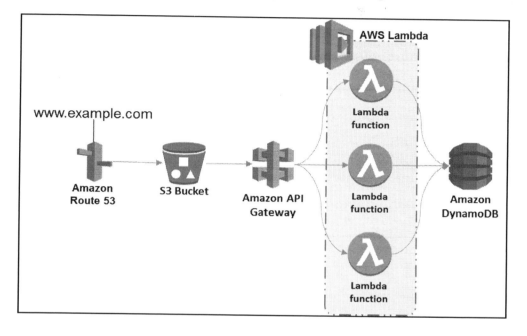

- **Real-time stream processing**: When we talk about streams and AWS, only one word comes to our mind and that is Kinesis. AWS Kinesis is a powerful and scalable solution that enables you to design and develop applications that can process as well as analyze large quantities of streaming data. Mix that with Lambda and you have yourselves a variety of use cases where this design becomes applicable such as transactions processing, log analysis, social media analytics, and much more!

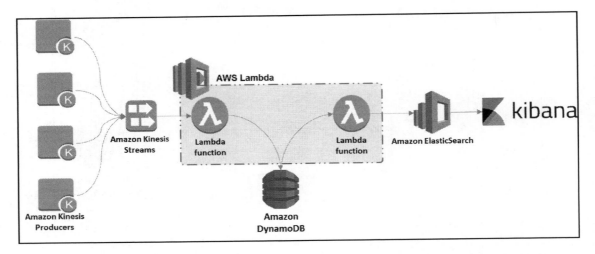

- **Backend services for mobile or IoT**: AWS Lambda can also be used to develop and support complete backend services for your IoT as well as mobile applications. You can use this pattern in conjunction with AWS API Gateway to create a REST API that invokes Lambda functions which in turn, performs some CRUD operations over data residing in DynamoDB or can even push notification messages to other users or systems using SNS as well.

With the architectural patterns done and dusted, let us move on to some seriously fun things by exploring some easy to use and practical event mapping examples!

Exploring Lambda and event mapping

We have already seen and learned a bit about how Lambda uses a notion called event mapping to map a particular AWS service to a corresponding Lambda function. In this section, we will be diving a bit further into event mapping with the help of some interesting real world use cases that most of you would find useful in your own AWS environments.

Mapping Lambda with S3

You can easily write and invoke Lambda functions for processing objects stored in an S3 bucket. The functions can be triggered using a set of notification configurations which trigger a corresponding Lambda function into action. The following is a list of few such notification configurations that can be used for triggering functions on S3 buckets:

- When an object is created in a bucket using either `put`, `post`, `copy` or a `completemultipartupload` operation
- When an object is deleted from a bucket using the `delete` operation
- When a bucket set with `ReducedRedundancy` storage option loses an object

How does it all work? Quite simple actually. When we first configure the event source mapping for a particular S3 bucket, we initially set the event source mapping of the bucket with it's corresponding Lambda function using the notification configuration we just talked about. Next, S3 begins to monitor the bucket for the particular event to be triggered. When the event is triggered, the corresponding notification configuration is activated which in turn invokes the assigned Lambda function.

Let us now look at a simple example of event source mapping between S3 and Lambda. In this scenario, we are going to simulate a simple image transformation example that gets triggered when a new object (image file) is uploaded or created in a particular S3 bucket (source bucket). This action, in turn, triggers a Lambda function that will first download the image from S3, transform it either to a grayscale, a negative image or a transparent image followed by uploading the new image into another S3 bucket (destination bucket).

This use case can be applied when you are hosting a simple website that runs some form of transformation techniques on images uploaded to it such as grayscale, creating thumbnail images and so on.

First up, let us explore the setup for this particular use case. We'll be using APEX to deploy the functions over to Lambda and I highly recommend you try out the same, although you could upload the following code snippets manually as well.

On my development server, I have already gone ahead and installed APEX.

 NOTE: You can read about installing and configuring APEX at `http://apex.run/`.

With APEX installed and set, you will now need to create a folder directory to work out of.

I have created a simple folder structure that makes it easy to work out APEX. You could follow a similar approach, or even try out something that suites your needs.

The folder structure I have for this use and other use cases to follow, looks something like this:

- `apex`: A primary working directory.
- `event_driven`: This is my project directory that will contain a `project.dev.json` (explained below) file.
- `functions`: This directory will contain all your Lambda functions that you are going to deploy for this chapter. The functions directory will have multiple sub folders, each one containing a master folder for our use cases. Since this is the first use case that we are performing, the only sub folder present in the functions directory is `myS3ToLambdaFunc`.
- Within the `myS3ToLambdaFunc` directory is where we will place the `index.js` (function code) and a `function.dev.json` file along with the `node_modules` directory as well:
    - `index.js`
    - `function.dev.json`
    - `node_modules/`

If the node modules directory is not present, simply copy and paste the `index.js` code and run the following command to install the necessary dependencies for the code to run:

```
# npm install async gm
```

The `index.js` file contains the actual Lambda function which will do the work of image transformation on the image that gets uploaded to a specified S3 bucket.

Here are a few key snippets of code for your understanding:

```
// dependencies
var async = require('async');
var AWS = require('aws-sdk');
var gm = require('gm')
          .subClass({ imageMagick: true });
```

The code starts off by declaring a few necessary variables, noticeably the `async Node.js` module and the `ImageMagick` module which is actually provided with the image transformation functions.

```
var transformFunc = process.env.TRANSFORM_FUNC;
```

In this example, we are setting the values of the image transformation function using Lambda's environment variables. You can select either `gray`, `negative`, or `transparent` based on your requirements.

```
exports.handler = function(event, context, callback) {
    // Read options from the event.
    console.log("Reading options from event:\n",
     util.inspect(event, {depth: 5}));
    var srcBucket = event.Records[0].s3.bucket.name;
    // Object key may have spaces or unicode non-ASCII characters.
    var srcKey = decodeURIComponent(event.Records[0].s3.object.key
     .replace(/\+/g, " "));
    var dstBucket = srcBucket + "-output";
    var dstKey    = "output-" + srcKey;
```

Here, we declare the handler function which Lambda invokes for execution. Our handler function will perform the following steps: download the image from S3 into a buffer, transform that image into the selected option (taken from the env variable), and then upload the image in the destination S3 bucket.

```
async.waterfall([
    function download(next) {
        // Download the image from S3 into a buffer.
        s3.getObject({
            Bucket: srcBucket,
            Key: srcKey
        },
        next);
    },
```

This is the transformation function which either generates a `gray`, `negative`, or `transparent` version of the uploaded image. A simple switch case will suffice.

```
function transform(response, next) {
        console.log("Here we have three option
         - negative, transparent and gray");
        console.log("Currently we have got the option of "
         + transformFunc+".");
        switch(transformFunc) {
            case "negative":
                gm(response.Body).negative()
```

```
            .toBuffer(imageType, function(err, buffer) {
                if (err) {
                    next(err);
                } else {
                    next(null, response.ContentType,
                     buffer);
                }
            });
        break;
```

You can find the complete code for this use case along with the other necessary files here: ht
tps://github.com/PacktPublishing/Mastering-AWS-Lambda

Your final folder structure should resemble something as shown:

Let us examine a few of the important files related with APEX as well as the function
deployment before moving on to the actual deployment process. First up is the
project.dev.json file. The file basically is a descriptor for your event_driven project
directory:

```
{
  "name": "eventDriven",
  "description": "event-driven use cases using pre-configured
    triggers",
  "profile": "example",
  "runtime": "nodejs4.3",
  "memory": 128,
  "timeout": 60,
  "role": "arn:aws:iam::<account-id>:role/myApexLambdaProjRole",
  "environment": {}
}
```

Here, you can set and modify default values that will be passed to your functions at runtime. For example, setting the default memory utilization, timeouts, as well as the role that Lambda functions will need to assume in order to get executed on your behalf. Here is a simple and minimalistic snippet of the `myApexLambdaProjRole` that we have used in this use case. Note that, in most cases, you will have to setup this role manually as APEX doesn't yet automate this for you. This proves yet another point: that there is a serious gap when it comes to Serverless Frameworks and tooling. For now, you could either do this manually or even use some automated deployment tool such as Terraform or Ansible to configure out this for you.

```
{
    "Version": "2012-10-17",
    "Statement": [
        {
            "Sid": "myLogsPermissions",
            "Effect": "Allow",
            "Action": [
                "logs:CreateLogGroup",
                "logs:CreateLogStream",
                "logs:PutLogEvents"
            ],
            "Resource": [
                "*"
            ]
        }
    ]
}
```

Now, the important point to note here is that, the `project.dev.json` file works at your project level, but what about my individual functions? That's where we have the `function.dev.json` file as described below. The `function.dev.json` file works very similarly to the `project.dev.json` file with the slight difference that here we pass the function's handler information along with the necessary information such as the environment variables that we need to pass to the function at runtime and the specific role required to run it.

```
{
    "description": "Node.js lambda function using S3 as a trigger to transform the uploaded image and then upload the new image in S3",
    "role": "arn:aws:iam::<account-id>:role/myLambdaS3FuncRole",
    "handler": "index.handler",
    "environment": {
        "TRANSFORM_FUNC" : "negative"
    }
}
```

In the `function.dev.json` case, we also need to create and assign a role that is going to be required by S3 to get and put objects along with write logs to Amazon CloudWatch. This task too could be automated using the likes of Terraform or Ansible or you could even do it out manually. The following is a snippet of the `function.dev.role` that you can use and modify according to your own needs:

```
{
    "Version": "2012-10-17",
    "Statement": [
        {
            "Sid": "myLogsPermissions",
            "Effect": "Allow",
            "Action": [
                "logs:CreateLogGroup",
                "logs:CreateLogStream",
                "logs:PutLogEvents"
            ],
            "Resource": "arn:aws:logs:*:*:*"
        },
        {
            "Sid": "myS3Permissions",
            "Effect": "Allow",
            "Action": [
                "s3:GetObject",
                "s3:PutObject"
            ],
            "Resource": "arn:aws:s3:::*"
        }
    ]
}
```

Phew, that was a lot to digest, but I am sure with a few rounds of practice you will get to assigning and working with roles in no time. Now, for the fun part! We deploy the function as a package to Lambda using APEX. To do so, simply type in the following command as shown:

```
# apex --env dev deploy myS3ToLambdaFunc
```

 You will need to run this command from the `project` directory.

With the deployment underway, you should see an output similar to the one shown below. Do note however that, with each deployment, APEX will automatically create a new version of your function just as it has done in my case (*version 2*)

```
ubuntu@ip-172-31-21-195:~/workdir/apex/event_driven$
ubuntu@ip-172-31-21-195:~/workdir/apex/event_driven$ apex deploy --env dev myS3ToLambdaFunc
   • creating function       env=dev function=myS3ToLambdaFunc
   • created alias current   env=dev function=myS3ToLambdaFunc version=1
   • function created        env=dev function=myS3ToLambdaFunc name=eventDriven_myS3ToLambdaFunc version=1
ubuntu@ip-172-31-21-195:~/workdir/apex/event_driven$
ubuntu@ip-172-31-21-195:~/workdir/apex/event_driven$
```

With the function deployed, the only thing left to do is configure the trigger mechanism out. To do this, you can login to the AWS Management Console or even use the AWS CLI or use Terraform to automate the process. We will use the simplest way to demonstrate the ease with which triggers can be created and set. First up, login to the AWS Management Console and Lambda service from the main landing page.

You should see your function already deployed out there. Select the function and click on the **Triggers** option as shown:

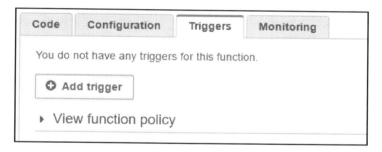

To create a new trigger, click on the **Add trigger** option. This will pop up an easy to use dialog box using which you can map a S3 bucket with your Lambda function.

Select the empty box adjacent to the Lambda function and from the drop down list provided and filter out **S3** as shown below. Select **S3** to view its corresponding event mapping properties:

- **Bucket name:** The bucket for which you wish to enable the trigger. In my case, I have already created a simple bucket with the name **image-processing-01**.
- **Event type:** From the dropdown, select the appropriate event for which you want to trigger the Lambda function. According to our use case, we want the function to run each time a new object/ image is uploaded to the S3 bucket. Hence, select the **Object Created (All)** option as shown as follows:

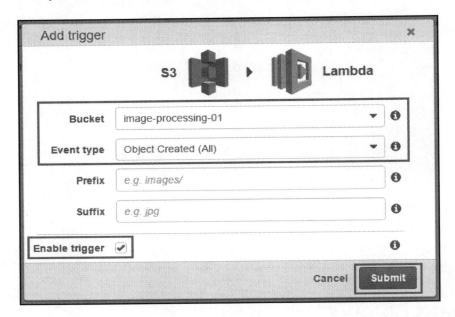

Leave the rest of the values to their defaults, but remember to check the **Enable trigger** option to yes before clicking on **Submit**. Your function is now mapped with the S3 bucket! It's that simple! With the trigger set, it's time to generate some events! In this case, simply upload an image (.jpg or .png) and watch the magic unfold. Depending on what was set in the function's environment variables during deployment (by default, its *negative*), the uploaded image will get transformed accordingly.

Go ahead and change the environment variable in the `function.dev.json` file from *negative* to *gray* to *transparent* and check the output in the S3 bucket that will be marked with the `*output*` keyword. Remember to deploy the updated functions using the same APEX command as done before. APEX will automatically handle the package uploads and the versioning for you! Here is a sample of an image I uploaded:

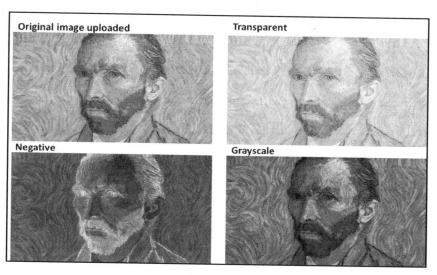

You can alternatively view the execution logs of your function using Amazon CloudWatch Logs.

Mapping Lambda with DynamoDB

Now that we've got a feel of mapping Lambda events with S3, let us give yet another service a go! This time its DynamoDB!

You can trigger Lambda functions in response to updates made to a particular DynamoDB table; for example, a new row that gets added in a table gets validated by a Lambda function, a row deletion operation resulting in Lambda sending a notification to a user, and so on. But, before you go ahead and implement triggers for DynamoDB, its important to note that, unlike S3, DynamoDB is a stream-based event source, which means that you first need to enable streams on your DynamoDB table before you create and map functions to it. Lambda actually polls the particular stream for events and when it finds one, it invokes the corresponding function mapped to it.

In the following use case, we shall see how to use a Lambda function to check a particular data column in the table for a pattern. If the pattern is invalid, the function should delete the entire data row, or else ignore it. Once again, I will be using APEX to deploy my functions, so first we need to get the folder directory all setup. Since we already have a work directory, and a project directory created, we will just go ahead and create a simple folder for this particular use case under the following folder structure:

```
# mkdir ~/workdir/apex/event_driven/functions/myDynamoToLambdaFunc
```

With the directory created, we only need to create a function.dev.json and index.js files here as well. Remember, the function.dev.json file is unique to each use case so in this case, the file will contain the following set of instructions:

```json
{
    "description": "Node.js lambda function using DynamoDB as a trigger to
validate the value of the inserted IP address and deletes it if it's
invalid.",
    "role": "arn:aws:iam::<account-id>:role/myLambdaDynamoFuncRole",
    "handler": "index.handler",
    "environment": {}
}
```

Once again, the code is self-explanatory. We once again have to create a corresponding IAM role to allow our Lambda function to interact and poll the DynamoDB table on our behalf. This includes providing Lambda with the necessary permissions to describe and list DynamoDB streams as well as get records from the table itself.

```json
{
  "Version": "2012-10-17",
  "Statement": [
  {
    "Sid": "myDynamodbPermissions",
    "Effect": "Allow",
    "Action": [
      "dynamodb:DescribeStream",
      "dynamodb:GetRecords",
      "dynamodb:GetShardIterator",
      "dynamodb:ListStreams",
      "dynamodb:DeleteItem"
    ],
    "Resource":
    [
      "arn:aws:dynamodb:us-east-1:<account-id>:table/LambdaTriggerDB*"
    ]
  },
  {
    "Sid": "myLogsPermissions",
```

```
    "Effect": "Allow",
    "Action": [
      "logs:CreateLogGroup",
      "logs:CreateLogStream",
      "logs:PutLogEvents"
    ],
    "Resource": "arn:aws:logs:*:*:*"
  }
  ]
}
```

With the configurations of the function out of way, let us now have a quick look at the function code itself:

```
function isValidIPAddress(ipAddr, cb){
  if(/^(25[0-5]|2[0-4][0-9]|[01]?[0-9][0-9]?)\.(25[0-5]|2[0-4][0-9]|
  [01]?[0-9][0-9]?)\.(25[0-5]|2[0-4][0-9]|[01]?[0-9][0-9]?)\
  .(25[0-5]|2[0-4][0-9]|[01]?[0-9][0-9]?)$/.test(ipAddr)){
    cb(null, "Valid IPv4 Address");
  }
  else{
    cb("Invalid");
  }
}
```

The following code snippet simply checks and validates whether a supplied IP address is a valid or an invalid IP address. We have used a regex expression to do the check.

```
exports.handler = (event, context, callback) => {
  var ipAddr, eventName;
  var tableName = "LambdaTriggerDB";
  event.Records.forEach((record) => {
    eventName = record.eventName;
    console.log("Event: "+eventName);
    switch(eventName){
      case "MODIFY":
      case "INSERT":
        ipAddr = record.dynamodb.Keys.IP_ADDRESS.S;
```

Here, we check the eventName that is, MODIFY, INSERT, or REMOVE, to decide the different execution paths. For Modify and Insert events, we will check for the validity of the IP address and if it's invalid then delete that particular record from the DynamoDB table. In case of a remove event, we don't want to do anything.

We have used a simple switch case to achieve this task.

You can find the complete code along with all the necessary config files for your reference here: `https://github.com/PacktPublishing/Mastering-AWS-Lambda`.

We will once again use APEX to deploy our function to Lambda. To do so, we execute the APEX deploy command from the project level directory as shown below:

```
# apex --env dev deploy myDynamoToLambdaFunc
```

With your function successfully packaged and deployed, you can now create the DynamoDB table and the associated Lambda trigger as well. The table creation is a straight forward process. Select the **DynamoDB** option from the AWS Management Console. Click on **Create new table** and fill out the necessary information as shown in the image below. Make sure to provide the same table name as provided in your Lambda IAM role. For the **Primary key**, type in IP_ADDRESS and select the attribute as **String**. Click on **Create** once done.

 Make sure the DynamoDB table and the lambda function reside in the same region

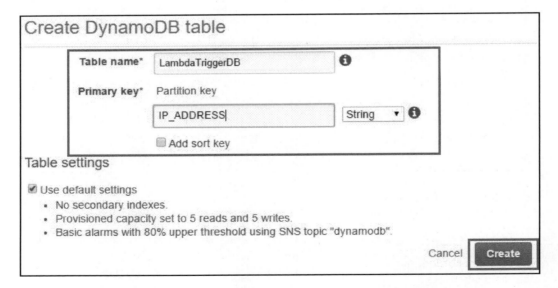

Once the table is copied, make sure to copy the table's stream ARN. The stream ARN will be required in the next steps when we map the table stream with our deployed Lambda function.

To configure the function's trigger, select the newly created function from Lambda's dashboard. Next, select the **Triggers** option to configure the event mapping. Click on the blank box adjacent to the Lambda function and choose the option **DynamoDB** as shown. Fill in the required details as described below:

- **DynamoDB table**: From the drop down list, select the stream enabled table that we just created a while back.
- **Batch size:** Provide a suitable value for the batch size operation. Here, I've opted for the default values.
- **Starting position:** Select the position from where the function must execute. In this case, we have gone with the **Latest** position marker.

Make sure the **Enable trigger** option is selected before you complete the configurations:

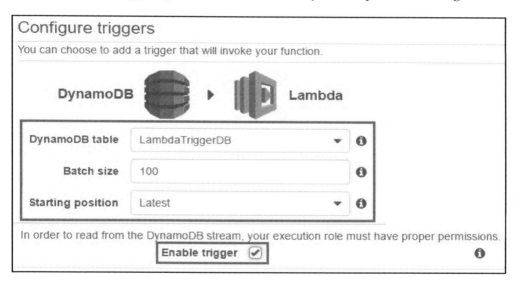

With this step completed, we are now ready to test our function. To do so, simply add a valid record in the DynamoDB table and check the function's logs using Amazon CloudWatch Logs. Once verified, try the same using an invalid IP address and see the results. You can use the same logic to verify data that is dumped into your DynamoDB table or even perform some level of processing over data in the table before it is either deleted or archived as a file to S3.

Mapping Lambda with SNS

Just as we have an event mapping for DynamoDB, AWS also provides event mapping for SNS and Lambda's integration. Lambda functions can get triggered each time a new message is published to an existing SNS topic. When triggered, a Lambda function can be used to perform tasks such as reading contents of the message payload, processing it or even forwarding it to other AWS services that can use the SNS notification to perform some action. An important thing to note here, while using SNS event mappings, is that, SNS will invoke Lambda functions in an asynchronous manner. If Lambda was successfully able to process the SNS event, it will send a successful delivery status. In the case of errors, SNS will try and invoke the particular function up to three times, post which, it will log an unsuccessful/failure message that can be viewed from Amazon CloudWatch.

Now, onward with the use case. This particular use case is a fairly simple representation of a simple user registration where a username is published via a SNS Topic which, in turn, triggers a Lambda function that reads the SNS Topic payload message, generates an MD5 checksum of the supplied username, and writes the first 10 characters of the MD5 checksum to a DynamoDB table.

To get started with the use case, we first create a corresponding directory structure. Type in the following command:

```
# mkdir ~/workdir/apex/event_driven/functions/mySnsToLambdaFunc
```

With the directory created, we only need to create a `function.dev.json` and our `index.js` files here as well. Remember, the `function.dev.json` file is unique to each use case so in this case, the file will contain the following set of instructions:

```
{
  "description": "Node.js lambda function using sns as a trigger to
    generate an md5 of the message received and store it in the
    database",
  "role": "arn:aws:iam::<account_id>:role/myLambdaSNSFuncRole",
  "handler": "index.handler",
  "environment": {}
}
```

Next, create the corresponding IAM role for providing permissions to the Lambda function to create and publish logs in CloudWatch as well as add items to a particular DynamoDB database:

```
{
  "Version": "2012-10-17",
  "Statement": [
  {
```

```
      "Sid": "myLogsPermissions",
      "Effect": "Allow",
      "Action": [
        "logs:CreateLogGroup",
        "logs:CreateLogStream",
        "logs:PutLogEvents"
      ],
      "Resource": [
        "*"
      ]
    },
    {
      "Sid": "myDynamodbPermissions",
      "Effect": "Allow",
      "Action": [
        "dynamodb:PutItem"
      ],
      "Resource": [
        "arn:aws:dynamodb:us-east-1:<account_id>:table/LambdaTriggerSNS"
      ]
    }
    ]
  }
}
```

Remember, the IAM role will not get pushed to AWS IAM by APEX. You will have to use some other means to achieve this action for now.

Finally, create the `index.js` file and paste the code as provided here: `https://github.com/PacktPublishing/Mastering-AWS-Lambda`.

The first section of the code is fairly understandable on its own. We check if the message string is not empty or undefined. If so, we simply return the `callback()` with a message. Else, we create an MD5 checksum of the supplied message and slice the first 10 characters off from it:

```
function getMessageHash(message, hashCB){
  if(message === ""){
    return hashCB("Message is empty");
  }
  else if((message === null) || (message === undefined)){
    return hashCB("Message is null or undefined");
  }
  else{
    var crypto = require('crypto');
    var messageHash =
     crypto.createHash('md5').update(message).digest("hex");
     return hashCB(null, messageHash.slice(0,10));
  }
```

```
}
```

The second piece is where we define the `insert` function that will populate the DynamoDB table.

```
function insertItem(insertParams, insertCB){
  var AWS = require('aws-sdk');
  AWS.config.update({
    region: "us-east-1",
    endpoint: "http://dynamodb.us-east-1.amazonaws.com"
  });
  var dynamodb = new AWS.DynamoDB({apiVersion: '2012-08-10'});
  dynamodb.putItem(insertParams, function(err, data) {
  if(err){
    insertCB(err);
  }
  else{
    insertCB(null, data);
  }
});
}
```

And finally, we have the handler of our function defined.

```
exports.handler = (event, context, callback) => {
var tableName = "LambdaTriggerSNS";
var message, recordVal;
```

With the basic steps done, your work directory should resemble the following screenshot a bit:

```
ubuntu@ip-172-31-21-195:~/workdir/apex$
ubuntu@ip-172-31-21-195:~/workdir/apex$ tree -L 4
.
└── event_driven
    ├── functions
    │   ├── myDynamoToLambdaFunc
    │   │   ├── function.dev.json
    │   │   └── index.js
    │   ├── myS3ToLambdaFunc
    │   │   ├── function.dev.json
    │   │   ├── index.js
    │   │   └── node_modules
    │   └── mySnsToLambdaFunc
    │       ├── function.dev.json
    │       └── index.js
    └── project.dev.json

6 directories, 7 files
ubuntu@ip-172-31-21-195:~/workdir/apex$
```

With this, we are ready to package and upload the function to Lambda. To do so, simply run the following command from your project directory:

```
# apex --env dev deploy mySnsToLambdaFunc
```

Next up, create a simple DynamoDB table and provide it with the same name as done in the function's role, that is, `LambdaTriggerSNS`. Make sure the **Primary key** of the table is set as `userName`. Accept the default settings for the table, and click on **Create** to complete the process.

Similarly, go ahead and create the corresponding SNS Topic. Login to the AWS Management Console and select the SNS service from the main landing page. Next, create a simple Topic by selecting the **Topics** option from the navigation pane to the left of the SNS Dashboard. Click on **Create topic** and fill out the **Topic name** and **Display name** for your **Topic** in the popup dialog box. Click **Create topic** once done.

With the topic created, the only thing left to do is subscribing the Lambda function to a particular topic. To do so, select the newly created Topic and from the **Actions** tab, select the option **Subscribe to topic**. This will bring up the **Create subscription** dialog, as shown as follows:

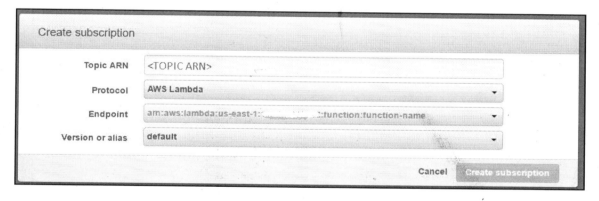

- **Topic ARN**: Provide the SNS Topic ARN here
- **Protocol**: Select AWS Lambda from the dropdown list
- **Endpoint**: From the drop down list, you will have to select the ARN of our deployed function
- **Version or alias**: You can leave this value to **default** as of now, however, you can always use the $LATEST flag to point to the latest version of your function code.

Verify that event mapping was indeed created successfully by viewing the **Triggers** tab of your function. You should see the SNS trigger configured there automatically as well. So, that should pretty much do it! You can now go ahead and test the event mapping. To do so, simply publish a username as a message in your Topic using the SNS dashboard itself. Back at Lambda, our deployed function will automatically get triggered once SNS publishes the message. It will read the contents of the message payload, create an MD5 checksum of the same, accept only the first 10 characters of the checksum and store that in the DynamoDB table we created a while back.

You can verify the output by viewing the logs of your functions' execution using Amazon CloudWatch as well:

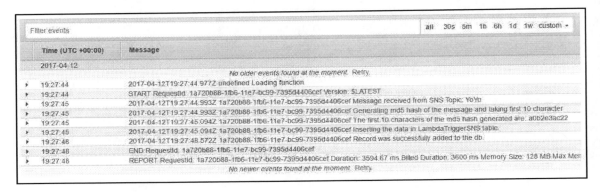

Mapping Lambda with CloudWatch events

CloudWatch offers easy event mapping integrations with Lambda using which you can execute Lambda functions either based on triggered events or even schedule their execution using CloudWatch events.

The following use case uses CloudWatch events to take periodic backups of data stored in a DynamoDB table over to S3. There are different ways to export data from your DynamoDB table and store it for later by using services such as data pipeline and EMR, but these approaches make sense when you have a really huge database consisting of millions of rows of data. What if you have a minimalistic DynamoDB table with a 100 or 200 rows of data only? In that case, it makes sense to write a simple function using Lambda that executes periodically, collecting the data from the table into a CSV file, and uploading the same to S3 for archival.

To get started with the use case, we once again create the necessary project directory folder for APEX:

```
# mkdir ~/workdir/apex/event_driven/functions/myCWScheduleToLambdaFunc
```

Next, we create the `function.dev.json` file that contains few descriptive elements with respect to the function code:

```
{
    "description": "Node.js lambda function using CloudWatch Scheduled
        events as a trigger to export a dynamodb table to s3",
    "role": "arn:aws:iam::<account_id>:role/myLambdaCWScheduleFuncRole",
    "handler": "index.handler",
    "environment": {}
}
```

Once created, go ahead and create the required IMA role as well. Remember to name the IAM role `myLambdaCWScheduleFuncRole` as done in the earlier step.

```
{
    "Version": "2012-10-17",
    "Statement": [
        {
            "Sid": "myLogsPermissions",
            "Effect": "Allow",
            "Action": [
                "logs:CreateLogGroup",
                "logs:CreateLogStream",
                "logs:PutLogEvents"
            ],
            "Resource": [
                "*"
            ]
        },
        {
            "Sid": "myS3Permissions",
            "Effect": "Allow",
            "Action": [
                "s3:PutObject"
            ],
            "Resource": [
                "arn:aws:s3:::dynamodb-backup-s3*"
            ]
        },
        {
            "Sid": "myDynamodbPermissions",
            "Effect": "Allow",
            "Action": [
```

```
                "dynamodb:Scan"
            ],
            "Resource": [
                "arn:aws:dynamodb:us-east-1:
                <account_id>:table/LambdaExportToS3*"
            ]
        }
    ]
}
```

Finally, we create the `index.js` file that will house the actual function's code. You can download the entire code and it's associated support files at `https://github.com/PacktPublishing/Mastering-AWS-Lambda`:

```
console.log('Loading function');
exports.handler = function(event, context, callback) {
  var csvExport = require('dynamodbexportcsv');
  var exporter = new csvExport(null, null, 'us-east-1');

  exporter.exportTable('LambdaExportToS3', ['userName'], 1,
  true, 250, 'dynamodb-backup-s3', '04-17-2017', function(err) {
    if(err){
      console.log("An error occurred while exporting the
        table to s3. The error is: "+err);
      return callback(err);
    }
    console.log("Succesfully exported the table to S3!");
    callback(null, "success");
  });
};
```

The function code is extremely streamlined and simple to use. Internally, we make use of a third-party npm module called `dynamodbexportcsv` that exports a DynamoDB table's records to a CSV and then writes that to local a file system or streams it to S3 as we are performing in this case. The module calls the `exportTable` function that takes the following parameters to execution:

- **table**: The name of DynamoDB table from which we need to export the contents.
- **columns**: The column name or names from where the data has to be extracted.
- **totalSegments**: The number of parallel scans to run on the table.
- **compressed**: The compresses the CSV file using GZIP compression.

- **filesize**: The maximum size of each file in megabytes. Once a file hits this size it is closed and a new file is created.
- **s3Bucket**: This is the name of the S3 bucket where you wish to stream the CSV file. If no value is provided, the file is streamed to a local directory instead.
- **s3Path**: Used as a prefix for the files created.
- **callback (err)**: A callback which is executed when finished and includes any errors that occurred.

Before we go ahead with the deployments, ensure that you compile the necessary npm modules into the project directory using the following command:

```
# node index.js
```

 To read more about the npm module and how to use it, check out its man page here: https://www.npmjs.com/package/dynamodbexportcsv.

With all the preparations completed, you can now go ahead and deploy your function to Lambda using the following command:

```
# apex --env dev deploy myLambdaCWScheduleFuncRole
```

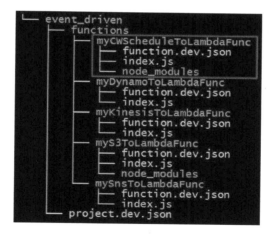

With the function deployed, let us move on the creation of the CloudWatch events that will schedule and execute the functions on our behalf. To do this, log on to the AWS Management Console and select the CloudWatch option from the main page.

In the CloudWatch dashboard, select **CloudWatch Events** to get started. Click on **Create rule** to bring up the scheduler wizard. Here, you can configure a particular event source based on which you would want your function to get triggered. In this case, I've opted to configure a **Schedule** with a **Fixed rate** of execution set as **1** day. You can, optionally, even configure an equivalent cron expression for the same:

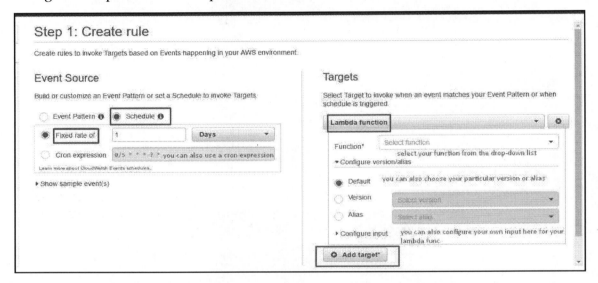

With the **Event Source** configured, we move on towards configuring the **Targets** that is, the Lambda functions. From the dropdown list, select **Lambda function** as the **Target**. Next, furnish the necessary details such as the name of the **Function** to trigger, the particular version/ alias of the function that you wish to invoke. Once completed, select **Next** to proceed. In the final step of the wizard, provide a suitable **Name** for the CloudWatch event and make sure to check the **State** option as **Enabled** before creating the rule.

You can now go ahead and run a few tests to make sure the code works as expected. First up, create a DynamoDB Simple Table named **LambdaExportToS3** containing a column called as **username**. Fill out few rows of the column and based on the scheduled time that you have specified during the CloudWatch event rule configuration, the associated Lambda function would then get triggered and export the contents of the table to a CSV in S3.

You can always verify the results by using the Function's CloudWatch Logs as shown as follows:

```
No older events found at the moment. Retry.
2017-04-22T20:56:53.373Z undefined Loading function
START RequestId: 366f4f9f-279e-11e7-8bca-a7dc5830a5a4 Version: $LATEST
2017-04-22T20:57:04.191Z 366f4f9f-279e-11e7-8bca-a7dc5830a5a4 Succesfully exported the table to S3!
END RequestId: 366f4f9f-279e-11e7-8bca-a7dc5830a5a4
REPORT RequestId: 366f4f9f-279e-11e7-8bca-a7dc5830a5a4 Duration: 10817.46 ms Billed Duration: 10900
```

The important point to note here again is that this technique is only going to be useful if you have a few set of records or at least the number of records that a function can consume within its maximum runtime limit of five minutes.

Mapping Lambda with Kinesis

The final use case in this chapter, but an equally interesting one, Kinesis is just one of another AWS services that provides stream based event sources just as we say with DynamoDB.

Kinesis and Lambda have by far the most exhaustive set of real world use cases; from log processing of streams of log data, to transactional processing, social media analytics and much more!

To get started with Kinesis and Lambda, we follow the same pattern as performed for DynamoDB. We start by creating a Kinesis Stream and mapping it to a particular Lambda function. Lambda then polls the stream for any new records and when it gets a new record (either a single record or in the form of a batch) it invokes the mapped function to execute its code. In the following example we will be using Kinesis to Stream Apache web server logs from a dummy EC2 instance. This log data is then processed by our trusty Lambda function that will send email notifications to a particular set of administrators each time an error is found in the Apache logs.

For simplicity, let's break this use case into two parts: the first is where we set up our dummy EC2 instance with Apache, a Kinesis Stream, and a Kinesis Agent, and the second part will contain the Lambda function code and how to deploy and package it using Apex.

Creating the Kinesis Stream

1. From the AWS Management Console or from the AWS CLI create a simple Kinesis Stream with the name `myKinesisStream`. Keep the **Number of shards** to the default value of **1** and create the steam. Make a note of the stream ARN as that will be required in subsequent steps.
2. Next, create a new **SNS Topic** as we performed in the earlier use case, however this time, in the **Create subscription** popup dialog, select the **Protocol** as **Email** as shown in the image below. This will enable our Lambda function to send out email based alerts whenever it gets an error log from our Kinesis Stream:

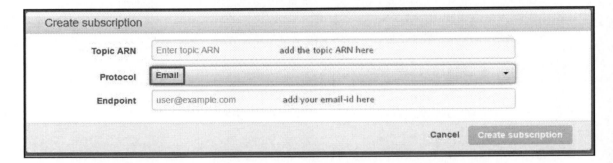

With this basic setup completed, move on to configuring our EC2 instance to send logs to this stream.

Setting up the log streaming

For this use case, I'll be using a simple EC2 instance with Apache web server installed in it. You could alternatively use any other software so long as it has the ability to produce logs.

1. Install `httpd` package:

    ```
    # sudo yum install httpd
    ```

2. Once the package is installed, edit the `httpd.conf` file to change the `error_log` file location to the `/tmp/ directory`:

    ```
    # sudo vi /etc/httpd/conf/httpd.conf
    ```

3. Search for `ErrorLog` and change the path to the `/tmp` directory as shown as follows:

```
ErrorLog /tmp/logs/error_log
```

4. With the changes done, restart the `httpd` service:

```
# sudo service httpd restart
```

5. The next step is to install the Kinesis agent on our instance. You can follow this straight forward link for the same: https://docs.aws.amazon.com/streams/latest/dev/writing-with-agents.html.

6. With the agent installed, the only thing left to do is edit the agent's config file so that you can set the file pattern as well as the Kinesis Stream name where the logs will get streamed to:

```
{
  "CloudWatch.emitMetrics": true,
  "kinesis.endpoint": "kinesis.us-east-1.amazonaws.com",
  "flows": [
  {
    "filePattern": "/tmp/logs/error_log",
    "kinesisStream": "myKinesisStream"
  }
  ]
}
```

Make sure the `kinesis.endpoint` points to the same region where your Lambda functions are going to get created.

7. With all the configurations out of the way, go ahead and start the agent:

```
# sudo kinesis-agent start
```

Remember, with each change you make in the Kinesis config file, you will need to restart the service once again for the changes to take effect.

8. You can tail the logs of the Kinesis agent:

```
# sudo tail -f /var/log/aws-kinesis-agent/aws-kinesis-agent.log
```

Packaging and uploading the function

With the log server set up along with the Kinesis Stream and the SNS based email notification, we can now move on to packaging and deploying the function using APEX.

Like always, we first start off by creating a directory for our code:

```
# mkdir ~/workdir/apex/event_driven/functions/mykinesisToLambdaFunc
```

Next, we create the `function.dev.json` file that contains few descriptive elements with respect to the function code:

```
{
  "description": "Node.js lambda function using Kinesis streams as
   a trigger to send an sns for error messages received from the
   stream",
  "role": "arn:aws:iam::<account_id>:role/myLambdaKinesisFuncRole",
  "handler": "index.handler",
  "environment": {}
}
```

Don't forget to create the associated `myLambdaKinesisFuncRole` IAM role as well. You can use either the AWS IAM Management Console or the AWS CLI to create this. The role will basically provide our Lambda function with the necessary access rights to describe and get records from the Kinesis Stream, as well as to create and add logs to Amazon CloudWatch and publish email notifications to an SNS topic.

```
{
  "Version": "2012-10-17",
  "Statement": [
  {
    "Sid": "myKinesisPermissions",
    "Effect": "Allow",
    "Action": [
      "kinesis:DescribeStream",
      "kinesis:GetRecords",
      "kinesis:GetShardIterator",
      "kinesis:ListStreams"
    ],
    "Resource": [
      "arn:aws:kinesis:us-east-1:<account_id>:stream/myKinesisStream"
    ]
  },
  {
    "Sid": "myLogsPermissions",
    "Effect": "Allow",
    "Action": [
```

```
          "logs:CreateLogGroup",
          "logs:CreateLogStream",
          "logs:PutLogEvents"
       ],
       "Resource": [
         "*"
       ]
    },
    {
      "Sid": "mySnsPermissions",
      "Effect": "Allow",
      "Action": [
        "sns:Publish"
      ],
      "Resource": [
        "arn:aws:sns:us-east-1:<account_id>:myHTTPSns"
      ]
    }
    ]
  }
```

Finally, we create the `index.js` file that will house the actual function's code. You can download the entire code and its associated support files at `https://github.com/PacktPublishing/Mastering-AWS-Lambda`.

The only place where you will be required to modify the code is in the handler section where you will have to provide your SNS topic's ARN as shown as follows:

```
exports.handler = function(event, context, callback) {
  event.Records.forEach(function(record) {
    var snsTopicArn = "arn:aws:sns:us-east-1:<account_id>:myHTTPSns";
    // Kinesis data is base64 encoded so decode here
    var payload = new Buffer(record.kinesis.data,
      'base64').toString('ascii');
    console.log("Decoded error log is: ", payload);
    console.log("Sending SNS topic - Alert to xyz@email.com");
    var snsParams = {
      Message: payload, /* required */
      Subject: 'HTTP Error',
      TopicArn: snsTopicArn
    };
```

With all the preparations completed, you can now go ahead and deploy your function to Lambda using the following command:

```
# apex --env dev deploy myKinesisToLambdaFunc
```

Remember to run this command from your project directory, as follows:

```
ubuntu@ip-172-31-21-195:~/workdir/apex/event_driven$ ll
total 16
drwxrwxr-x 3 ubuntu ubuntu 4096 Apr 10 12:12 ./
drwxrwxr-x 3 ubuntu ubuntu 4096 Apr  9 19:51 ../
drwxr-xr-x 6 ubuntu ubuntu 4096 Apr 10 12:12 functions/
-rw-rw-r-- 1 ubuntu ubuntu  285 Apr 10 12:12 project.dev.json
ubuntu@ip-172-31-21-195:~/workdir/apex/event_driven$
ubuntu@ip-172-31-21-195:~/workdir/apex/event_driven$ apex --env dev deploy myKinesisToLambdaFunc
   • creating function         env=dev function=myKinesisToLambdaFunc
   • created alias current     env=dev function=myKinesisToLambdaFunc version=1
   • function created          env=dev function=myKinesisToLambdaFunc name=eventDriven_myKinesisToLambdaFunc version=1
ubuntu@ip-172-31-21-195:~/workdir/apex/event_driven$
```

With the function now deployed, the final step involves setting up the event mapping of your function with the Kinesis Stream. To do so, from the AWS Lambda dashboard, select your newly deployed function and click on the **Triggers** tab. Next, select the **Add trigger** option. This will pop up the **Add trigger** configuration page where just as before, we select the appropriate service we wish to map to this particular Lambda function. Next, provide the details as shown below:

- **Kinesis Stream**: Provide the name of the Kinesis Stream that we created. Remember the stream has to be in the same region as your Lambda function to work.
- **Batchsize**: Keep it to it's default value of 100 for now.
- **Startingposition**: Select **latest** as the starting position.

Remember to select the option **Enable trigger** before completing the trigger configuration.

That's it! We are all ready to test now! Open up a browser window and type in the URL of your Apache web server. You should see the default welcome page. Now, go ahead and type in some additional parameters in the URL that will force the Apache server to send out an error in the logs as shown as follows:

Each error message that gets streamed triggers the Lambda function to send an email notification to the people who have subscribed to the Topic. In this way, you can leverage Kinesis and Lambda to perform similar tasks on your transactional data, as well as social data for real time analytics.

With this we come towards the end of this chapter, but before we close out and move on to the next chapter, here are a few key pointers to try out and explore AWS Lambda.

Planning your next steps

Although we have covered quite a few interesting use cases, there are still a lot more event mappings that you can work with when it comes to Lambda, including services such as AWS CodeCommit, AWS Config, Amazon Echo, Amazon Lex and Amazon API Gateway. Try exploring a few of these services and coming up with simple, reusable functions on your own for starters.

The second important thing worth mentioning here is the availability of sample events based on the supported event sources by Lambda. You can use these sample events as base templates when it comes to testing your code with event mappings. This enables you to effectively test your code out without having to enable the trigger in the first place. To know more, check out the sample events page here: `http://docs.aws.amazon.com/lambda/latest/dg/eventsources.html`.

Remember, although the event mapping and triggers are taken care by AWS, you still need to monitor your functions' execution and logs.

Summary

So, yet another chapter comes to an end! We have come a small way from where we started off in the first chapter. By now, you should have understood and got a good feel of Lambda's true capabilities and potential as well! So, before we finish off this chapter, let us conclude by summarizing all that we have learned.

We started off by understanding what an event-based system is and how it actually works. Later we saw a few simple and easy to understand Lambda architecture patterns. Finally, we took a deep dive into how Lambda works with events with the help of event mappings and a few easy-to-replicate real world use cases as well.

In the next chapter, we will take the event mappings a step further by exploring few third party tools and services that can also trigger Lambda functions to perform some set of tasks. So, stay tuned for much more is coming your way!

5
Extending AWS Lambda with External Services

In the previous chapter, we learned how to leverage and execute few Lambda functions based on triggers. However, one key aspect of that chapter was that the events were generated by sources or services residing within AWS. But, what if the triggers are generated by an external service provider or a third-party tool? Is Lambda even capable of handling such external services and events? Well, that's exactly what we are going to discuss and talk about in this chapter!

In this chapter, we will be covering the following topics:

- Understanding the concept of Webhooks and how they can be used to trigger Lambda functions remotely
- Triggering Lambda functions with the help of a few commonly used third-party tools and services, such as Git, Teamwork, and Slack
- Triggering Lambda functions from an external application

Introducing Webhooks

Webhooks are simple callbacks that are rapidly growing in popularity with a lot of developers. Webhooks work in a very similar way to Lambda functions; they are invoked when a particular event is fired by an application on the web. This makes them highly applicable to a variety of web development use cases where, rather than having a traditional API that polls for data on a frequent basis, you use a Webhook to get data at real time.

With most APIs there's a request followed by a response, whereas in the case of Webhooks, they simply send the data whenever it's available.

The way a Webhook works is quite simple! To use a Webhook, you register a URL with the Webhook provider, for example IFTTT or Zapier. The URL is a place within your application that will accept the data and do something with it. In some cases, you can tell the provider the situations when you'd like to receive data. Whenever there's something new, the Webhook will send it to your URL.

Here's a common example of a Webhook--open up any of your GitHub pages from your browser. There, in your repository's **Setting** page, you will see a **Webhooks** section as shown in the following image. You can always add a new Webhook to your repository by selecting the **Add webhook** option. There, you can provide a URL that will receive an event each time you either push or commit code into your repository and so on. On the event getting triggered, GitHub sends a POST request to the URL with details of the subscribed events. You can also specify which data format you would like to receive the request in, for example, JSON or x-www-form-urlencoded. In this way, you can easily create open ended integrations with other arbitrary web services without having to spin up any new infrastructure or manage any complex code integrations as well.

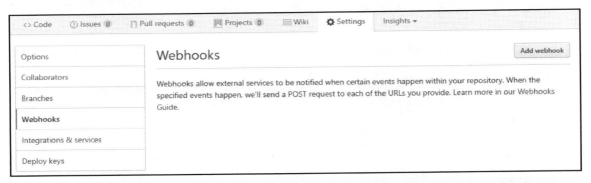

This is the exact same case that we are going to explore and learn about in this chapter. We will learn how to effectively use Webhooks to hook into third-party services and sites, and trigger some Lambda action on it's behalf. Since we have already taken up the topic of GitHub, let us look at how Lambda, Webhooks and a GitHub repository can be tied together functionally with minimal efforts.

Integrating GitHub with AWS Lambda

Before we begin with the actual integration, let us take some time to understand the purpose of this particular use case. For starters, we will be using two third-party tools, namely GitHub and Teamwork. For those of you who don't know or haven't used Teamwork before; it is basically a productivity and communication tool that helps with project management activities. You can read up more about Teamwork here at `https://www.teamwork.com/`.

The end goal of this exercise is to simulate the automated creation tasks in Teamwork each time a new issue is created in GitHub with the help of AWS Lambda. So, each issue created will in turn create a corresponding task in our Teamwork project for the team to work on:

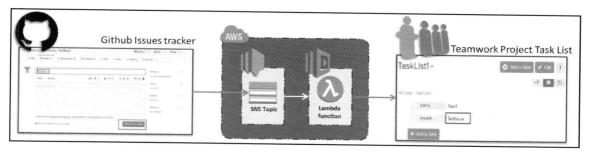

To begin with ,you will require a GitHub account along with a Teamwork account. You can sign up for a Teamwork account for 30 days absolutely free of charge. So, without further ado, let's get started!

The first step that we are going to start off with is the creation of an SNS topic. Why SNS? Well, it's simple. Lambda functions do not have an endpoint or unique URL on which we can send event payloads, and hence we need an AWS service that provides some form of notification services that other third-party services like GitHub can subscribe to, but also can be used as a trigger in combination with Lambda--enter SNS!

Following are steps to create a topic:

1. Log in to the AWS Management Console and select the **SNS** service from the main landing page.
2. Next, create a simple topic by selecting the **Topics** option from the navigation pane to the left of the SNS dashboard.

3. Click on **Create topic** and fill out the **Topic name** and **Display name** for your topic in the popup dialog box. Click **Create topic** once done.

4. Select the newly created topic and make a note of its **Topic ARN**:

With the SNS created, we move ahead with the next step of creating a separate user which will be used to publish messages from GitHub to our SNS topic:

1. From the IAM console, select the **Users** option from the panel. Click on the **Add user** option.

2. Provide the user's name and make sure to check the **Programmatic access** checkbox before you proceed any further with the wizard.

3. Once done, click on **Next** and it will ask you for permissions to be given to this user. Click on the **Create Policy** option. Provide the policy with a suitable **Name** and **Description**.

4. Paste the following code in the policy window. Make sure to edit the **Resource** field with the correct SNS ARN:

```
{
  "Version": "2012-10-17",
  "Statement": [
  {
    "Sid": "mySnsPermissions",
    "Effect": "Allow",
    "Action": [
      "sns:Publish"
    ],
    "Resource": [
      "arn:aws:sns:us-east-1:<account-id>:myGitSNS"
    ]
  }
  ]
}
```

5. With the policy created, go back to **IAM User Permissions** and choose the **Attach existing policies** option and select the policy we just created. Complete the user creation process by reviewing the user settings and selecting the **Create user** option.

With the basics configured, let us now focus our attention to configuring the GitHub repository.

Login into your GitHub account and select your repository for which you wish to enable the integration:

1. Go to the **Settings** tab in your repository and, from the left-hand side panel, select the **Integration and services** option.
2. Click on **Add service** and select **Amazon SNS** option as shown in the following screenshot:

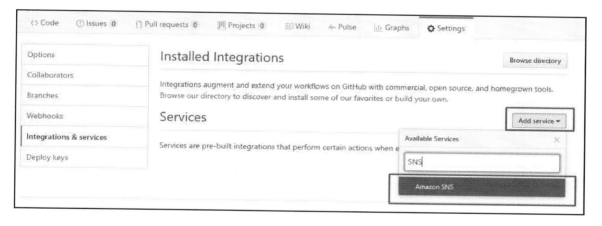

3. In the **Add service** dialog box, provide the AWS GitHub user's **Aws key**, **SNS topic** ARN, and **Sns region** details. Once done, click on **Add service**. Make sure the **Active** checkbox is selected before you add the service. This will enable the service to run when a corresponding trigger is invoked.

An important point to note here is that the service integration responds only to push events, however, we need responses for any **Issues** and **Pull request** events as well. For that, we will have to create a hook using *GitHub API*. Here is a simple Node.js script which will create the hook for us in our repository, but before we do that we will need a GitHub **Personal access tokens** to be able to authenticate and create the hook. For this, follow these simple steps from your GitHub account:

1. Go to your GitHub **Settings**. On the left hand-side panel, you will see **Personal access tokens**. Click on **Generate new token** as shown in the following screenshot:

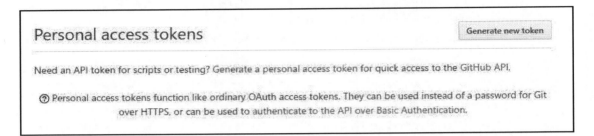

2. In the next dialog box, provide a suitable description for the token and select **repo** and **gist** options from the list of scopes. Once completed, you will receive the token from GitHub. Make sure you save it safely somewhere!

Creating the hook Node.js code:

```
var GitHubApi = require("github") // npm i github
var github = new GitHubApi({version: "3.0.0"})
var gitToken = process.env.gitToken;
github.authenticate({type:"oauth", token: gitToken})
github.repos.createHook({
  owner : process.env.owner,
  user: process.env.user,
  repo: process.env.repoName,
  name: "amazonsns",
  config: {
    "aws_key": process.env.awsAccessKey,
    "aws_secret": process.env.awsSecretKey,
    "sns_topic": process.env.snsTopicARN,
    "sns_region": process.env.AWS_SNS_REGION || "us-east-1"
  },
  events: ["pull_request", "issues"]
}, function(err, result) {
console.log(arguments)
```

```
});
```

The code is pretty self-explanatory. All we have done is added all the variable details like `aws_key`, `gitToken`, and so on as environment variables for our function. We have also used the `createHook` call and in the events, we have passed the `pull request` and `issues` objects to the same.

With this step completed, we now move on to creating the all-important lambda function. Start by creating a role for our function:

```json
{
    "Version": "2012-10-17",
    "Statement": [
    {
      "Sid": "myLogsPermissions",
      "Effect": "Allow",
      "Action": [
        "logs:CreateLogGroup",
        "logs:CreateLogStream",
        "logs:PutLogEvents"
      ],
      "Resource": [
        "*"
      ]
    },
    {
      "Sid": "myKMSPermissions",
      "Effect": "Allow",
      "Action": [
        "kms:Decrypt"
      ],
      "Resource": [
        "*"
      ]
    }
    ]
}
```

The role is basically required for two things--adding the function's logs to CloudWatch and decrypting the API key that we will be using to create tasks in Teamwork.

Why encrypt the keys in the first place? Since API keys are sensitive data, we will be encrypting those using KMS keys and then decrypt the same key in our code before using it. This is more or less a best practice when it comes to handling keys in Lambda functions. Once the role is created, make a note of it's ARN value.

As we have been using APEX till now to create our Lambda functions, we will use APEX once again to create this Lambda function too.

To get started, create the necessary project directory folder for APEX:

```
# mkdir ~/workdir/apex/event_driven/functions/myGitAWSIntegration
```

Next, we create the necessary `function.dev.json` file that contains few descriptive elements with respect to the function code:

```json
{
    "description": "Node.js lambda function to show integration
      between Git and lambda via SNS service",
    "role": "arn:aws:iam::<accountid>:role/myGitRole",
    "handler": "index.handler",
    "environment": {
      "kmsEncryptedAPIKey" : "<your API key>",
      "taskListID" : "<Task List ID>",
      "teamworkCompany" : "<Teamwork company name>"
    }
}
```

You can obtain the `taskListID` by searching the in the URL of our Teamwork webpage

Next, we create the `index.js` file that will house the actual function's code. You can download the entire code and it's associated support files from `https://github.com/Packt Publishing/Mastering-AWS-Lambda`.

The code has two parts--a `handler` function and a `createTask` function.

The `handler` function first checks whether the trigger was for an *issue* or something else. If it was for an *issue* then it checks whether the KMS encrypted API key is present or not. If yes, then it decrypts it and sends the event and the API key to the `createTask` function:

```javascript
'use strict';
const request = require('request');
const AWS = require('aws-sdk');
const company = process.env.teamworkCompany;
const kmsEncryptedAPIKey = process.env.kmsEncryptedAPIKey;
const taskListID = process.env.taskListID;
let teamworkAPIKey;
exports.handler = function(event, context, callback) {
  var githubEvent = JSON.parse(event.Records[0].Sns.Message);
  console.log('Received GitHub event:', githubEvent);
```

```
if (!githubEvent.hasOwnProperty('issue') || githubEvent.action
 !== 'opened') {
  // Not an event for opening an issue
  console.log("Event isn't for issue opening!");
  callback(null, "Event isn't for issue opening!");
}
else{
  // Event for opening an issue
  console.log("Issue was opened!");
  if(teamworkAPIKey){
    // Container re-use
    createTask(githubEvent, callback);
  }
  else if (kmsEncryptedAPIKey && kmsEncryptedAPIKey !==
   '<kmsEncryptedAPIKey>') {
    const encryptedBuf = new Buffer(kmsEncryptedAPIKey, 'base64');
    const cipherText = { CiphertextBlob: encryptedBuf };
    const kms = new AWS.KMS();
    kms.decrypt(cipherText, (err, data) => {
      if (err) {
        console.log('Decrypt error:', err);
        return callback(err);
      }
      teamworkAPIKey = data.Plaintext.toString('ascii');
      createTask(githubEvent, callback);
    });
  }
  else{
    console.error("API Key has not been set.");
    callback("API Key has not been set.");
  }
}
};
```

Now, the `createTask` function takes the event and the API key, forms the request URL to be hit, and sends a POST request to the Teamwork API. Using this, it creates the corresponding task in Teamwork which our project team can work on:

```
function createTask(githubEvent, callback){
  let taskName = githubEvent.issue.title;
  let path = "/tasklists/" + taskListID + "/tasks.json";
  let date = new Date();
  let month = date.getMonth();
  let day = date.getDate();
  let endDate = date.getFullYear() + ((month+2) < 10 ? '0' : '')
   + (month+2) + (day < 10 ? '0' : '') + day;
  let startDate = date.getFullYear() + ((month+1) < 10 ? '0' : '')
   + (month+1) + (day < 10 ? '0' : '') + day;
```

```
let base64 = new Buffer(teamworkAPIKey + ":xxx").toString("base64");
let json = {"todo-item": {"content": taskName,
 "startdate": startDate, "enddate": endDate }};
let options = {
  uri: "https://"+ company + ".teamwork.com" + path,
  hostname: company + ".teamwork.com",
  method: "POST",
  encoding: "utf8",
  followRedirect: true,
  headers: {
    "Authorization": "BASIC " + base64,
    "Content-Type": "application/json"
  },
  json: json
};
request(options, function (error, res, body) {
  if(error){
    console.error("Request Error: " + error);
    callback(error);
  }
  else{
    console.log("STATUS: " + res.statusCode);
    res.setEncoding("utf8");
    console.log("body: " + body);
    callback(null, "Task Created!");
  }
});
}
```

As you can see, our code has used some of the environment variables, so don't forget to add those to the function.dev.json file's environment section as shown in the following snippet:

```
"environment": {
  "kmsEncryptedAPIKey" : "<your API key>",
  "taskListID" : "<you Task List ID>",
  "teamworkCompany" : "<your company>"
}
```

Next, deploy the function to Lambda using the apex deploy command:

```
# apex deploy --env dev myGitAWSIntegration
```

With the function deployed, log in to the AWS Lambda web console and verify whether the environment variables were added successfully or not. Click on the **Enable encryption helpers** checkbox and encrypt the `kmsEncryptedAPIKey` key value as shown in the following screenshot:

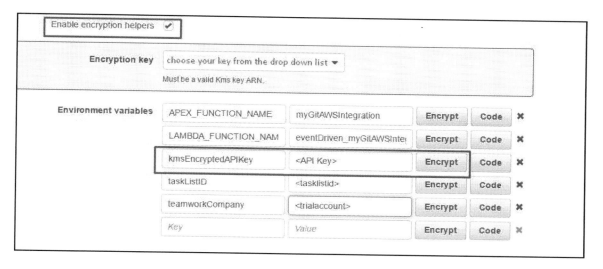

TO create your own KMS key, visit `http://docs.aws.amazon.com/lambda/latest/dg/tutorial-env_console.html`.

With the function deployed, go ahead and configure the SNS trigger for the function. Select the **Trigger** tab from the AWS Lambda console, select the **SNS** service from the trigger and populate the **SNS topic** field with the SNS we created in our earlier steps. Remember to check the **Enable trigger** option before you click on **Submit**:

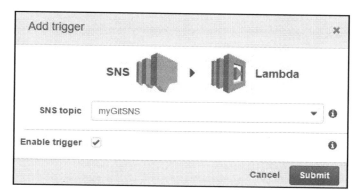

If you made it this far, then the only thing left is to test the setup! Go ahead and create an issue in your GitHub repository. If all settings were done correctly, you should have a new task created within Teamwork, as shown in the following screenshot:

You can use a similar setup to trigger actions from GitHub to other services, such as Jenkins, for triggering automated code builds and deploys as well.

In the next use case, we are going to explore yet another very commonly used team collaboration and communication tool that uses interactive notifications to inform us of the health of our EC2 instances.

Integrating Slack with AWS Lambda

I'm a big fan of Slack and have been using it for quite some time now. It's perhaps one of the trendiest collaboration tools, just because of it's intuitiveness and ability to program things around it! Perhaps that's why this particular use case is also one of my favorites. In this scenario, we will be using Slack as our custom EC2 alerting dashboard by integrating it with AWS Lambda and a few other services. The alerts will be sent out to a custom made Slack channel that the IT team will use to track alerts and other important notifications.

In a broader sense, here are the list of things that we plan to do for this activity:

- Create SNS topic which will act as the Lambda trigger.
- Create a CloudWatch alarm for one of our EC2 machines. Say if CPU utilization goes higher than 80% then, trigger the alarm.
- The CloudWatch alarm will post the notification to an SNS topic.

- The SNS topic will act as a trigger to our Lambda function.
- As soon as the Lambda function gets a trigger, it will post the notification to our Slack channel.

Sounds simple? Let's get down to implementing it then.

We will once again begin by creating an SNS topic which will act as a trigger for the Lambda function. A CloudWatch alarm would hit this SNS topic which will in turn set in motion the Lambda function that publishes the CloudWatch alert on Slack.

Go ahead and create another simple SNS topic as we did in our earlier use case. Once completed, make a note of the SNS topic's ARN as well. In this case, our SNS is configured to send a simple notification to an IT admin email alias.

Next up, we create our CloudWatch alarm. To do so, select the **CloudWatch** service from the AWS Management Console and click on **Alarms** in the left-hand side panel. Select the option **Create alarm** to get started.

Since we will be monitoring the EC2 instances in our environment, I've gone ahead and selected the **EC2 Metrics** option. Alternatively, you can select any other metric, as per your requirements.

In our case, we have gone ahead and configured a simple **CPUUtilization** alarm as shown in the following screenshot:

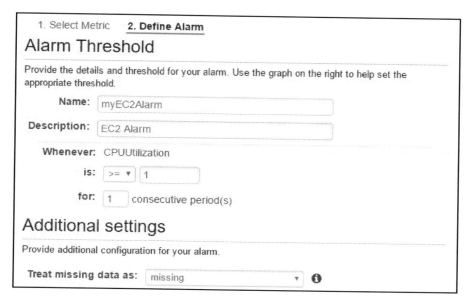

Make sure to set up a notification for the alerts and point it to the newly created SNS topic as shown in the following screenshot:

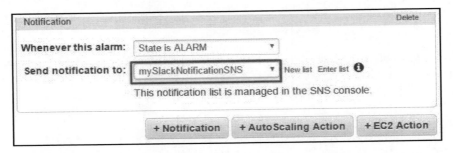

Once the alarm is created, it will show up as it's in **OK** state in CloudWatch's dashboard.

Next, we need to configure a Slack channel where the notifications will be posted. For that we will need an incoming Webhook to be set and a hook URL that will be used to post the notifications. To do so, go to your Slack team's settings page and select the **Apps & integrations** option as shown in the following screenshot:

Once you click on **Apps & integrations**, it will take you to a new page of apps. Search for `Incoming` and select the **Incoming WebHooks** from the options that show up.

Next, click on **Add Configuration**. It will ask you to select the channel to post to along with a few other necessary parameters. Make sure to copy and save the *Webhook URL* before you proceed any further with the next steps.

Now that we have our Slack hook URL ready, we can finally get started with deploying our Lambda function. Since the hook URL is sensitive data, we will be encrypting it the same way we did in the earlier use case and then decrypt it in our code before using it. For this exercise, we will be using an existing AWS Lambda function blueprint designed for Slack integration using Node.js 4.3 version.

Since we already have the AWS template, here is a quick explanation of what it does.

The code has three functions: `handler`, `processEvent`, and `postMessage`.

The `handler` function is where the execution will start. It checks whether the KMS encrypted key is present or not. If yes, it decrypts it and forms the hook URL.

After that, it calls the `processEvent` function:

```
const AWS = require('aws-sdk');
const url = require('url');
const https = require('https');
// The base-64 encoded, encrypted key (CiphertextBlob) stored in the
  kmsEncryptedHookUrl environment variable
const kmsEncryptedHookUrl = process.env.kmsEncryptedHookUrl;
// The Slack channel to send a message to stored in the slackChannel
  environment variable
const slackChannel = process.env.slackChannel;
let hookUrl;
exports.handler = (event, context, callback) => {
  console.log("EVENT: ", JSON.stringify(event));
    if (hookUrl) {
      // Container reuse, simply process the event with the key
      in memory
      processEvent(event, callback);
    }
    else if (kmsEncryptedHookUrl && kmsEncryptedHookUrl !==
    '<kmsEncryptedHookUrl>') {
      const encryptedBuf = new Buffer(kmsEncryptedHookUrl, 'base64');
      const cipherText = { CiphertextBlob: encryptedBuf };
      const kms = new AWS.KMS();
      kms.decrypt(cipherText, (err, data) => {
        if (err) {
          console.log('Decrypt error:', err);
          return callback(err);
        }
        hookUrl = `https://${data.Plaintext.toString('ascii')}`;
```

```
        processEvent(event, callback);
      });
    }
    else {
      callback('Hook URL has not been set.');
    }
};
```

Now, the `processEvent` function extracts the required information from the event and forms the Slack message that's going to be posted on the Slack channel. Once the message is formed, it calls the `postMessage` function:

```
function processEvent(event, callback) {
  const message = JSON.parse(event.Records[0].Sns.Message);
  const alarmName = message.AlarmName;
  const newState = message.NewStateValue;
  const reason = message.NewStateReason;
  const slackMessage = {
    channel: slackChannel,
    text: `${alarmName} state is now ${newState}: ${reason}`,
  };
  console.log("slack msg: ", slackMessage);
  postMessage(slackMessage, (response) => {
    if (response.statusCode < 400) {
      console.info('Message posted successfully');
      callback(null);
    }
    else if (response.statusCode < 500) {
      console.error(`Error posting message to Slack API:
        ${response.statusCode} - ${response.statusMessage}`);
      callback(null);
      // Don't retry because the error is due to a problem with
      the request
    }
    else {
      // Let Lambda retry
      callback(`Server error when processing message:
        ${response.statusCode} - ${response.statusMessage}`);
    }
  });
}
```

The `postMessage` function uses the `https` and `url` npm modules to form the `options` to hit the Slack URL. We are doing a `POST` request in this case. The syntax of these modules is very simple and can be obtained from the documentation itself:

```
function postMessage(message, callback) {
  const body = JSON.stringify(message);
  const options = url.parse(hookUrl);
  options.method = 'POST';
  options.headers = {
    'Content-Type': 'application/json',
    'Content-Length': Buffer.byteLength(body),
  };
  //console.log("options: ", options);
  const postReq = https.request(options, (res) => {
    const chunks = [];
    res.setEncoding('utf8');
    res.on('data', (chunk) => chunks.push(chunk));
    res.on('end', () => {
      if (callback) {
        callback({
          body: chunks.join(''),
          statusCode: res.statusCode,
          statusMessage: res.statusMessage,
        });
      }
    });
    return res;
  });
  postReq.write(body);
  postReq.end();
}
```

The function takes two environment variables: `hookUrl` and the slack channel name. Add those to the `function.dev.json` file. Also, make sure the hook's URL environment variables in `function.dev.json` file doesn't contain the `https` protocol appended to it:

```
{
  "description": "Node.js lambda function to show integration
    between lambda and Slack via SNS service",
  "role": "arn:aws:iam::<account_id>:role/mySlackBotRole",
  "handler": "index.handler",
  "environment": {
    "slackChannel" : "<channel name>",
    "kmsEncryptedHookUrl" : "<slack_hook_url_without_protocol>"
  }
}
```

As we have been following APEX to deploy Lambda functions, we will be doing the same this time too. First, let's create a role for the Lambda function to assume when it executes:

```
{
  "Version": "2012-10-17",
  "Statement": [
    {
      "Sid": "myLogsPermissions",
      "Effect": "Allow",
      "Action": [
        "logs:CreateLogGroup",
        "logs:CreateLogStream",
        "logs:PutLogEvents"
      ],
      "Resource": [
        "*"
      ]
    },
    {
      "Sid": "myKMSPermissions",
      "Effect": "Allow",
      "Action": [
        "kms:Decrypt"
      ],
      "Resource": [
        "*"
      ]
    }
  ]
}
```

With the role created, we are now ready to deploy the Lambda function using APEX.

Run the following command to get the deployment started:

```
# apex deploy --env dev mySlackLambdaIntegration
```

Once the function is deployed, using the **Lambda Management Console**, encrypt the hookURL environment variable just as we performed in the earlier use case. Review the configurations and remember to **Save** your changes:

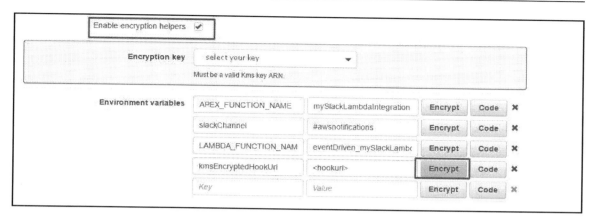

With the function ready to deploy, you can now go ahead and configure the function's trigger using the **Trigger** tab from the **Lambda Management Console**. Select the **SNS** service and make sure you populate the correct **SNS topic** for this exercise as created earlier. Don't forget the check the **Enable trigger** checkbox before selecting **Submit**.

Now our function and Slack integration is ready and primed! All that is required is increasing the CPU load on our EC2 instance and we should start getting custom alert notifications on our Slack channel. In our case, we used an open source CPU load testing tool called as **stress** to generate a synthetic load on our instance. When the CloudWatch alarm thresholds were crossed, the alert was triggered from CloudWatch and the corresponding SNS event was generated. The SNS triggered Lambda to publish the alert to our Slack channel as depicted in the following screenshot:

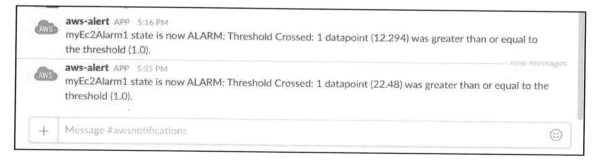

You can use a similar set of notifications and alert mechanisms to provide your IT admins with a more intuitive and customizable response rather than the traditional alerting via email approach.

Invoking Lambda using an external application

So far, we have seen how to integrate third-party services such as GitHub and Slack with Lambda functions. In this section, we will be looking into yet another simple example where an application is used to invoke a particular Lambda function.

The use case is pretty straightforward--we have a simple Node.js application that accepts any city's name as a parameter and as a response, provides you with the detailed weather conditions of that city. The city name is passed to the Lambda function in the form of an event using SNS. Once the event is provided to the function, it makes a call to an open sourced API called as openweather by passing the city name as a parameter. The API in turn returns the current temperature as well as other miscellaneous weather details of that city. If the current temperature of the city is greater than say 25 degrees, the function automatically sends a customized SNS email to the specific user. Sounds simple? Then let's see how it all fits together.

 To learn more about the openweather API and how to use it, check out it's main documentation at https://openweathermap.org/api.

Once again, like all our examples, we will begin by creating a simple SNS topic for our Lambda functions to send the email notifications out. Make sure you copy the ARN of the SNS topic as we will be requiring that in the later steps.

With the SNS topic created, let us go ahead and create the Lambda function. First up, creating the IAM role for our function to execute.

Here is the role:

```
{
  "Version": "2012-10-17",
  "Statement": [
  {
    "Sid": "myLogsPermissions",
    "Effect": "Allow",
    "Action": [
      "logs:CreateLogGroup",
      "logs:CreateLogStream",
      "logs:PutLogEvents"
    ],
    "Resource": [
      "*"
```

```
      ]
    },
    {
      "Sid": "myKMSPermissions",
      "Effect": "Allow",
      "Action": [
        "kms:Decrypt"
      ],
      "Resource": [
        "*"
      ]
    },
    {
      "Sid": "mySNSPermissions",
      "Effect": "Allow",
      "Action": [
        "sns:Publish"
      ],
      "Resource": [
        "arn:aws:sns:us-east-1:<account-id>:myWeatherSNS"
      ]
    }
    ]
  }
```

As you can see we have logs permissions, as usual, but we also have KMS decrypt along with SNS publish permissions. Since the code uses the openweather API, we will be requiring an API key for the same. So just as we did in our previous use cases, we are encrypting the API key and then decrypting it by our code before using it.

 The SNS publish permission is present because we will be publishing an SNS to the email address if the temperature is greater than 25 degrees Celsius.

Next, create a new folder structure for our new Lambda function and copy the following contents into the function.dev.json file:

```
{
  "description": "Node.js lambda function to show lambda invocation
    from a custom application",
  "role": "arn:aws:iam::<account-id>:role/myWeatherLambdaRole",
  "handler": "index.handler",
  "environment": {
    "snsTopicARN": "arn:aws:sns:us-east-1:<account-id>:myWeatherSNS",
    "kmsEncryptedAPIKey": "<API key>",
    "language" : "en",
```

```
          "units" : "metric"
     }
  }
```

Finally, go ahead and create the `index.js` file that will house the code that will pass the `city` parameter to the `openweather` API. The code is divided into two functions--one is the `handler` function and the other is the `processEvent` function.

The `handler` function first checks whether the encrypted API key is present or not. If it is, then it decrypts the key and sends the event for further processing to the `processEvent` function. The `processEvent` function then takes the event which has the city name mentioned and gets the required info using the `openweather` API. It also checks whether the temperature of that particular city is greater than 25 degrees Celsius or not. If it is, then it will send an SNS alert to the subscribed SNS topic.

```javascript
'use strict';
const weather = require('openweather-apis');
const AWS = require('aws-sdk');
const sns = new AWS.SNS({apiVersion: '2010-03-31'});
const kmsEncryptedAPIKey = process.env.kmsEncryptedAPIKey;
const snsTopicARN = process.env.snsTopicARN;
let language = process.env.language;
let units = process.env.units;
let apiKey;

function processEvent(event, callback) {
  let city = event.city;
  weather.setAPPID(apiKey);
  weather.setLang(language);
  weather.setUnits(units);
  weather.setCity(city);
  weather.getSmartJSON(function(err, smart){
    if(err){
      console.log("An error occurred: ", err);
      callback(err);
    }
    else{
      if(Number(smart.temp) > 25){
        console.log("Temperature is greater than 25 degree celsius!!");
        let snsParams = {
          Message: "Its Hot outside!! Avoid wearing too many layers!
          WEATHER UPDATE: "+ JSON.stringify(smart),
          Subject: 'WEATHER UPDATE',
          TopicArn: snsTopicARN
        };
        sns.publish(snsParams, function(snsErr, data) {
          if (snsErr){
```

```
          console.log("An error occurred while sending SNS Alert:
            "+snsErr, snsErr.stack); // an error occurred
          callback(snsErr);
        }
        else{
          console.log("SNS Alert sent successfully:
            ", snsParams.Message); // successful response
          callback(null, "Done");
        }
      });
    }
    else{
      console.log("WEATHER UPDATE: ", smart);
      callback(null, "Done");
    }
  }
 });
}

exports.handler = function(event, context, callback) {
  //var weatherEvent = JSON.parse(event);
  console.log('Received custom event:', event);
  if (apiKey) {
   // Container reuse, simply process the event with the key in memory
    processEvent(event, callback);
  }
  else if (kmsEncryptedAPIKey && kmsEncryptedAPIKey
   !== '<kmsEncryptedAPIKey>') {
    const encryptedBuf = new Buffer(kmsEncryptedAPIKey, 'base64');
    const cipherText = { CiphertextBlob: encryptedBuf };
    const kms = new AWS.KMS();
    kms.decrypt(cipherText, (err, data) => {
      if (err) {
        console.log('Decrypt error:', err);
        return callback(err);
      }
      apiKey = data.Plaintext.toString('ascii');
      processEvent(event, callback);
    });
  }
  else {
    callback('API Key has not been set.');
  }
};
```

Make sure to run the following command before you deploy the function to Lambda. Since the code uses the `openweather-apis` npm module, you will also need to install the same locally:

```
# npm install -save openweather-apis
```

With the function and it's necessary dependencies sorted out, go ahead and upload the package using the following command:

```
# apex deploy --env dev myCustomAppToLambda
```

The following screenshot shows the output for the preceding command:

```
ubuntu@ip-172-31-21-195:~/workdir/apex/event_driven$
ubuntu@ip-172-31-21-195:~/workdir/apex/event_driven$ apex deploy --env dev myCustomAppToLambda
   • creating function        env=dev function=myCustomAppToLambda
   • created alias current     env=dev function=myCustomAppToLambda version=1
   • function created          env=dev function=myCustomAppToLambda name=eventDriven_myCustomAppToLambd
a version=1
ubuntu@ip-172-31-21-195:~/workdir/apex/event_driven$
```

With the function deployed, you will need to enable the encryption enablers for encrypting the API key using the Lambda Management Console. Select the checkbox **Enable encryption helpers** and encrypt the API key as shown in the following screenshot:

Remember to save the changes before proceeding further with the configurations.

Now that our function is in place, we need to create our custom application and invoke the Lambda function from it. The application will simply accept a parameter (`city`) from the user and invoke the function with the following event in JSON format:

```
{
    "city":"<city_entered_by_user>"
}
```

The code is really simple to understand. We are will be using an npm module named `prompt` which will help us prompt our users to enter a city name and then we send it to our Lambda function using the `invoke` function from the AWS SDK itself.

 The only required parameter is the function name; the rest all are optional. You can read more about this from the AWS SDK documentation.

```javascript
const AWS = require('aws-sdk');
AWS.config.update({
  region: 'us-east-1',
  maxRetries: 20
});
const lambda = new AWS.Lambda({apiVersion: '2015-03-31'});
const prompt = require('prompt');
console.log("Greetings!!");
console.log("Please enter the city name for weather updates.");
// Start the prompt
prompt.start();
// Get city
prompt.get(['city'], function (err, result) {
  // Log the results
  console.log('Command-line input received:');
  console.log('city: ' + result.city);
  // Create lambda event
  var event = "{\"city\":\""+ result.city + "\"}";
  // Form lambda params
  var params = {
    FunctionName: "<lambda_function_name>", /* required */
    InvocationType: "Event",
    Payload: event
  };
  // invoke lambda function
  lambda.invoke(params, function(err, data) {
    if (err) console.log(err, err.stack); // an error occurred
    else console.log(data);                // successful response
```

```
    });
  });
```

With the application created, simply run it using the following command:

```
# node weatherApp.js
```

When prompted, type in the city name for which you would like to check the weather. In our case, we have given the city as Mumbai as it's really nice and hot during the summers.

You can verify the output of the application's output by viewing the CloudWatch Logs for the same:

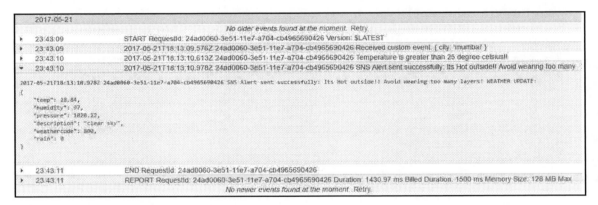

Also, since you can see that the temperature is greater than 25 in Mumbai, we received an email stating the same! The following screenshot depicts this:

In this way, you can also create custom applications and integrate them with SNS and Lambda functions to perform some backend processing. With this use case, we come towards the end of this chapter, but before concluding, let us look at some important next steps, recommendations, and best practices to keep in mind when working with Webhooks and external service integrations with Lambda.

Planning your next steps

Although we have just scratched the surface when it comes to integrating and leveraging AWS Lambda with other external services, the use cases and implementations are practically endless. There are however few simpler ways to try out these integrations as well with the help of a few third-party service integration providers such as Zapier, or IFTTT. Zapier provides easy to use and out of the box integrations of Lambda with other services such as Slack, Teamwork, and Twilio. With a few simple clicks and configurations your connection is established securely and you can get up and running with your integration in a matter of minutes.

 Zapier provides AWS Lambda on a premium basis; however, you can sign up and use certain services for free.

The other step worth trying out is building your own Webhooks as well. If the third-party service has an API (which most of them do today) you could even create and run your own Webhook server to accept the Webhook posts, transform them, and then post it back to the third-party API. This is a bit of a long shot, but if you are a developer and wish to create customized and more secure Webhooks, then this is probably a good way to go.

Recommendations and best practices

Here are a few key recommendations and best practices that you ought to keep in mind when working with integration services as well as with Webhooks:

- **Secure your Webhooks**: As Webhooks deliver data to publicly available URLs in your application, there are chances that a spoofer may provide your URL with false data. The easiest way to safeguard against such events is by forcing TLS connections. You can even secure the Webhook further by adding tokens to the URL that act as unique identification marker and then rotate these tokens on a regular basis.
- **Securing your API**: Make sure you always encrypt secret keys and API keys using KMS service and the encryption helpers provided by Lambda. The decrypting logic can be written in your Lambda function itself and invoked using the AWS SDKs.

Summary

With this, we come towards the end of yet another chapter. But before we move on to the next, here's a quick summary of the things we covered so far!

We started off by understanding the basic concepts of Webhooks and how they can be leveraged to connect your applications with any third-party services. We later looked at a few real world use cases where we integrated Lambda functions with a host of services such as Teamwork, GitHub, Slack and finally even with a custom made application. Towards the end we also covered a few key best practices and recommendations that you should keep in mind when invoking Lambda with external services.

In the next chapter, we will be exploring few new services that have been rolled out by AWS and we will also learn how to build serverless applications using them! So, don't go anywhere! More Lambda use cases and how-tos are just a page away!

6
Build and Deploy Serverless Applications with AWS Lambda

In the previous chapter, we saw how easy it is to build and integrate your applications and third party services with AWS Lambda functions. In this chapter, we will be taking things up a notch by learning how to design and build simple serverless applications with Lambda and a few other AWS services in the form of **Serverless Application Model (SAM)** and a newly launched service called as Step Functions.

In this chapter we will be learning:

- What the SAM template is and how to build serverless applications with it
- Using SAM to build and deploy serverless applications using simple examples
- Introducing AWS step functions
- Building coordinated Lambda services using step function's visual workflows

So without any further delays, let's get started!

Introducing SAM

The story of SAM starts back with few of the caveats faced by AWS CloudFormations. Although immensely powerful in it's automated infrastructure deployment capabilities, CloudFormations is still a tool that's not that easy to work with and maintain. A simple infrastructure deployment template can range anywhere from a 100 lines to even a 1,000 lines depending on the way the template is authored. More so, CloudFormation lacked the specialized resource types optimized for defining serverless applications which is why project Flourish was established which later on became known as SAM.

SAM is an extension of CloudFormation and basically provides developers with a really simplified way of writing CloudFormation-like templates for serverless services such as API Gateway, DynamoDB and even Lambda.

 NOTE: SAM is released under the Apache 2.0 License

The main goal of SAM is to define a standard application model for serverless applications which in turn helps developers design, deploy, and manage these applications using CloudFormation templates.

SAM is structured similarly to CloudFormation and just like it's counterpart, provides template support using both JSON and YAML. You can easily define and create S3 buckets to store the individual Lambda function deployment packages, create an API Gateway with the necessary configurations, create Simple DBs, configure SNS notifications, and much more using simple **commandlets** that make it far easier to read and manage your templates.

Writing SAM templates

Before we get going with writing our own SAM templates, it is important to understand a few SAM terms and terminologies. For starters; SAM is built on top of the standard CloudFormation service itself, so most of the SAM templates are nothing more than simplified CloudFormation templates that you can deploy just as you would deploy a standard CloudFormation stack! Even the concepts of resources, parameters, properties, and so on are all reused in SAM as well. The main difference however, is that simplified support for serverless AWS services namely API Gateway, Lambda functions, and DynamoDB makes these templates far easier to write and maintain than traditional CloudFormation ones.

Writing a SAM template starts off just as any other CloudFormation template does, with an `AWSTemplateFormatVersion` followed by a transform section that is specific to SAM. The transform section takes a value of `AWS::Serverless-2016-10-31` as shown in the snippet below:

```
AWSTemplateFormatVersion: '2010-09-09'
Transform: 'AWS::Serverless-2016-10-31'
```

After the transform section, you can have the resources section where you can define one or more serverless resource types. While writing this book, SAM supports three resource types namely:

- AWS::Serverless::Function
- AWS::Serverless::Api
- AWS::Serverless::SimpleTable

AWS::Serverless::Function

The AWS::Serverless::Function resource type is used to define and create Lambda functions and it's associated event source mappings which trigger the function.

Consider the flowing example snippet for creating a simple Lambda function using SAM:

```
Handler: index.js
Runtime: nodejs4.3
CodeUri: 's3://myS3Bucket/function.zip'
Description: A simple function for demonstrating SAM
MemorySize: 128
Timeout: 15
Policies:
 - LambdaFunctionExecutePolicy
 - Version: '2012-10-17'
   Statement:
     - Effect: Allow
       Action:
         - s3:GetObject
         - s3:GetObjectACL
       Resource: 'arn:aws:s3:::myS3Bucket/*'
Environment:
  Variables:
    key1: Hello
    key2: World
```

From the following snippet, most of the properties should be well known by now, including the Handler, Runtime, MemorySize, Timeout, and so on. The CodeUri refers to the S3 URI or any other valid location from where SAM will obtain the Lambda function for deployment. It's important to note, however, that this has to be a packaged Lambda function (.zip) even if it contains just a single index.js file.

The Policies section contains the names of either the AWS managed IAM policies or IAM policy documents that this function will require for execution; and finally we have the Environment section that can be used to set the function's environment variables as well.

AWS::Serverless::Api

You can use the `AWS::Serverless::API` resource type to define one or more Amazon API Gateway resources and methods that can be invoked through HTTPS endpoints. SAM supports two ways of creating API Gateways; both are explained as follows:

- **Implicitly**: In this case, the API is created implicitly by combining one or more API events defined using the `AWS::Serverless::Function` resource. For example, consider this simple example where we create an API Gateway using the `Events` parameter of the `AWS::Serverless::Function` resource. In this case, SAM will auto-generate that API for you. The API that is going to be generated from the three API events above looks like the following:

```
Resources:
  GetFunction:
    Type: AWS::Serverless::Function
    Properties:
      Handler: index.js
      Runtime: nodejs4.3
      Policies: myAWSLambdaReadOnlyPolicy
      Environment:
        Variables:
          Key: Hello
      Events:
        GetSomeResource:
          Type: Api
          Properties:
            Path: /resource/{resourceId}
            Method: get
```

- **Explicitly**: You can additionally create and configure API Gateway resources by using the `AWS::Serverless::Api` resource type followed by a valid Swagger file and a Stage name as shown in the example below:

```
Resources:
  ApiGatewayApi:
    Type: AWS::Serverless::Api
    Properties:
      DefinitionUri: s3://myS3Bucket/swagger.yaml
      StageName: Dev
```

The `StageName` parameter is used by the API Gateway as the first path segment for the invocation of the URI.

AWS::Serverless::SimpleTable

You can use the `AWS::Serverless::SimpleTable` resource to create a DynamoDB table with a single attribute primary key (hence the name `SimpleTable`). You can additionally provide the name and type of your primary key along with the table's provisioned throughput as parameters, as shown in the following example:

```
MySimpleTable:
    Type: AWS::Serverless::SimpleTable
    Properties:
        PrimaryKey:
            Name: userId
            Type: String
        ProvisionedThroughput:
            ReadCapacityUnits: 5
            WriteCapacityUnits: 5
```

You can optionally even use the `AWS::DynamoDB::Table` resource instead of the `SimpleTable` if, you require more advanced functionalities for your tables.

Putting it all together, you will end up with a ready to use template that can deploy a simple serverless application based on API Gateway, Lambda functions, and a simple backend in the form of DynamoDB as described in the next section.

Building serverless applications with SAM

Now that we have the basics covered, let us stitch together and deploy a simple application using SAM. To do so, we are going to use a readymade template provided by Lambda itself. Go to the AWS Lambda dashboard and select the option **Create a Lambda function**. Next, from the **Select blueprint** page, type in the filter **microservice** as shown below. Select the download icon adjoining to the blueprint and download the associated `microservice-http-endpoint.zip` on your workstation.

The following blueprint will provide a simple backend service using API Gateway that is able to read and write data to a particular DynamoDB table using a simple Lambda function!

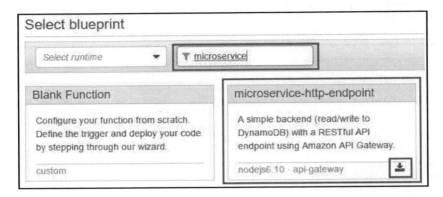

Once the zip is downloaded, extract it's contents to a folder. You will now have two files present namely `index.js` and `template.yaml`. The SAM template is declaring a Lambda resource and we are using the same to create an API (implicit) as well. The `index.js` file contains the necessary code that queries any DynamoDB table based on the parameters (`PUT`, `GET`, `DELETE`, `POST` and so on) that are passed to it via the API Gateway.

Have a look at the `template.yaml` file. You will notice that the `CodeUri` parameter under the `AWS::Serverless::Function` resource simply has a dot provided in it. Leave this as it is for now, we will be explaining that in a short while. The rest of the template should be pretty self-explanatory.

Now there are two ways in which we could have deployed this entire template. First up is by using the Lambda dashboard itself. You can simply select the `microservice-http-endpoint` blueprint and continue to setup the Lambda function just as you would have done during the initial deployment chapters. The second way is by uploading the template file to CloudFormation and executing it from there. We will give the second way a try by using AWS CLI.

For this setup, you will need AWS CLI installed and configured on your workstation. Make sure the CLI is the latest by either upgrading it by using python pip, or manually by installing a latest version of the CLI from here: `https://aws.amazon.com/cli/`.

 NOTE: You can refer to the following site for configuring the AWS CLI: `http://docs.aws.amazon.com/cli/latest/userguide/cli-chap-getting-started.html`

Next, cd into the `microservice-http-endpoint` directory and run the following command:

```
# aws cloudformation package \
--template-file template.yaml \
--output-template-file output.yaml
--s3-bucket sam-codebase
```

The following code simply takes the existing `template.yaml` file and packages it for the CloudFormation stack by replacing the `CodeUri` with the one that will be used for the deployment. You can clearly see the difference in the `template.yaml` and the `output.yaml` file as shown below:

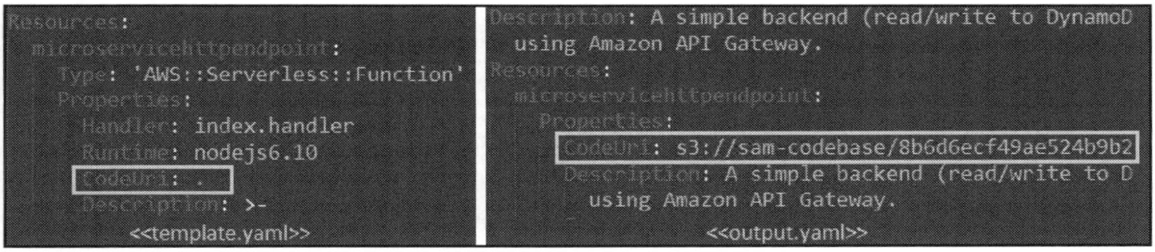

This comes in really handy when we want to implement a CICD pipeline for our Lambda functions. The CloudFormation `package` command does all the work for us by zipping the files, uploading them to the required S3 bucket, and even updating the `CodeUri` parameter with the correct URI. In this way, you can package your code and create multiple versions of the deployment packages without having to manually go and change the `CodeUri` each time. Simple, isn't it?

With the code uploaded, the next step is to deploy the code using the newly generated `output.yaml` as a CloudFormation stack. Type in the following command:

```
# aws cloudformation deploy \
--template-file output.yaml \
--stack-name MyFirstSAMDeployment \
--capabilities CAPABILITY_IAM
```

The `--capabilities CAPABILITY_IAM` parameter enables CloudFormation to create roles on our behalf for executing the Lambda function. If all goes well, your new application should be deployed over to CloudFormation as a Stack. Verify this by viewing the newly created Stack from the CloudFormation dashboard as shown below:

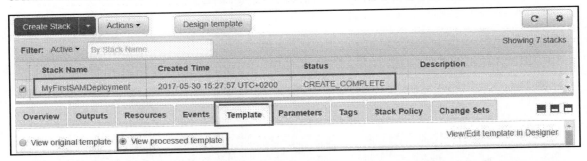

Select the newly deployed Stack and click on the **Template** tab as shown. You will see two checkboxes here: **View original template** and **View processed template**. Selecting the second option shows you just how few of the necessary permissions, as well as event parameters, were auto-filled by CloudFormations to ensure that Lambda Function executes properly.

With the stack deployed, you will now need the API Gateway URL to send POST or GET requests. You can obtain that by going over to the Lambda Dashboard, selecting the newly deployed Lambda function (`MyFirstSAMDeployment-microservicehttpendpoint-15L1RPRD4QGZ` in my case) and then selecting the **Triggers** tab, as shown:

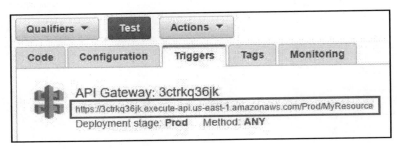

Make a note of the API Gateway URL that is displayed there. You can now use a tool such as Postman (`https://www.getpostman.com/`) to fire queries at the URL. You can pass the **TableName** of your DynamoDB table as a key-value pair and **Send** the request.

Corresponding to your table, you will be provided with a list of the table's items as shown below:

```
1 ▾ {
2 ▾    "Items": [
3 ▾        {
4              "IP_ADDRESS": "10.0.0.0"
5          },
6 ▾        {
7              "IP_ADDRESS": "192.168.76.90"
8          }
9      ],
10     "Count": 2,
11     "ScannedCount": 2
12 }
```

You can use the same steps to build and deploy your own serverless applications using SAM. Let us look at yet another example where we take our trusty calculator code and modify it to accept the operator and operands using an API Gateway. When a user posts these values using the gateway, it triggers the Lambda function that calculates the answer and stores the relevant data in a simple DynamoDB table.

First up, let us have a look at the calculator function code. The code is modified a bit to accept parameters from the API Gateway and write the output to a DynamoDB table:

```
'use strict';
console.log('Loading the Calc function');
let doc = require('dynamodb-doc');
let dynamo = new doc.DynamoDB();
const tableName = process.env.TABLE_NAME;
const createResponse = (statusCode, body) => {
    return {
        "statusCode": statusCode,
        "body": body || ""
```

```
        }
};
let response;

exports.handler = function(event, context, callback) {
    console.log('Received event:', JSON.stringify(event, null, 2));
    let operand1 = event.pathParameters.operand1;
    let operand2 = event.pathParameters.operand2;
    let operator = event.pathParameters.operator;

    if (operand1 === undefined || operand2 === undefined
    || operator === undefined) {
        console.log("400 Invalid Input");
        response = createResponse(400, "400 Invalid Input");
        return callback(null, response);
    }
    let res = {};
    res.a = Number(operand1);
    res.b = Number(operand2);
    res.op = operator;
    if (isNaN(operand1) || isNaN(operand2)) {
        console.log("400 Invalid Operand");
        response = createResponse(400, "400 Invalid Operand");
        return callback(null, response);
    }

    switch(operator)
    {
        case "add":
            res.c = res.a + res.b;
            break;
        case "sub":
            res.c = res.a - res.b;
            break;
        case "mul":
            res.c = res.a * res.b;
            break;
        case "div":
            if(res.b === 0){
                console.log("The divisor cannot be 0");
                response = createResponse(400, "400 The
                 divisor cannot be 0");
                return callback(null, response);
            }
            else{
                res.c = res.a/res.b;
            }
            break;
```

```
            default:
                console.log("400 Invalid Operator");
                response = createResponse(400, "400 Invalid Operator");
                return callback(null, response);
                break;
        }
        console.log("result: "+res.c);
        console.log("Writing to DynamoDB");

        let item = {
            "calcAnswer": res.c,
            "operand1": res.a,
            "operand2": res.b,
            "operator": res.op
        };

        let params = {
            "TableName": tableName,
            "Item": item
        };

        dynamo.putItem(params, (err, data) => {
            if (err){
                console.log("An error occured while writing to Db: ",err);
                response = createResponse(500, err);
            }
            else{
                console.log("Successfully wrote result to DB");
                response = createResponse(200, JSON.stringify(res));
            }
            callback(null, response);
        });
    };
```

Copy and save the code in an index.js file. Next up, we will create the all-important SAM file (template.yaml) for our calculator application.

```
AWSTemplateFormatVersion: '2010-09-09'
Transform: AWS::Serverless-2016-10-31
Description: Simple Calc web service. State is stored in a DynamoDB table.
Resources:
  CalcGetFunction:
    Type: AWS::Serverless::Function
    Properties:
      Handler: index.handler
      Policies: AmazonDynamoDBFullAccess
      Runtime: nodejs4.3
      Role: <role arn>
```

```
        Environment:
          Variables:
            TABLE_NAME: !Ref: Table
        Events:
          GetResource:
            Type: Api
            Properties:
              Method: get
              Path: /calc/{operand1}/{operand2}/{operator}
  Table:
    Type: AWS::Serverless::SimpleTable
    Properties:
      PrimaryKey:
        Name: calcAnswer
        Type: Number
      ProvisionedThroughput:
        ReadCapacityUnits: 5
        WriteCapacityUnits: 5
```

With the SAM all set up, let us run a few commands to generate the all-important
`output.yaml` file and later deploy our application using CloudFormation as well. First up,
we package the `template.yaml` with the command as shown below:

Change into the calculator application directory where the `index.js` file and the
`template.yaml` file are saved and run the following command:

```
# aws cloudformation package \
--template-file template.yaml \
--output-template-file output.yaml \
--s3-bucket sam-codebase
```

The output of this packaging command will be an `output.yaml` file. The output file will
have the `CodeUri` parameter autofilled with a unique S3 URI.

With the code uploaded, the next step is to deploy the code using the newly generated
`output.yaml` as a CloudFormation stack. Type in the following command as shown:

```
# aws cloudformation deploy \
--template-file output.yaml \
--stack-name MyCalcSAMDeployment \
--capabilities CAPABILITY_IAM
```

Remember to add the `--capabilities CAPABILITY_IAM` parameter that enables CloudFormation to create roles on our behalf for executing the Lambda function. A few minutes later, you should have your application stack created. You can verify the same using the CloudFormation dashboard as shown below:

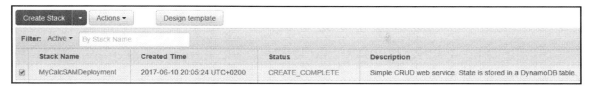

Now, over to the fun part! Testing and making sure the entire application setup works as expected or not. To do so, we will first require the API Gateway URL for posting the requests. You can obtain the same using either the API Gateway dashboard or even by using the Lambda dashboard as explained in the steps below.

First up, open up the Lambda management dashboard and select the newly created functions from the **Functions** page. The function name will be prefixed by the CloudFormation Stack name followed by some random string of characters; for example: `MyCalcSAMDeployment-CalcGetFunction-18T7IJLS4F53L`

Next, select the **Triggers** option and copy the API Gateway URL as shown in the image below:

You can use a tool such as Postman to send the requests to the API Gateway URL. To download the latest version of Postman, click here: `https://www.getpostman.com/`

Paste the API Gateway URL and substitute the {Operator1}, {Operator2}, and the {Operand} with your own values as shown in the image below. Once done, click on **Send** to send the request. If the application is setup correctly, you should see the output displayed in the **Body** section as shown. You can even verify the output by checking against the application's table from DynamoDB. The **Table** will have a similar naming convention as used for the Lambda function; prefixed by the name of the CloudFormation Stack and ending with some randomly added set of characters, for example: MyCalcSAMDeployment-Table-9G02RMWZ9O4M.

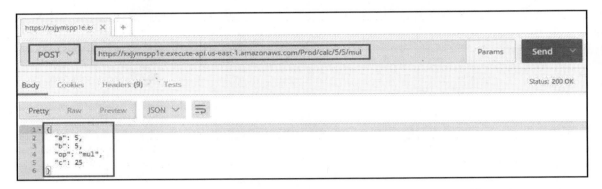

In similar ways, you can easily build out and deploy complete serverless applications such as this, using a standardized SAM template. But, as your applications gains in complexity with the introduction of more and more Lambda functions, it becomes even more difficult to write and coordinate the interactions among all these components. But fret not! You will be really happy to know that there's yet another AWS service that makes building and orchestrating serverless apps a breeze! Here's introducing AWS step functions!

Introducing AWS step functions

Working with Lambda functions so far has been really great for us and I hope it's been a similar experience for you as well! But there's a slight hitch that the Lambda service alone cannot help solve: how do you effectively coordinate and orchestrate Lambda functions so that they form a backbone for some really distributed applications that rely on complex workflows for execution? For most of you, working with AWS for a long time, the obvious answer would be to use something like AWS **Simple Workflow Service (SWF)** or maybe even create a single Lambda function that acts as an orchestrator for some other worker functions, but both these techniques have their own sets of pros and cons. To solve this, AWS unfolded the Step Functions web service during the *AWS re:Invent* 2016 event!

AWS Step Functions is basically an orchestration service for Lambda functions, using which you can orchestrate and control multiple Lambda function executions. Using Step Functions, you build individual functions that perform a particular "task", with each task being capable of scaling independently of each other. The scaling, retries in case of failure, and the coordination among other components is all taken care of, by Step Functions itself, leaving you to design the workflows as you see fit.

Under the hood

Under the hood, AWS step functions mainly relies on two things apart from few other essential components: tasks and state machines. Let us take a quick peek into what each of these component performs:

- **State machine**: State machine is basically a JSON-based structured language used to define one or more "states". States can be used to perform some specific set of tasks, for example, the "task states" can be used to perform some activity, the "choice states" determine which states to transition to next, the "Fail states" are designed to stop an execution with an error, and so on. States can run in a sequence or even in parallel with each copy of the state machine called as an "execution." Multiple executions can run independently at any given point in time.

    Here is a simple representational example of a state machine:

    ```
    {
        "Comment": "A Hello World example of the Amazon
          States Language using a Pass state",
        "StartAt": "HelloWorld",
        "States": {
          "HelloWorld": {
            "Type": "Pass",
            "Result": "Hello World!",
            "End": true
          }
        }
    }
    ```

- **States**: States are individual elements or helper functions that together combine to form the state machine. They can be used to perform a variety of functions in your state machine such as:
- **Task state**: Used to perform activities in your state machine.

- **Choice state:** Used to make decisions between multiple executions.
- **Pass state:** Simply used to pass some data from one point to another.
- **Wait state:** Used to provide a timed delay between executions.
- **Parallel state:** Starts a parallel execution of tasks.
- **Succeed/ fail state:** Used to stop an execution based on it's success or failure.
- **Tasks and activities:** Each work performed by your state machine is termed as a Task. Tasks can be further subdivided into two categories: A Lambda function that performs some task based on the code that's written and a second category called as activities which is basically any and all code that's either hosted on EC2, ECS containers, physical infrastructure, or even mobile devices!
- **Transitions**: Transitions are points in your state machine's execution that define the next state that step functions have to advance to. In some states, you can provide only a single transition rule however, this does not hold true if you are using the choice state which can require more than one transition rules.

Besides these concepts, step functions also provide a really simple and easy to use visual workflow editor of sorts that provides you with a color coded representation of your workflow during it's execution. This comes in real handy during debugging of your workflows as well as helps to view the various input and output values passed by the State Machine.

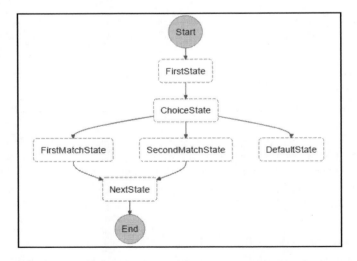

Let us now look at a couple of examples on how we can leverage Step Functions to co-ordinate and organize our Lambda functions.

Getting started with step functions

In this section, we are going to walk you through a fairly simple example of how to set up and get started with your very first step function state machine.

The scenario is fairly straight forward: I have two Lambda functions that are used to either switch on or switch off the light bulbs in my house! Don't worry, we are not going to set up any AWS IoT out here! The functions simply simulate the actions of switching on and off the light bulbs; the real idea here is to understand how to create a minimalistic state machine that will help you do so.

Before we go ahead and create the state machine, the first order of business is to create our Lambda functions. In this case, the functions are really just place holders, so you can actually use the same function with a slight modification for simulating both the switch on and off of the light bulbs.

```
'use strict';
console.log('Loading function');
exports.handler = (event, context, callback) => {
    console.log('Some magical code to turn on my lightbulb goes
     here!', event.onoff);
    callback(null, "Light Bulb is switched on");
};
```

The function simply takes an event parameter and returns a message in it's `callback()`. Go ahead and deploy this function to Lambda by providing it a meaningful name (in my case, I named it `switchOn`). The event for triggering the `switchOn` function is supplied in the following format:

```
{
    "onoff": "on"
}
```

With the code deployed, make a note of it's ARN as well, this will be required during the state machine creation phase. Similarly, go ahead and create the `switchOff` function as well. With our functions created, it's time to move on to the second part of this exercise which is basically creating the state machine itself.

To do so, from the AWS Management Console, filter and select the service **Step Functions**. Select the **Get started** option on the dashboard. This will bring you to the **Create State Machine** page as shown below. Here, we provide a suitable name for your **State Machine**:

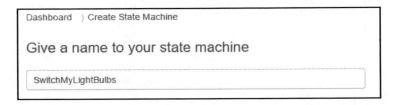

Next, scroll down towards the **Code** section and paste the following machine state code there:

```
{
    "Comment": "Change Power State of my light bulbs",
    "StartAt": "SwitchState",
    "States": {
        "SwitchState": {
            "Choices": [
                {
                    "Next": "OnSwitch",
                    "StringEquals": "on",
                    "Variable": "$.onoff"
                },
                {
                    "Next": "OffSwitch",
                    "StringEquals": "off",
                    "Variable": "$.onoff"
                }
            ],
            "Default": "DefaultState",
            "Type": "Choice"
        },
        "DefaultState": {
            "Cause": "No Matches!",
            "Type": "Fail"
        },
        "OffSwitch": {
            "End": true,
            "Resource": "arn:aws:lambda:us-east-1:12345678910:
              function:switchOff",
            "Type": "Task"
        },
        "OnSwitch": {
            "End": true,
```

```
        "Resource": "arn:aws:lambda:us-east-1:12345678910:
           function:switchOn",
        "Type": "Task"
      }
    }
  }
```

Lets us understand what we pasted into the **Code** section a bit. First up, is the all-important **StartAt** parameter that defines the start of our state machine code. This is followed up by the **Choices** parameter that provides us with one or more choices to follow; in this case, what choice do I need to take if the function receives an *on* or an *off* event. Within each **Choice** we also pass a **Next** parameter that defines the name of the next logical step that the state machine has to follow in case that particular choice is met. We can also see a **Default** state being created which basically handles the actions that are required to be performed if neither of the choices are met. In this case the default state will simply fail with an error message if no match is found during the choices state.

Towards the end of the State Machine is where we have actually defined the actionable states (**OffSwitch** and **OnSwitch**) that call the necessary Lambda functions when invoked. Replace the ARN of your Lambda functions with the ones shown in the above state machine and click on the **Preview** button to visually view the state machine. You will end up with a similar flowchart as shown as follows:

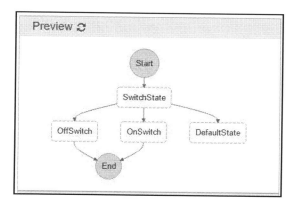

Click on **Create State Machine** option to complete the creation process. At this point, you will be prompted to select an IAM role for your task. To do so, you will need to create an IAM Role with the following policy:

```
{
    "Version": "2012-10-17",
    "Statement": [{
        "Effect": "Allow",
```

```
        "Action": [
            "lambda:InvokeFunction"
        ],
        "Resource": ["*"]
    }]
}
CODE:
```

Once the Role is created, you will also need to establish a trust relationship of that role with Step Functions. To do so, copy the following policy in the "Trusted entities" section of your Role:

```
{
  "Version": "2012-10-17",
  "Statement": [
    {
      "Sid": "",
      "Effect": "Allow",
      "Principal": {
        "Service": "states.us-east-1.amazonaws.com"
      },
      "Action": "sts:AssumeRole"
    }
  ]
}
```

Once completed, you should be able to select your newly created role and complete the creation of your first state machine, as shown below:

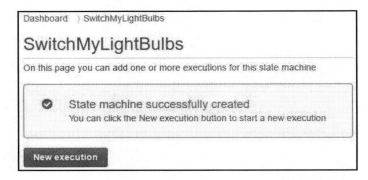

To test and execute the state machine, select the **New execution** option, as shown. This will provide you with a JSON editor where you can type in the required event you want to pass to the state machine. In this case, the event should look something like this:

```
{
    "onoff": "on"
}
```

Once done, click on **Start Execution** to begin your state machine. If all goes according to plan, you should see a successful execution of your state machine as shown in the image below. You can select the **SwitchState** and the **OnSwitch** states to view more details about them. For example, selecting the **Output** tab from the **OnSwitch** state will display the message **Light bulb is switched on** and so on.

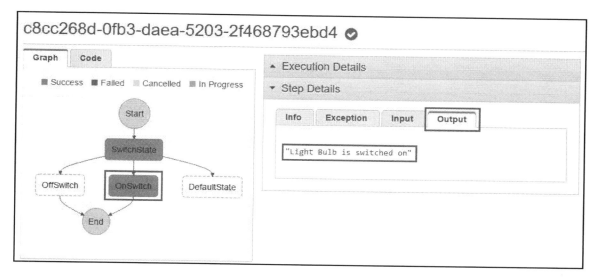

You can additionally drill down into your state machine's execution by selecting other tasks and checking the input and output parameters supplied. Remember, however, that each time you wish to run the state machine; you will have to create new executions of the same.

With this, we come towards the end of this section. In the next section, we will take what we have learned so far with step functions and apply it to our calculator example.

Building distributed applications with step functions

The whole idea behind step functions is to make it easier for developers to write and orchestrate multiple Lambda functions with ease. This comes in really handy when you have a really large number of Lambda functions, each performing a very specific task, and you wish to coordinate the actions among them. In this scenario, we will be taking our monolithic calculator example code from the earlier deployed SAM template and re-engineer it to work with Step Functions. To begin with, let us examine the Lambda functions that we have created for this scenario. First up, are the basic addition, subtraction, and multiplication functions that all follow the same code as shown below:

```
'use strict';
console.log('Loading the Addition function');

exports.handler = function(event, context, callback) {
    console.log('Received event:', JSON.stringify(event, null, 2));
    let operand1 = event.a;
    let operand2 = event.b;
    let operator = event.op;

    let res = {};
    res.a = Number(operand1);
    res.b = Number(operand2);
    res.op = operator;

    res.c = res.a + res.b;
    console.log("result: "+res.c);
    callback(null, res);
};
```

The function is very simple to understand and implement. It takes three parameters (operand1, operand2 and operator) as events, calculates the results, and simply passes all the details to an object as a callback().

The function code for dividing is a bit different, in the sense that it does a few checks before actually running a divide operation on the two operands as shown in the snippet below:

```
function ZeroDivisorError(message) {
    this.name = "ZeroDivisorError";
    this.message = message;
}

    if(res.b === 0){
        console.log("The divisor cannot be 0");
```

```
        const zeroDivisortError =
          new ZeroDivisorError("The divisor cannot be 0!");
        callback(zeroDivisortError);
    }
    else{
        res.c = res.a/res.b;
        console.log("result: "+res.c);
        callback(null, res);
    }
```

Apart from these two functions, we have also gone ahead and created a function that basically checks whether all the required values are entered or not, as well as, whether the operands are numbers or not. If the operands clear the checks, they are then passed to the respective Lambda function for further calculation.

```
'use strict';
console.log('Loading the Calc function');

function InvalidInputError(message) {
    this.name = "InvalidInputError";
    this.message = message;
}

function InvalidOperandError(message) {
    this.name = "InvalidOperandError";
    this.message = message;
}

exports.handler = function(event, context, callback) {
    console.log('Received event:', JSON.stringify(event, null, 2));
    let operand1 = event.operand1;
    let operand2 = event.operand2;
    let operator = event.operator;

    InvalidInputError.prototype = new Error();
    if (operand1 === undefined || operand2 === undefined
     || operator === undefined) {
        console.log("Invalid Input");
        const invalidInputError =
          new InvalidInputError("Invalid Input!");
        return callback(invalidInputError);
    }
    let res = {};
    res.a = Number(operand1);
    res.b = Number(operand2);
    res.op = operator;
    InvalidOperandError.prototype = new Error();
```

```
        if (isNaN(operand1) || isNaN(operand2)) {
            console.log("Invalid Operand");
            const invalidOperandError =
              new InvalidOperandError("Invalid Operand!");
            return callback(invalidOperandError);
        }

        callback(null, res);
};
```

Once the calculations are all completed, the final results are stored in a predefined DynamoDB table using the final function code snippet as shown below:

```
let item = {
        "calcAnswer": event.c,
        "operand1": event.a,
        "operand2": event.b,
        "operator": event.op
    };

let params = {
        "TableName": tableName,
        "Item": item
    };

dynamo.putItem(params, (err, data) => {
        if (err){
            console.log("An error occured while writing to Db: ",err);
            callback(err);
        }
        else{
            console.log("Successfully wrote result to DB");
            callback(null, "success!");
        }
```

So, all in all, we have taken our standard calculator code and split it's functionality into six different Lambda functions! Once all the functions are deployed to Lambda, the last thing left is to go ahead and create the associated state machine for step functions! Let us have a look at the state machine one section at a time:

The first section is where we are defining the starting state `FetchAndCheck` that will basically accept the operands and operator as events and pass them through a series of validation checks. If an error is found, the `FailState` is invoked with the appropriate error message else the execution continues with the invocation of the `ChoiceStateX`.

```
{
    "Comment": "An example of the Amazon States Language using
```

```
    an AWS Lambda Functions",
  "StartAt": "FetchAndCheck",
  "States": {
    "FetchAndCheck": {
      "Type": "Task",
      "Resource": "arn:aws:lambda:us-east-1:12345678910:
        function:fetchandCheckLambda",
      "Next": "ChoiceStateX",
      "Catch": [
            {
              "ErrorEquals": ["InvalidInputError",
                "InvalidOperandError"],
              "Next": "FailState"
            }
        ]
    },
```

The `ChoiceStateX` state decides the task to invoke, based on the operator parameter passed during the state machine's execution

```
    "ChoiceStateX": {
      "Type": "Choice",
      "Choices": [
        {
          "Variable": "$.op",
          "StringEquals": "add",
          "Next": "Addition"
        },
        {
          "Variable": "$.op",
          "StringEquals": "sub",
          "Next": "Subtraction"
        },
        {
          "Variable": "$.op",
          "StringEquals": "mul",
          "Next": "Multiplication"
        },
        {
          "Variable": "$.op",
          "StringEquals": "div",
          "Next": "Division"
        }
      ],
      "Default": "DefaultState"
    },
```

With the choice state defined, the next step in the state machine's definition is the individual task itself. Here, we will provide the individual Lambda function ARN's that we created earlier:

```
"Addition": {
  "Type" : "Task",
  "Resource": "arn:aws:lambda:us-east-1:12345678910:
    function:additionLambda",
  "Next": "InsertInDB"
},

"Subtraction": {
  "Type" : "Task",
  "Resource": "arn:aws:lambda:us-east-1:12345678910:
    function:subtractionLambda",
  "Next": "InsertInDB"
},

"Multiplication": {
  "Type" : "Task",
  "Resource": "arn:aws:lambda:us-east-1:12345678910:
    function:multiplication",
  "Next": "InsertInDB"
},

"Division": {
  "Type" : "Task",
  "Resource": "arn:aws:lambda:us-east-1:12345678910:
    function:divisionLambda",
  "Next": "InsertInDB",
  "Catch": [
        {
            "ErrorEquals": ["ZeroDivisorError"],
            "Next": "FailState"
        }
     ]
},

"DefaultState": {
  "Type": "Pass",
  "Next": "FailState"
},
```

The `InsertInDB` state is the final state in the state machine's execution where the operands, the operator, and the calculated value are stored in a pre-defined DynamoDB table:

```
"InsertInDB": {
  "Type": "Task",
  "Resource": "arn:aws:lambda:us-east-1:12345678910:
    function:insertInDBLambda",
  "Next": "SuccessState",
  "Catch": [
        {
            "ErrorEquals": ["States.ALL"],
            "Next": "FailState"
        }
     ]
},

"FailState": {
  "Type": "Fail"
},

"SuccessState": {
  "Type": "Succeed"
  }
 }
}
```

With the code pasted, click on the **Preview** option to visually see the state machine. You should see a flowchart similar to the one shown as follows:

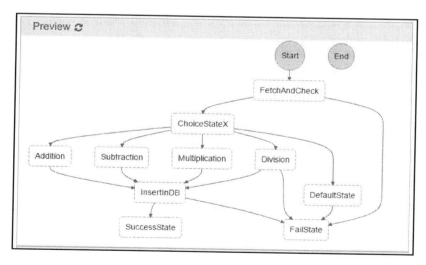

Once completed, click on **Create State Machine** option to select the IAM role for our state machine. Unlike the previous IAM role for our example, we need to add few specific policies for logging the events to CloudWatch, as well as inserting items to a specific DynamoDB table. Note that, in my case, I'm reusing one of my table's for this exercise.

```json
{
    "Version": "2012-10-17",
    "Statement": [
        {
            "Sid": "Stmt1497293444000",
            "Effect": "Allow",
            "Action": [
                "logs:CreateLogGroup",
                "logs:CreateLogStream",
                "logs:PutLogEvents"
            ],
            "Resource": [
                "*"
            ]
        },
        {
            "Sid": "Stmt1497293498000",
            "Effect": "Allow",
            "Action": [
                "dynamodb:PutItem"
            ],
            "Resource": [
                "arn:aws:dynamodb:us-east-1:12345678910:
                table/myCalcResults"
            ]
        }
    ]
}
```

With the IAM role created and assigned to the state machine, you can now go ahead and create an execution for the same.

Click on the **New execution** option and pass the following event in the events pane as shown:

```json
{
  "operand1": "3",
  "operand2": "5",
  "operator": "mul"
}
```

With the event parameters passed, you should see a flowchart along with the **Input** and **Output** values as shown in the following flowchart:

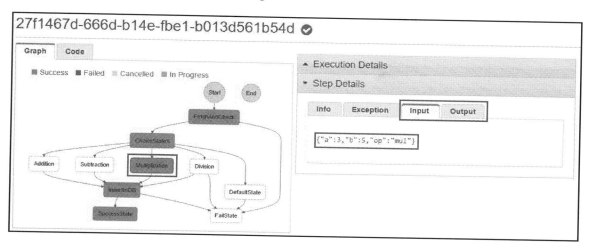

You can run similar permutations and combinations of executions on the following state machine as per your requirements. Make sure to check the DynamoDB table whether the records are inserted or not, as well as the CloudWatch logs of your individual Lambda functions for troubleshooting and error checking.

Planning your next steps

There's a lot you can achieve by working with SAM as well as with Step Functions when it comes to building and deploying Lambda applications. But besides these services, you can still use other AWS services such as AWS Code Build and AWS Code Deploy. Code Build can be leveraged to build, locally test, and package your serverless application, whereas Code Deploy can be used to automate the steps for your application's release management. You can find detailed implementation steps for the same using this link: `http://docs.aws.amazon.com/lambda/latest/dg/automating-deployment.html`

The second AWS service worth trying out is Amazon Simple Workflow Service or SWF. Although step functions are a small part of SWF's overall functionality, it greatly enhances the overall experience of orchestrating and running distributed serverless apps when compared to the latter service. But in that case, when do we use SWF and when do we use step functions? Well, there's no simple way of putting it. Both the services have their own pros and cons but the ultimate choice, according to me, depends on the complexity of the tasks that you plan to execute. For example, SWF can be better off suited for tasks that involve intervention of your processes by any external application as by design, SWF uses a concept called as a "Decider" program that separates the decision making steps from the actual steps that perform some activity. In case of step functions, there is no need for your application to communicate with this type of orchestration service and this makes step functions ideal for simpler applications that just need some form of managed orchestration. You can even give SWF a try out using the steps mentioned in this guide here: `http://docs .aws.amazon.com/amazonswf/latest/developerguide/lambda-task.html`

Summary

So, here we are again! The end of yet another chapter! By now I'm pretty sure you will have gotten a good handle over Lambda functions and how to work with them! So, before we move on to the next chapter, here's a quick summary of the things we have covered so far.

This chapter was all about how to leverage AWS services such as SAM and Step Functions to build, deploy, and orchestrate serverless applications that are predominantly run by a combination of AWS services such as DynamoDB, API Gateway, and Lambda. We created few SAM templates and learnt how to effectively deploy them, as well as took a crash course into AWS step functions with a few handy deployment examples as well. Towards the end of the chapter, we topped it all off with some interesting next steps that I would really recommend that you try out as well.

In the next chapter, we will be covering yet another very important section related to working with Lambda functions, which is how you can effectively monitor and troubleshoot your functions. So, stay tuned; there's still a lot more to learn!

7
Monitoring and Troubleshooting AWS Lambda

So far, we have been learning about how to write, test, and build serverless applications using the AWS Lambda service. This chapter is going to cover few different aspects with regards to Lambda functions, namely: how to effectively monitor and troubleshoot your functions and applications using a combination of both AWS CloudWatch, as well as a few third-party tools in the form Datadog and Loggly.

In this chapter we will be learning:

- How to monitor Lambda functions using CloudWatch
- How to leverage AWS X-Ray for monitoring your serverless applications
- How to get started on monitoring your Lambda functions using Datadog
- How to log and analyze your application as well as your functions logs to Loggly
- Some basic steps and tricks to troubleshoot your Lambda functions

So, without any further delays, let's get started!

Monitoring Lambda functions using CloudWatch

Throughout the book we have been talking about checking and monitoring your Lambda functions using CloudWatch. It's really not that difficult to set it up and once you have the base ready, you can reuse the same setup for monitoring almost all of your functions. So, let us quickly recap on how to monitor Lambda functions using CloudWatch!

To start off, we first need to prepare the base that we talked about. The base here is nothing more that the correct set of policies that allow your function to send its logs to CloudWatch. In most cases, your functions will require rights to create log groups and streams in CloudWatch, as well as to put log events into that particular stream. The log group creation, as well as the stream creation, is all taken care of by CloudWatch itself. Here is a simple IAM policy that will basically allow your functions to dump their logs into CloudWatch. Remember, this is just a template so you should always follow the practice of creating specific IAM policies and roles for your functions, especially if they are going to be running on a live production environment:

```
{
    "Version": "2012-10-17",
    "Statement": [
    {
      "Effect": "Allow",
      "Action": [
        "logs:CreateLogGroup",
        "logs:CreateLogStream",
        "logs:PutLogEvents"
      ],
      "Resource": "*"
    }
    ]
}
```

Once the base is ready, you can write, package, and upload your functions to Lambda and when your functions get triggered, they will ideally start pumping logs to CloudWatch. You can view your function's logs by selecting CloudWatch Logs option from the CloudWatch dashboard and typing the name of your function in the filter text as shown as follows:

```
/aws/lambda/<Name_Of_Your_Function>
```

Select your function and you should see a log stream created already for you. If you don't see a log stream, it is probably because you haven't configured the IAM role to grant the necessary permissions to write the logs to CloudWatch.

You can then use the CloudWatch Logs dashboard to scroll and filter your application logs as you see fit. Here's a sample CloudWatch Logs dashboard view for one of our calculator functions that we created in the previous chapter:

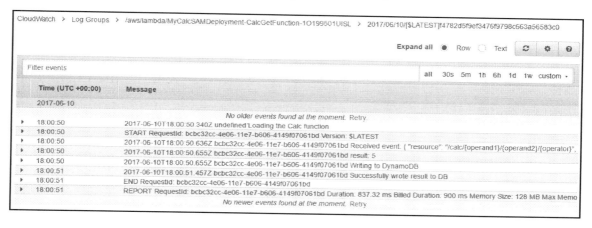

Apart from the standard logs, you can also use CloudWatch metrics to view and analyze a few of your function's runtime parameters, such as **Errors**, **Invocations**, **Duration**, and **Throttles**; each is explained briefly as follows:

- **Invocations**: This metric measures the number of times a particular function was invoked either by an API call or an event response.
- **Errors**: The errors metric only counts the number of invocations that failed due to errors present in the function. It does not take into account internal service errors or errors caused by other AWS services connected to Lambda functions.
- **Duration**: This metric measures the elapsed time from when a function is invoked to run till the time it stops execution.
- **Throttles**: This metric counts the number of invocations that are throttled in case the invocation rates exceed the set concurrent execution limit.

To view your function's metrics, simply select the **Metrics** option from the CloudWatch dashboard. Next, search for the **Lambda** metrics group from the **All metrics** tab. You can now drill further down to your individual functions by selecting either the **By Resource** or **By Function Name** options. You can alternatively view the collective metrics for all your functions using the **Across All Functions** option as well.

In this case, I have opted for the **By Function Name** option and selected the **Error, Throttles, Invocations**, and **Duration** metrics for the calculator function that we deployed from our earlier chapter. You can select any of the function metrics as you see fit. Once the metrics are selected, you will automatically be shown a simple **Line** graph that depicts the overall duration of the function's execution, as well as whether there were any error or throttle events. You can switch between **Line** graphs or **Stacked area** graphs by selecting the **Graph options** tab provided beneath your graph area:

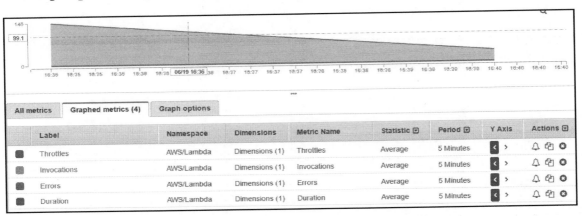

Alternatively, you can even configure CloudWatch alarms by selecting the individual metric from the **Graphed metrics** tab and clicking on the adjoining alarm icon as depicted in the previous image.

Although CloudWatch provides a good assortment of services for monitoring your Lambda functions, it still had some clinks in its armor. First up, as we know, Lambda functions are more or less designed around the principles of microservices, where each service gets its own functional container for hosting. However, unlike the traditional EC2 instances that hosted monolithic apps, thousands of containers can be spun up within fractions of seconds using Lambda. This, along with the large number of other moving parts in the form of AWS services such as DynamoDB and API Gateway, can prove too much for even CloudWatch to handle. A specialized tool was required that could effectively trace each request made by functions against other services and also that could be used to analyze performance bottlenecks and remediate against them. Enter the newest kid on the block! AWS X-Ray!

Introducing AWS X-Ray

AWS X-Ray was first introduced during *AWS re:Invent 2016* as a tool that would enable developers to debug their distributed applications by analyzing and tracing the calls that occur between the application and its various components. By analyzing this performance, you can easily isolate and remediate issues caused either due to bottlenecks or errors. The best part of X-Ray is its ability to work with a wide variety of applications and services; for example, your application maybe running on a single EC2 instance or it might even be a highly distributed application containing thousands of Lambda functions! X-Ray can easily get integrated with your code; whether it is written in Node.js, .NET, or Java, and start providing performance metrics for the same. This, along with the support for tracing requests from services such as EC2, ECS, Beanstalk, DynamoDB, SNS, SQS, and Lambda makes, X-Ray a really important tool from an application performance management perspective.

How does it all work? X-Ray provides an SDK that you will be required to incorporate in your applications for performance monitoring. You can even leverage an X-Ray agent provided by X-Ray that can be installed on applications hosted on EC2 instances. If your application is hosted on an Elastic Beanstalk environment, the agent comes pre-installed so the only activity that you need to do is plug in the SDK with your app and you can get started with the traces immediately. The traces are used to track each request made to your application. The data that passes through each of the services or application component is recorded as a trace and displayed using a visual map format using the X-Ray dashboard:

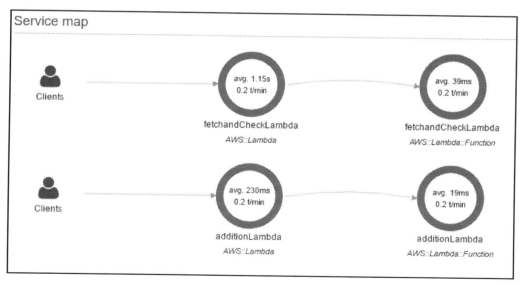

Before we begin with the actual monitoring of your application, we need to have a quick understanding of some of the concepts and terminologies that are commonly used in X-Ray:

- **Segments**: Segments are small work units that contains data about your running application. Segments with common requests are grouped into what we call traces. A segment provides the resource's name, details about the request, the response, and details about the work done.
- **Subsegments**: Subsegments are smaller groups of more granular data present within one segment. They provide more information about a particular response that your application might make against a request.
- **Service graph**: Service graphs are generated by X-Ray using the metrics that are passed by your application. Each AWS resource that sends data to X-Ray appears as a service in the graph.
- **Trace**: A trace, as the name suggests, tracks the path of a request made through your application. A single trace can be a collection of requests (GET/ POST) that propagate all the way from the time your application was invoked either by a Load Balancer, all the way to the code itself, and finally to some other AWS service or an external API.

With the basics out of the way, let us look at how to enable your serverless applications for monitoring using X-Ray.

To demonstrate X-Ray's usage for tracing purposes, we are going to re-use the same calculator code that leveraged an API Gateway, a single Lambda function and a DynamoDB as a backend. You can refer to `Chapter 6`, *Build and Deploy Serverless Applications with AWS Lambda* for this code's explanation and details. That being said, we are going to look into using X-Ray for our Lambda functions. The good thing here is, it's as easy as checking a box to activate X-Ray tracing for your Lambda function! No, I am not kidding! It's literally a checkbox on your Lambda console. To enable X-Ray monitoring for your functions, select the **Configuration** tab and under **Advanced settings**, you should be able to see a checkbox that reads **Enable active tracing**. Go ahead and select that and remember to **Save** the configuration settings before running your function code.

Additionally, you will also need to provide your Lambda function with an IAM role that enables Lambda to create traces in X-Ray for you.

This is a predefined policy provided by AWS under the name `AWSXrayWriteOnlyAccess` as shown as follows:

```
{
  "Version": "2012-10-17",
  "Statement": [
    {
      "Effect": "Allow",
      "Action": [
        "xray:PutTraceSegments",
        "xray:PutTelemetryRecords"
      ],
      "Resource": [
        "*"
      ]
    }
  ]
}
```

So, remember to add this to your Lambda execution role before you start using X-Ray's tracing.

Now, if you go through the extensive X-Ray documentation, you will see that X-Ray has three types of nodes on the service map for requests served by Lambda:

- Lambda service (`AWS::Lambda`)
- Lambda function (`AWS::Lambda::Function`)
- Downstream service calls

The trace will display the in-depth info regarding the Lambda function in the form of segments and subsegments. Now there are various kinds of segments and subsegments depending on the event type--synchronous or asynchronous, and so on. By default, once you activate X-Ray on your function, the basic segments and subsegments are visible in the trace view but if you want to see custom segments, annotations, or subsegments for downstream calls, you might need to include additional libraries and annotate your code.

In our example, we do have a downstream call made to DynamoDB and hence we will be including the additional libraries. To do so, you first need to include the AWS X-Ray SDK for Node.js in your deployment package. In addition, you will also need to wrap your AWS SDK's `require` statement as depicted in the snippet below:

```
'use strict';
console.log('Loading the Calc function');
var AWSXRay = require('aws-xray-sdk-core');
var AWS = AWSXRay.captureAWS(require('aws-sdk'));
```

Then, use the AWS variable defined in the preceding example to initialize any service client that you want to trace with X-Ray, for example:

```
s3Client = AWS.S3();
```

 These additional capabilities of custom segments, annotations and subsegments for downstream calls are only present for Java and Node.js runtimes.

The rest of the code remains practically unchanged. Here too, we are going to use the SAM template to deploy our entire calculator code. Remember, this is the same SAM template as we used back in Chapter 6, *Build and Deploy Serverless Applications with AWS Lambda*, so, if you ever need to understand the steps a bit better, just revisit the previous chapter for more details.

```
AWSTemplateFormatVersion: '2010-09-09'
Transform: AWS::Serverless-2016-10-31
Description: Simple Calc web service. State is stored in a DynamoDB table.
Resources:
  CalcGetFunction:
    Type: AWS::Serverless::Function
    Properties:
      Handler: index.handler
      Runtime: nodejs4.3
      Policies: AmazonDynamoDBReadOnlyAccess
      Role:
        arn:aws:iam::012345678910:
        role/MyCalcSAMDeployment-CalcGetFunctionRole-1JSUDGR70YYON
      Environment:
        Variables:
          TABLE_NAME: !Ref Table
      Events:
        GetResource:
          Type: Api
          Properties:
```

```
        Path: /calc/{operand1}/{operand2}/{operator}
        Method: post
Table:
  Type: AWS::Serverless::SimpleTable
  Properties:
    PrimaryKey:
      Name: calcAnswer
      Type: Number
    ProvisionedThroughput:
      ReadCapacityUnits: 5
      WriteCapacityUnits: 5
```

Here are the CLI commands to deploy the SAM template. Replace the content in the brackets < > with your values:

```
# aws cloudformation package --template-file <templateName.yaml> --s3-
bucket <bucketName> --output-template-file <packaged-templateName.yaml>
# aws cloudformation deploy --template-file <packaged-templateName.yaml> --
stack-name <stackName>
```

Once the stack gets deployed, go to the Lambda function and activate the X-Ray tracing as shown in the following screenshot:

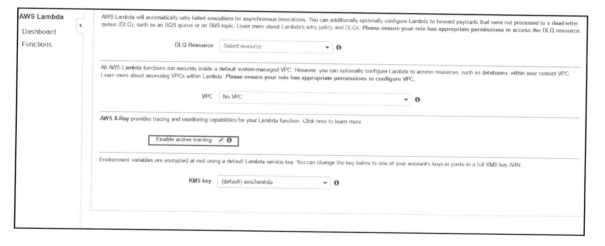

Go ahead and pass a few values to the deployed application using the API Gateway. Next, jump on to the X-Ray console and select the **Service map** tab on the left-hand side panel. You should see a graph populated as shown in the following screenshot:

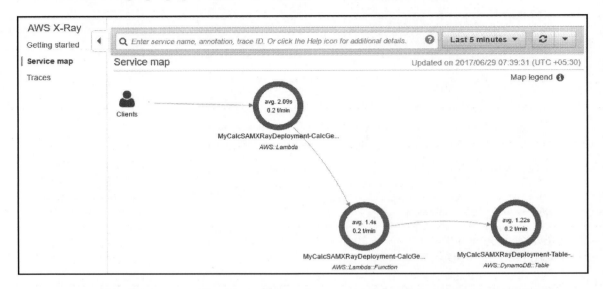

Select the **Traces** tab to view the trace list for this particular application. Select the trace **ID** to view an in-depth analysis of your application's performance and traces as shown in the following screenshot:

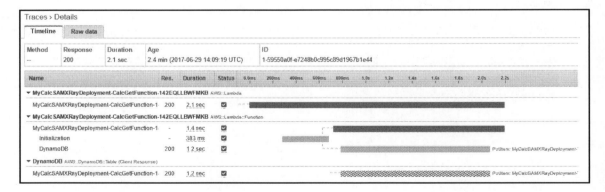

This is just one of the ways using which you can effectively analyze and monitor the performance of your serverless applications using one or more combinations of AWS services such as CloudWatch and X-Ray. In the next section, we will be exploring some really awesome third-party tools that are real handy when it comes to monitoring and analyzing performances of your serverless applications.

Monitoring Lambda functions using Datadog

Although CloudWatch and X-Ray are really awesome tools, there are times when these tools are simply not enough to work with at an *enterprise* level. This can hold true for a variety of reasons; take for example maturity--now, although X-Ray provides you with some real time trace statistics, it's still a very young service and will take time to evolve, into say, something provided by an enterprise transaction monitoring tool such as Dynatrace. Dynatrace actually leverages artificial intelligence to detect performance and availability issues and pinpoints their root causes; something that X-Ray doesn't support today. The same can be said for CloudWatch as well. Although you can monitor your AWS infrastructure using CloudWatch, sometimes you may require some extra tools such as Datadog, New Relic, Splunk, and so on to do some customized monitoring for you. Mind you, this doesn't mean there's something wrong in using AWS services for monitoring or performance tuning. It's simply a matter of perspective and your requirements.

So, that's what this section will cover mostly! We will understand how to leverage third-party tools for monitoring your serverless applications and infrastructure. We begin with a small walkthrough of Datadog!

Datadog is cloud infrastructure and an application monitoring service that comes packaged with an intuitive dashboard for viewing performance metrics along with notifications and alert capabilities. In this section, we will walk through few simple scenarios using which you can integrate Datadog with your own AWS environment and start monitoring your Lambda and rest of the serverless services with ease.

To start off with Datadog, you will first need to sign up for it's services. Datadog offers a 14-day trial period in which you can get complete access to all of its services for free. You can read about the entire integration process by visiting the site `http://docs.datadoghq.com/integrations/aws/`. With the integration completed, all you need to do is filter and select the **AWS Lambda** dashboard from the **List Dashboard** section. This is a prebuilt dashboard that you can start using immediately out of the box for your Lambda function monitoring. You can, alternatively, copy or **Clone Dashboard** into a new custom dashboard and add more metrics for monitoring, or change the overall setup of the dashboard as well:

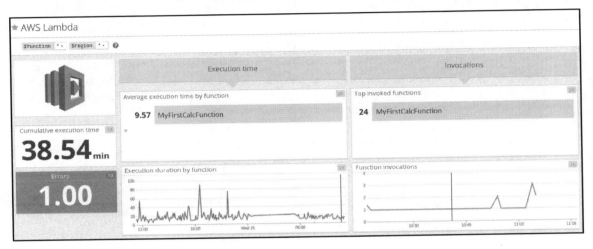

Simple enough, isn't it? There's still a lot more you can do and achieve with the dashboard, so feel free to give it a few tries.

With the basics out of the way, let us try something a bit different with Lambda as well. In this use case, we will be using a Lambda function to report our custom metrics obtained from monitoring a sample website running on an EC2 instance. These metrics will then be sent to Datadog for visualizations.

You can start of by installing a simple Apache web server on an EC2 instance with it's default `index.html` page being able to load when invoked by the instance's URL. The function's code will check whether it's getting a successful `200` response code from the website that you just created. If yes, then the function will send a `gauge` metric called `websiteCheck = 1` back to Datadog for visualization, else it will send a `gauge` metric called `websiteCheck = 0`.

Before we begin with the actual setup, here are a few pointers to keep in mind when working with Lambda and Datadog integration:

- At time of writing, Datadog supports only `gauge` and `count` metrics for Lambda
- Datadog Agent monitors our AWS account and sends metrics every 10 minutes
- Most of the service integrations with dashboards are already provided out of the box in Datadog, so you don't have to go around creating dashboards for your custom metrics as well

To get started, we first need to integrate our AWS account with Datadog. For this, we will be installing a Datadog Agent on an EC2 instance in our AWS account. This agent will monitor the AWS resources and periodically send metric data back to Datadog. The Agent requires certain permissions to be provided to it so that it is able to collect the metrics and send it back to Datadog. You will be required to create AWS role using the steps provided in this link: `http://docs.datadoghq.com/integrations/aws/`.

The role can be modified as per your requirements, but make sure the role in this case has at least permissions to describe and get EC2 instance details as well as logs.

We can create a role with the following snippet:

```json
{
  "Version": "2012-10-17",
  "Statement": [
  {
    "Action": [
      "ec2:Describe*",
      "ec2:Get*",
      "logs:Get*",
      "logs:Describe*",
      "logs:FilterLogEvents",
      "logs:TestMetricFilter"
    ],
    "Effect": "Allow",
    "Resource": "*"
  }
  ]
}
```

With the role created, you now need to install the Datadog Agent in your AWS environment. If you already have an account in Datadog, then simply go to **Integrations** and select the **Agent** option from there. Here, you can select the option **Amazon Linux**, and click on **Next** to continue.

This will bring up a few extremely easy to follow and straightforward steps using which you can install and configure your Datadog Agent on the Amazon Linux EC2 instance.

For installing the Datadog Agent on the Amazon Linux instance, login to your Datadog account and follow the steps mentioned at `https://app.da tadoghq.com/account/settings#agent/aws`.

With the Datadog Agent installed, the final steps required are simply to configure your service and Agent integration. This can be achieved by selecting the **Integrations** option from the Datadog dashboard and selecting the **Amazon Web Services** integration tile. Next, filter and select **Lambda** from the services list as shown in the following screenshot. You will also need to select the **Collect custom metrics** option for this case. Finally, fill in the required AWS account information along with the Datadog Agent role that we created at the beginning of this use case. With all settings completed, select the **Update Configuration** option to complete the Agent's configuration:

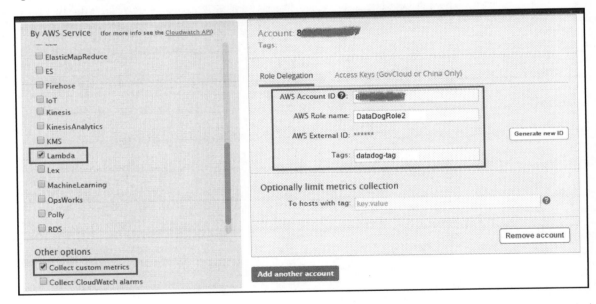

Now that you are done with AWS and Datadog integration, the next steps are all going to be Lambda specific configurations. First up, we need to understand how the metric data is going to be sent to Datadog by our Lambda function.

To send custom metrics to Datadog, you must print a log line from your Lambda, using the following format:

```
MONITORING|unix_epoch_timestamp|value|metric_type|my.metric.name|#tag1:value,tag2
```

In the preceding code:

- `unix_epoch_timestamp`: It is a timestamp value calculated in seconds.
- `value`: It is the actual value of the metric.
- `metric_type`: It defines the type of metric. While writing, only `gauge` and `count` metrics are supported.
- `metric.name`: It is your custom name. In our case it is `websiteCheckMetric`.
- `tag`: is the tag name you wish to give to your custom metric so that you can filter out from the Datadog dashboard.

Here's a quick look at the metrics provided by Datadog for monitoring Lambda functions:

`aws.lambda.duration` (gauge)	Measures the average elapsed wall clock time from when the function code starts executing as a result of an invocation to when it stops executing. It is shown in millisecond.
`aws.lambda.duration.maximum` (gauge)	Measures the maximum elapsed wall clock time from when the function code starts executing as a result of an invocation to when it stops executing. It is shown in millisecond.
`aws.lambda.duration.minimum` (gauge)	Measures the minimum elapsed wall clock time from when the function code starts executing as a result of an invocation to when it stops executing. It is shown as millisecond.
`aws.lambda.duration.sum` (gauge)	Measures the total execution time of the lambda function executing. It is shown in millisecond.
`aws.lambda.errors` (count every 60 seconds)	Measures the number of invocations that failed due to errors in the function (response code `4XX`).

aws.lambda.invocations (count every 60 seconds)	Measures the number of times a function is invoked in response to an event or invocation API call.
aws.lambda.throttles (count every 60 seconds)	Measures the number of Lambda function invocation attempts that were throttled due to invocation rates exceeding the customer's concurrent limits (error code 429). Failed invocations may trigger a retry attempt that succeeds.

Table source: Datadog Lambda integration (http://docs.datadoghq.com/integrations/awslambda/)

 Make sure that your IAM role contains the following permissions in order for the function to collect and send metric data to Datadog: logs:describeloggroups, logs:describelogstreams, and logs:filterlogevents.

Next, we prepare our Lambda function code that will be monitoring our simple website whether it is up and running, or down. Make sure to replace the `<Your_URL>` field with the URL of your website that you wish to monitor:

```
'use strict';
const request = require('request');
let target = "<Your_URL>";
let metric_value, tags;
exports.handler = (event, context, callback) => {
  // TODO implement
  let unix_epoch_timeshtamp = Math.floor(new Date() / 1000);
  // Parameters required for DataDog custom Metrics
  let metric_type = "gauge";
  // Only gauge or count are supported as of now.
  let my_metric_name = "websiteCheckMetric";
  // custom name given by us.
  request(target, function (error, response, body) {
    // successful response
    if(!error && response.statusCode === 200) {
      metric_value = 1;
      tags = ['websiteCheck:'+metric_value, 'websiteCheck'];
      console.log("MONITORING|" +unix_epoch_timeshtamp+ "|" +metric_value+
        "|"+ metric_type +"|"+ my_metric_name+ "|"+ tags.join());
      callback(null, "UP!");
    }
    // erroneous response
    else{
      console.log("Error: ",error);
      if(response){
```

```
        console.log(response.statusCode);
    }
    metric_value = 0;
    tags = ['websiteCheck:'+metric_value,'websiteCheck'];
    console.log("MONITORING|" +unix_epoch_timeshtamp+ "|" +metric_value+
        "|"+ metric_type +"|"+ my_metric_name+ "|"+ tags.join());
    callback(null, "DOWN!");
        });
    };
```

With the code in place, package, and upload the same to Lambda. Make sure you build the code at least once so that the necessary npm modules are downloaded as well. With this step completed, we can now test our custom metrics by simply accessing the web URL of our Apache web server instance. If the page loads successfully, it will send a 200 response code that is interpreted by our Lambda function as a custom metric of value 1 to Datadog. You can even verify the output by viewing the functions' logs either from the Lambda dashboard or from CloudWatch as shown as follows:

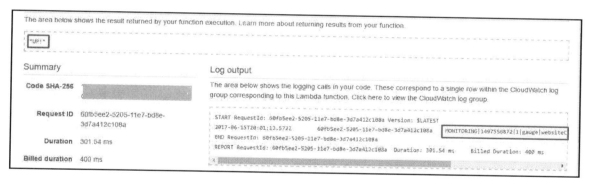

Coming back to Datadog, to view your custom metrics, Datadog provides out-of-the-box dashboards that are able to display the custom metrics as well. You could alternatively even use the existing pre-created Lambda monitoring dashboard and add a new widget specifically for these custom metrics as well.

To view the custom metrics, select the **Custom Metrics (**no namespace) dashboard from Datadog's **List Dashboard**. Here, you can edit the graph's properties and provide customized values as per your requirements. To do so, click on the **Edit this graph** option:

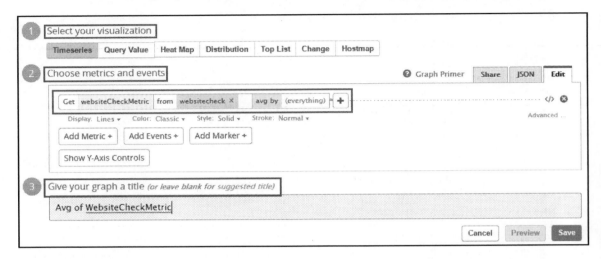

Here, you can edit the graph's visualization type from **Timeseries** to **Heat Map** as well as configuring the graph to display the outcome of our custom metric using the **Choose metrics and events** section. In our case, the query string is pretty straightforward: where we simply get the metric value by providing the metric name that we configured a while back in our Lambda function. Once you are done with your changes, remember to click on **Save** and exit the graph properties window. You should automatically see your custom metric get populated here after a short while. Remember, it can take time to display the metric as the Datadog Agent sends metrics in 10 minute intervals, so be patient! By default, the graph will show the average value of the metric. However you can always clone the dashboard and then make changes to the graph as you see fit. Here are a few examples of what the graph looks like once it is configured correctly:

In this case, we are displaying the *average* as well as the *maximum* occurrence of the `websiteCheckMetric` over a period of 4 hours. In similar ways, you can configure custom metrics using more than one Lambda functions and visualize the same using Datadog's custom dashboards. Once the dashboards are all setup, you can even configure advanced alerts and notification mechanisms that trigger out in case an error or threshold value is detected.

In the next and final section of this chapter, we take a look at yet another popular tool that can prove to be a real life saver when it comes to churning through your functions logs and making some sense of your applications as well. Welcome to the world of Loggly!

Logging your functions with Loggly

You might have already used CloudWatch log streams since the time we have started working with Lambda functions in this book. Although a pretty neat tool; CloudWatch still lacks a good interface for performing log filtering and analysis. That's where Loggly steps in! Loggly is a centralized logging solution that offers powerful filtering capabilities along with the ability to analyze historical data to help detect anomalies within log data.

In this section, we will be exploring two simple use cases where Lambda functions and Loggly can be used together--the first is where we use Lambda to pump logs from CloudWatch all the way to Loggly and the second is by leveraging a few npm modules supported by Loggly for sending your application's logs to Loggly. So, without further ado; let get started!

First up, register for a Loggly account. You can sign up for one free of charge for a period of one month. You can sign up by visiting `https://www.loggly.com/signup/`.

Once you have signed up, you will need to generate a unique token called as **Customer Token** that will basically authenticate and send your CloudWatch logs from your AWS account over to your newly created Loggly account. To do so, select the **Source Setup** tab on the navigation bar and select **Customer Tokens** option from under it as shown:

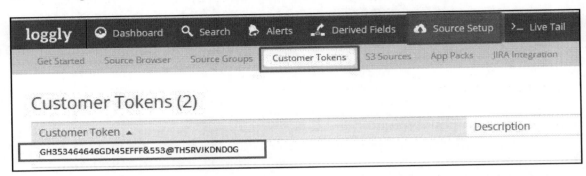

With the token created, move over to your Lambda dashboard and filter out a blueprint with the name of `cloudwatch-logs-to-loggly`. This is perhaps the best part of working with Lambda! You have readymade starter templates for connecting to almost any service you can think of! Let us go ahead and deploy a function from this template.

In the **Configure triggers** page, select a log group whose logs you wish to send to Loggly for analysis. You can optionally provide a suitable **Filter Name** and **Filter Pattern** as well for your logs here. Once completed, click on **Next** to proceed with the next steps. Remember to select the **Enable trigger** option as well before you continue further.

In the **Configure function** page, provide a suitable **Name** for your function. Next, scroll down to the **Environment variables** section and provide the following information as shown in the following screenshot:

- `kmsEncryptedCustomerToken`: Provide the customer token that you created using Loggly dashboard here. Remember to encrypt the same using the KMS **Encryption key**.
- `logglyTags`: These are simple tags to identify your logs using Loggly.
- `logglyHostName`: Provide a suitable hostname for your Loggly function here. The name can be any meaningful identifier.

Finally, create, and assign your function an execution role. The role only needs to have full access to the logs as shown in the following snippet:

```
{
    "Version": "2012-10-17",
    "Statement": [
    {
        "Action": [
            "logs:*"
        ],
        "Effect": "Allow",
        "Resource": "*"
    }
    ]
}
```

Review the function's configurations and finally go ahead and create the function. You can simulate tests on your new function by simply selecting the **Test** option and passing the sample **CloudWatch Logs** as shown in the following screenshot:

Use the editor below to enter an event to test your function with. You can edit the event again by choosing **Configure test event** in the Actions list. Note that changes to the event will only be saved locally.

Sample event template: CloudWatch Logs

```
1 {
2    "awslogs": {
3        "data": "H4sIAAAAAAAAAHWPwQqCQBCGX0Xm7EFtK+smZBEUgXoLCdMhFtKV3akI8d0bLYmibvPPN3wz00CJxmQnT
4    }
5 }
```

To verify whether the events were passed to Loggly or not, log in to your Loggly account and select the **Search** tab and pass the `tag` name that you provided during the lambda function's creation as shown as follows:

```
tag:CloudWatch2Loggly
```

You should see the sample events passed during the tests as shown in the following screenshot:

Simple, isn't it? With this part over, let us move on to the second part of this section where we use a Loggly provided npm module and send our application logs over to Loggly for analysis.

For this scenario, we will be looking at a few communities provided npm modules that actually, make logging your application's logs to Loggly a breeze. To start with, here are four of the most commonly used npm modules that comply with Loggly's API:

- **Node-Loggly**: Node-Loggly can be used to send log data, search within log data, and retrieve relevant information as well. The Node-Loggly module is also capable of logging data with tags and supports sending log messages either as simple or as complex JSON objects.
- **Winston**: Winston is the most preferred out of the lot when it comes to logging and is also a recommended module by Loggly themselves. It is capable of accomplishing much more than the Node-Loggly module. It has the ability to perform profiling, handle logging exceptions, create custom error levels, and much more.
- **Bunyan**: Bunyan is also a very similar tool, in terms of functionality, to Winston. For this scenario we will be using Bunyan's logging module.
- **Morgan**: Unlike it's counterparts, Morgan is not very powerful or flexible. However it is specifically designed to work best with Express.js applications.

To know more about Bunyan, check out its documentation here: `https ://github.com/trentm/node-bunyan`.

First up, we will need to create an IAM role for our application to be able to create and put logs into CloudWatch as well as permissions to decrypt the KMS keys. Here's a small snippet of the same:

```
{
  "Version": "2012-10-17",
  "Statement": [
    {
      "Sid": "myLogsPermissions",
      "Effect": "Allow",
      "Action": [
        "logs:CreateLogGroup",
        "logs:CreateLogStream",
        "logs:PutLogEvents"
      ],
      "Resource": [
        "*"
      ]
    },
    {
      "Sid": "myKMSPermissions",
      "Effect": "Allow",
      "Action": [
        "kms:Decrypt"
      ],
      "Resource": [
        "*"
      ]
    }
  ]
}
```

With the IAM role created, we can now move on to our application and injecting the Bunyan code within it as well. Copy the code to an `index.js` file and install the `bunyan` and `bunyan-loggly` npm modules using the `npm install` command. Once the code is up and ready, create a zip and upload the same to Lambda either manually, or by using APEX as performed in our earlier chapters.

The code relies on two environment variables; one for customer token and another for the Loggly subdomain. During execution, the code simply creates a new logger stream named `mylogglylog`. We specify our customer token (which is first decrypted) and our Loggly subdomain during configuring the environment variables for the function:

```
'use strict';
const bunyan = require('bunyan');
const Bunyan2Loggly = require('bunyan-loggly');
const AWS = require('aws-sdk');
const kms = new AWS.KMS({ apiVersion: '2014-11-01' });
const decryptParams = {
  CiphertextBlob: new Buffer(process.env.kmsEncryptedCustomerToken,
  'base64'),
};
let customerToken;
let log;
exports.handler = (event, context, callback) => {
  kms.decrypt(decryptParams, (error, data) => {
    if (error) {
      console.log(error);
      return callback(error);
    }
    else {
      customerToken = data.Plaintext.toString('ascii');
      log = bunyan.createLogger({
        name: 'mylogglylog',
        streams: [
        {
          type: 'raw',
          stream: new Bunyan2Loggly({
            token: customerToken,
            subdomain: process.env.logglySubDomain,
            json: true
          })
        }
        ]
      });
      log.info("My first log in loggly!!!");
      return callback(null, "all events sent to loggly!");
    }
  });
};
```

With the code uploaded, make sure you check **Enable encryption helpers** and fill out the **Environment variables,** namely the customer token and the Loggly subdomain as shown in the following screenshot:

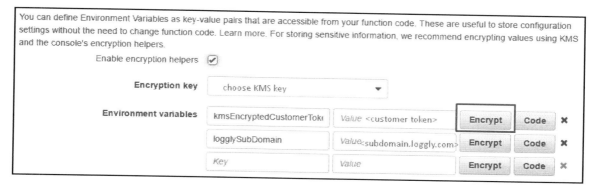

With this step completed, you can now test the application. The code doesn't require any specific events to be passed during execution. You should see the output in your function's logs, as shown in the following screenshot:

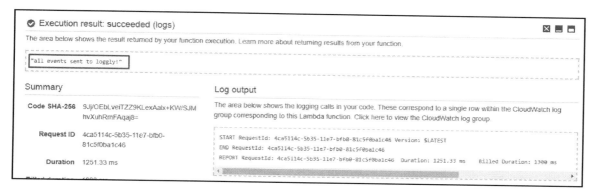

Bunyan in it's output to Loggly includes the **process id (pid)**, hostname, and timestamp, along with the log message as shown in the following screenshot:

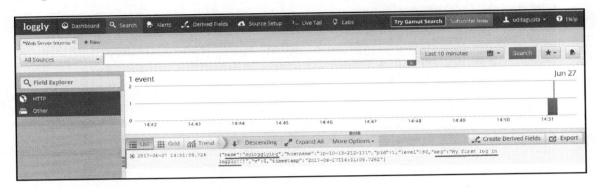

Using such npm modules or other third-party libraries written in languages such as C#, Java, and so on, you can easily create and send logs to Loggly for analysis.

With this section completed, let us review some good to keep, best practices, and recommendations when it comes to monitoring, logging, and troubleshooting your serverless applications.

Recommendations and best practices

Here are a few key recommendations and best practices that you ought to keep in mind when working with monitoring and logging services:

- **Leverage AWS services for monitoring**: Although still a long way from a fully potent monitoring solution, CloudWatch and X-Ray still are a good choice for starting out with monitoring your serverless applications. The ideal case would always be to leverage both these services together for a complete monitoring experience.
- **Provide the correct IAM permissions**: Most of the time the issues are not with your function's code, but rather caused due to incorrect or missing IAM policies and permissions. Always make sure you provide the IAM policies that follow the least privileged requirement in order to run your function and periodically ensure that unwanted or unused IAM roles and policies are removed from the environment.

- **Log everything**: A good practice towards identifying application performance bottlenecks is always enabling logging for the AWS service as well as your application; at least during the development and test stages. This helps in identifying potential bugs as well as performance improvements that can be implemented before the application is pushed to production.
- **Visualize logs with Elasticsearch**: Since we are talking about logs and all, it's equally important to visualize the logs in order to make some meaningful sense of it. That's where you can leverage the built integration between AWS CloudWatch and AWS Elasticsearch to accomplish this.

Summary

With this, we come to yet another chapter's completion. Here's a quick round up of all the things covered in this chapter so far. We first started out by looking at how you can effectively monitor Lambda functions using CloudWatch metrics and graphs. Later, we also explored the newest performance monitoring service on the block: AWS X-Ray. We learnt a few simple terms and terminologies used by X-Ray and then enabled X-Ray monitoring for a custom serverless application as well. Towards the end, we looked at two really awesome monitoring and logging third-party services in the form of Datadog and Loggly and how you can effectively use both of them for your requirements. And finally, topped it all off with some keen and useful best practices and handy recommendations.

In the next chapter, we will be exploring yet another extremely useful and upcoming framework for deploying your serverless applications on the cloud, so stay tuned!

8

Introducing the Serverless Application Framework

Throughout this book, we have seen quite a few tool sets and platforms readily available in the market that can help with the deployment and life cycle management of your Lambda functions. In my quest to find something better, I happened to stumble across a unique framework that I feel is worth talking about and exploring: introducing the Serverless Framework!

In this chapter, we will cover the following topics:

- What the Serverless Framework is all about and why it is important
- Setting up the Serverless Framework locally for development
- Getting started with Serverless Frameworks using a few examples

What is the Serverless Framework?

When it comes to developing and deploying serverless applications, one thing's certain! Developers don't want to waste a lot of their time and effort on setting up the development environments, nor do they want to be concerned with the burden of deploying and managing different versions of their functions. What makes things more complicated is the fact that, sometimes, you end up with a large number of Lambda functions to be used along with other AWS services such as API gateways and DynamoDBs. Looking at this, developers soon realized that there was a strong need for some standardization and structure toward deploying serverless applications, especially when orchestrating multiple functions and complex service integration.

With this in mind and a goal of creating a smooth transition for developers, the greater AWS community started working on developing a framework that would ease and help others when it comes to building functions or backend services for web, mobile, and IoT applications.

And that's how the Serverless Framework was born! The Serverless Framework is basically a rich CLI that helps you develop and deploy your serverless functions along with other native Cloud services. It provides developers with structure, automation, and best practices out of the box, allowing you to focus on building the applications rather than focusing on other activities. The best part is that, apart from AWS support, the Serverless Framework additionally supports the following cloud providers as well:

- **Google Cloud Functions**: As of today, Google Cloud Functions are still in the beta stage and support Node.js as a runtime environment
- **Microsoft Azure Functions**: Azure Functions support a wide variety of languages, including JavaScript, C#, Python, PHP, Bash, Batch, and PowerShell
- **IBM Bluemix OpenWhisk**: OpenWhisk supports Node.js, Swift, and arbitrary binary programs encapsulated within Docker containers

The Serverless Framework helps developers in two ways: firstly, by providing a minimal and clear organization for your serverless functions. The organization helps you manage and maintain functions while adhering to all forms of serverless best practices such as versioning, aliases, stages, variables, IAM roles, and so on.

The second way in which the framework helps out is by doing all the heavy lifting in terms of your function's actual deployments. This really proves to be handy when dealing with multiple functions and a complex setup that involves API Gateways and databases as well.

Getting started with the Serverless Framework

Before we get going with some hands-on code, we first need to understand a few essential concepts and terminologies provided by the Serverless Framework:

- **Projects**: Projects are, as the name suggests, independent serverless projects that you can either create from scratch or by importing a pre-created one as well. Projects are shared using standard npm modules.

- **Functions**: Just as with AWS Lambda, functions form the core of your projects. Similar to the concepts of Lambda functions, here too, you can create small independent pieces of code that perform a certain type of role in your serverless application. Although you can have a single function performing all the tasks, it is highly recommended that you leverage the Serverless Framework to create smaller, more independent pieces of code that can be organized and executed by the Serverless Framework itself.

- **Events**: The concept of events is also the same as what we have been learning throughout this chapter. The functions can get invoked based on some event that can be triggered by one or more AWS services such as **Simple Notification Service (SNS)**, S3, Kinesis Streams, and so on. The best part of events in the Serverless Framework is that on defining an event for your Lambda function using the Serverless Framework, the framework automatically creates the underlying AWS resource necessary to run that event and automatically configures your function to listen to it as well.

- **Resources**: Resources in the Serverless Framework terms can be any component, such as IAM roles, policies, SNS topics, S3 buckets, and so on. Once again, the Serverless Framework takes care of the creation of all these resources for you so you don't have to waste your time in setting up the infrastructure necessary to support your functions.

- **Services**: Services are logical grouping or organizations that together contain your function, the event that triggers the function, as well as the list of resources necessary to execute the function. Services are declared in a file called `serverless.yml/json`.

- **Plugins**: One of the key features of the Serverless Framework is its support for extensibility using a rich set of plugins that add useful functionalities to the core framework. These plugins can be used for a variety of purposes, such as testing your functions locally, simulating AWS services locally for development and tests to store your function's encrypted variables, and a lot more. You can even create and publish your own plugins on the plugins registry.

 Note that you can read more about the Serverless Framework's Plugin Registry at `https://github.com/serverless/plugins`.

With the theory done and dusted, let's move on to the fun part: working with the Serverless Framework!

Working with the Serverless Framework

In this section, we will be exploring the ins and out of the Serverless Framework using a few cool and easy-to-replicate examples. Here's a quick summary of the use cases that we will be covering in this section:

- Our traditional *hello world* example, where we will explore how to use Serverless to package and deploy your functions. You will also learn how to include environment variables and other function-related configurations in the Serverless YAML file.
- A more complex example, where we will include other AWS resources to our example in the form of DynamoDB and API Gateway as well.
- Use serverless offline plugins to simulate a DynamoDB, an API Gateway, and Lambda stack offline. This use case is particularly good for developers who wish to test their functions locally and then do the actual deployment on AWS.

So, let's get the show on the road! First up, let's talk about installing the Serverless Framework. In this case, I'll be using a simple Linux server hosted on AWS itself; however, you can very well run the same commands on a Linux box setup locally as well:

```
# npm install -g serverless
```

 An important point to note here is that serverless runs only on Node v4 or higher, so make sure you have the latest Node version installed on your Linux system.

With the installation completed, you can test the serverless CLI by simply typing the following command on your terminal:

```
# sls --help
```

The output of this command will show you a bunch of really useful commands that we will require in order to manage the overall framework. Here's a quick list of a few of these commands:

- `config`: Configures the Serverless Framework
- `configcredentials`: Configures a new provider profile for the Serverless Framework
- `create`: Creates new serverless service
- `deploy`: Deploys the newly created serverless service

- `deploy function`: Deploys a particular or single function from the service
- `info`: Displays information about a particular service
- `install`: Used to install a serverless service from GitHub; these services are packaged as npm modules
- `invoke`: Invokes a deployed function
- `invokelocal`: Invokes a function locally; this comes in handy in testing your functions before actually deploying them to Lambda
- `logs`: Displays the logs of a particularly deployed function

With the installation done, we now have to write a configuration YAML file, which will help us in stating the function as well as its associated configurations we want.

A typical configuration YAML file will consist of services, functions, and resources. The configuration will also require a `provider`, which is essentially the cloud provider that will provide a runtime for your functions. In this case, it is going to be all AWS!

Here's what a standard `serverless.yml` file looks like:

```
service: my-helloWorld-service

provider:
  name: aws
  runtime: nodejs6.10

  iamRoleStatements:
  - Effect: "Allow"
    Action:
      - "logs:CreateLogGroup"
      - "logs:CreateLogStream"
      - "logs:PutLogEvents"
    Resource: "*"

functions:
  hello:
    handler: handler.hello

    events:
     - schedule: rate(1 minute)

    environment:
      testEnvVariable: "it works!"
```

As you can see, the file is structured pretty straightforwardly with the `service` name upfront, followed by the `provider`, which in this case is AWS. The best part of the `provider` is that you can additionally pass IAM roles to your functions right here. And don't worry about the creation of the IAM role; it's all taken care of by the Serverless Framework! Once the `provider` section is completed, the `functions` section is where you can define one or more of your serverless functions along with their `handler`, `events`, and even pass `environment` variables as well.

To create `serverless.yml`, you can use the Serverless Framework command line itself. Here's a simple example of how you can create the `hello world` example:

```
# sls create --template "hello-world"
```

The `--template` parameter is mandatory when it comes to creating your configuration file. This essentially tells the framework which boilerplate or template to use to create your configuration file.

The `--template` parameter supports these values as of writing this book: `"aws-nodejs"`, `"aws-python"`, `"aws-python3"`, `"aws-groovy-gradle"`, `"aws-java-maven"`, `"aws-java-gradle"`, `"aws-scala-sbt"`, `"aws-csharp"`, `"aws-fsharp"`, `"azure-nodejs"`, `"openwhisk-nodejs"`, `"openwhisk-python"`, `"openwhisk-swift"`, `"google-nodejs"`, `"plugin"`, and `"hello-world"`.

Executing this command will result in the creation of two files: `serverless.yml` and `handler.js`:

```
[ec2-user@ip-172-31-70-9 ~]$ sls create --template "hello-world"
Serverless: Generating boilerplate...



           _____     _____ _____ _____
          |       |   |       |       |       |
          |    ___|   |   _   |   _   |   _   |
          |   |___    |  | |  |  | |  |  | |  |
          |    ___|   |  |_|  |  |_|  |  |_|  |

                The Serverless Application Framework
                      serverless.com, v1.17.0


Serverless: Successfully generated boilerplate for template: "hello-world"
Serverless: NOTE: Please update the "service" property in serverless.yml with your service name
[ec2-user@ip-172-31-70-9 ~]$
```

Here is the snippet of the `handler.js` file:

```
'use strict';

module.exports.hello = (event, context, callback) => {
  console.log(process.env.testEnvVariable);
  const response = {
    statusCode: 200,
    body: JSON.stringify({
      message: 'Your function executed successfully!',
      input: event,
    }),
  };

  callback(null, response);

  // Use this code if you don't use the http event with the
   LAMBDA-PROXY integration
  // callback(null, { message: 'Go Serverless v1.0! Your
     function executed successfully!', event });
};
```

With this, you are now ready to deploy your function over to AWS. This is also a pretty simple process as the Serverless Framework does all the heavy lifting for you! Simply type in the following command and watch as the magic unfolds:

```
# serverless deploy --verbose
```

 Note that the **--verbose** parameter is optional.

```
[ec2-user@ip-172-31-70-9 ~]$
[ec2-user@ip-172-31-70-9 ~]$ serverless deploy --verbose
Serverless: Packaging service...
Serverless: Creating Stack...
Serverless: Checking Stack create progress...
CloudFormation - CREATE_IN_PROGRESS - AWS::CloudFormation::Stack - serverless-hello-world-dev
CloudFormation - CREATE_IN_PROGRESS - AWS::S3::Bucket - ServerlessDeploymentBucket
CloudFormation - CREATE_IN_PROGRESS - AWS::S3::Bucket - ServerlessDeploymentBucket
CloudFormation - CREATE_COMPLETE - AWS::S3::Bucket - ServerlessDeploymentBucket
CloudFormation - CREATE_COMPLETE - AWS::CloudFormation::Stack - serverless-hello-world-dev
Serverless: Stack create finished...
```

The code takes a few minutes to complete its execution, but the interesting thing to note here is the way serverless actually deployed your function over to AWS Lambda! Behind the scenes, serverless leverages a single CloudFormation template to create, update, and deploy your entire serverless stack. This means that in case of errors during deployment, CloudFormation will simply roll back all the changes that it performed, leaving you with a clean slate to start over from. The template first starts off by creating an S3: : Bucket, which will store the ZIP file of your code along with any dependencies, if present. Next, any associated IAM roles, events, and other resources are added to the CloudFormation template. Once the deployment is completed, you will be provided with the following deployment information:

```
Service Information
service: my-helloWorld-service
stage: dev
region: us-east-1
api keys:
  None
endpoints:
  None
functions:
  hello: my-helloWorld-service-dev-hello
```

 Note that the stage and region parameters can be updated under the provider section of your serverless.yml file. By default, the values are set to dev and us-east-1.

Log in to the AWS Lambda management console and locate your function. Go ahead and pass a few parameters to your function and test its output. You should see the following log messages:

```
{
  "testEnvVariable": "Serverless is fun!"
}
```

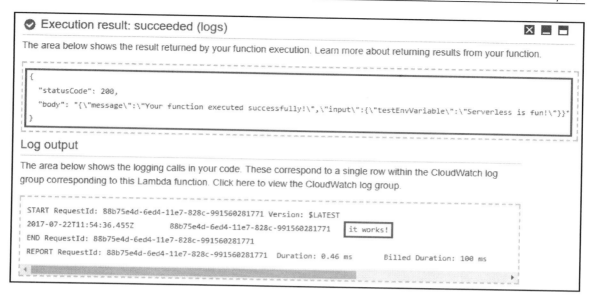

You can alternatively use the `sls` CLI to invoke your function from your local Linux server as well. Give the example a couple of tries by varying the `sls invoke` parameters and passing different environment variables as well.

With the basic deployments out of the way, let's look at a slightly more complex example where we leverage AWS DynamoDB, API Gateway, and Lambda to build a simple food descriptor application!

To begin, repeat the same steps that we performed earlier for creating our `serverless.yml` file using the `sls create` command and paste the following code snippet in it:

```
service: my-serverless-app

provider:
  name: aws
  runtime: nodejs6.10
  stage: dev
  region: us-east-1

  iamRoleStatements:
  - Effect: Allow
    Action:
      - logs:CreateLogGroup
      - logs:CreateLogStream
```

```
            - logs:PutLogEvents
            - dynamodb:PutItem
        Resource: "*"

functions:
  hello:
    handler: index.handler
    name: serverless-apiGW-Dynamodb
    events:
      - http:
          path: /food/{name}/{description}
          method: post
    environment:
      TABLE_NAME:
        ${self:resources.Resources.foodTable.Properties.TableName}

# you can add CloudFormation resource templates here
resources:
  Resources:
    foodTable:
      Type: AWS::DynamoDB::Table
      Properties:
        TableName: foodTable-serverless
        AttributeDefinitions:
          - AttributeName: id
            AttributeType: S
          - AttributeName: name
            AttributeType: S
        KeySchema:
          - AttributeName: id
            KeyType: HASH
          - AttributeName: name
            KeyType: RANGE
        ProvisionedThroughput:
          ReadCapacityUnits: 5
          WriteCapacityUnits: 5
```

 Here's a handy tip. Run the `sls create` command from a new folder. In this way, you will have a much cleaner organization of your functions that can be easily sorted out by their names.

So, remember a couple of things here. First up, we have explicitly passed the `stage` and `region` parameters in the `provider` section, as discussed a bit earlier. You can modify the values as per your requirements. Next are the all important IAM role policies followed by the `events` section. As you can see, we have added the `http` event and provided a `path` to it, which is pretty similar to what we had done in our chapter on working with SAM template. This automatically creates the necessary API Gateway with the set configurations so that you don't have to do any work for the same.

In the `environment` section, we pass the table name of our DynamoDB table using a special variable that references the resource that will be created by the CloudFormation template in the `resource` section. The overall schema of the variable is as follows:

```
${self:resources.Resources.<Resource_name>.<Resource_property>.<resource_at
tribute>}
```

These "self-reference" properties in `serverless.yml`, use the `${self:}` syntax and can go as deep in the object tree as you want.

In the `resource` section, we have added a DynamoDB table and specified its configuration, including its key schema. Also, ensure that your `iamRoleStatements` parameter contains the DynamoDB `PutItem` permission so that our function can write to it.

With the `serverless.yml` done, we can now move on to the `index.js` creation, which is really straight forward. The only point that you need to know here is that the function leverages the `uuid` npm module to generate a unique ID for every entry in our table, so make sure your npm modules directory is created before you deploy the code over to AWS.

Here is the snippet for the `index.js` file:

```
'use strict';
console.log('Loading the Calc function');
let doc = require('dynamodb-doc');
let dynamo = new doc.DynamoDB();
const uuidv4 = require('uuid/v4');
const tableName = process.env.TABLE_NAME;
const createResponse = (statusCode, body) => {
    return {
        "statusCode": statusCode,
        "body": body || ""
    }
};
let response;

module.exports.handler = function(event, context, callback) {
    console.log('Received event:', JSON.stringify(event, null, 2));
```

```
let name = event.pathParameters.name;
let description = event.pathParameters.description;
console.log("Writing to DynamoDB");

let item = {
    "id": uuidv4(),
    "name": name,
    "description": description
};

let params = {
    "TableName": tableName,
    "Item": item
};

dynamo.putItem(params, (err, data) => {
    if (err){
        console.log("An error occured while writing to Db: ",err);
        response = createResponse(500, err);
    }
    else{
        console.log("Successfully wrote result to DB");
        response = createResponse(200, JSON.stringify(params));
    }
    callback(null, response);
});
};
```

With the code in place, go ahead and deploy the code using the following command:

```
# sls deploy --verbose
```

Once again, the Serverless Framework takes care of creating the AWS resources and packaging and uploading your code over to AWS Lambda. With the code successfully uploaded, make a note of the Service Information section, as shown here:

```
Service Information
service: my-serverless-app
stage: dev
region: us-east-1
api keys:
  None
endpoints:
  POST - https://cv5s19ba56.execute-api.us-east-1.amazonaws.com/dev/food/{name}/{description}
functions:
  hello: my-serverless-app-dev-hello
```

You will notice that the output will also contain the URL of your newly created API Gateway under the `endpoints` section. Use this URL to post the description of your favorite food. On posting, the associated Lambda function should get triggered, and that will write the values within the newly created DynamoDB as well. Here is an example of the API Gateway :

```
# curl -X POST
https://1234567.execute-api.us-east-1.amazonaws.com/dev/food/Burgers/Awesom
e
```

You can verify the output by checking your DynamoDB table for the corresponding entries, as shown in the following screenshot:

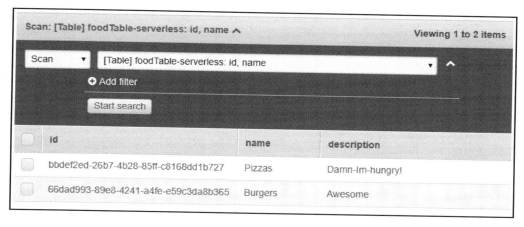

With this, we come toward the end of yet another Serverless Framework use case. The third and final use case is all about leveraging third-party plugins for extending the Serverless Framework. We will leverage the same example as the earlier use case, where we created a food descriptor service using AWS DynamoDB, API Gateway, and Lambda. The only difference here is that we will be using serverless offline plugins to first test our function locally using an offline DynamoDB and API Gateway simulator and then deploy it to AWS.

To start off, we first need to set up a local DynamoDB for which we will be using the `serverless-dynamodb-local` module. You can read more about the plugin at `https://github.com/99xt/serverless-dynamodb-local`.

Similarly, we have the `serverless-offline` plugin for simulating the calling of your Lambda functions offline by an API Gateway. To learn more about the `serverless-offline` plugin, check out `https://github.com/dherault/serverless-offline`.

To install the plugins, simply execute the following commands in your terminal:

```
# npm install serverless-offline --save-dev
# npm install --save serverless-dynamodb-local
```

Now, add both the `serverless-offline` plugin and the `serverless-dynamodb-local` plugin to our `serverless.yml` file under a new section called as `plugins`, as shown here:

```
plugins:
    - serverless-dynamodb-local
    - serverless-offline
```

The order of mentioning the plugins is important, as we want our local DynamoDB to load first, followed by the serverless plugins. After adding this to our existing `serverless.yml` file from the earlier example, run the following command:

```
# sls
```

You should see these two plugins in the plugins list that gets displayed in the output.

The final `serverless.yml` file now looks something like this:

```
service: serverless-offline-plugins-service

frameworkVersion: ">=1.1.0 <2.0.0"

provider:
  name: aws
  runtime: nodejs4.3
  environment:
    TABLE_NAME:
      ${self:resources.Resources.foodTable.Properties.TableName}
  iamRoleStatements:
    - Effect: Allow
      Action:
        - dynamodb:PutItem
      Resource: "arn:aws:dynamodb:${opt:region,self:provider.region}:
        *:table/${self:provider.environment.TABLE_NAME}"
    - Effect: Allow
      Action:
        - logs:CreateLogGroup
        - logs:CreateLogStream
        - logs:PutLogEvents
```

```
        Resource: "*"

plugins:
  - serverless-dynamodb-local
  - serverless-offline

custom:
  dynamodb:
    start:
      port: 8000
      inMemory: true
      migrate: true

functions:
  create:
    handler: todos/create.handler
    events:
      - http:
          path: /food/{name}/{description}
          method: post
          cors: true

resources:
  Resources:
    foodTable:
      Type: AWS::DynamoDB::Table
      Properties:
        TableName: foodTable-serverless-plugins
        AttributeDefinitions:
          - AttributeName: id
            AttributeType: S
          - AttributeName: name
            AttributeType: S
        KeySchema:
          - AttributeName: id
            KeyType: HASH
          - AttributeName: name
            KeyType: RANGE
        ProvisionedThroughput:
          ReadCapacityUnits: 5
          WriteCapacityUnits: 5
```

As you can see, we have added the `plugins` section and have also added a custom section in which we have defined the port on which our local DynamoDB will run along with other options, such as `migrate` = `true`.

In our `create.js` file, instead of using AWS SDK, we have now used a Node.js package `serverless-dynamodb-client`. The issue here is that if we use the AWS SDK, then we would be required to configure the same in our code, however it will cause issues when we run the same code locally. So our goal is to use to deploy to AWS as well as locally. Hence, we have `serverless-dynamo-client`. This takes care of such configurations by automatically detecting whether we are using the local server or an AWS platform to deploy the code.

Besides this, the rest of the code remains unchanged:

```
// food name and description
'use strict';
console.log('Loading the foodFeedback function');
var AWS = require("aws-sdk");
var dynamodb = require('serverless-dynamodb-client');
var docClient = dynamodb.doc;
const uuidv4 = require('uuid/v4');
const tableName = process.env.TABLE_NAME;
const createResponse = (statusCode, body) => {
    return {
        "statusCode": statusCode,
        "body": body || ""
    }
};
let response;

module.exports.handler = function(event, context, callback) {
    console.log('Received event:', JSON.stringify(event, null, 2));
    let name = event.pathParameters.name;
    let description = event.pathParameters.description;
    console.log("Writing to DynamoDB");

    let item = {
        "id": uuidv4(),
        "name": name,
        "description": description
    };

    let params = {
        "TableName": tableName,
        "Item": item
    };

    docClient.put(params, (err, data) => {
        if (err){
            console.log("An error occured while writing to Db: ",err);
            response = createResponse(500, err);
```

```
    }
    else{
        console.log("Successfully wrote result to DB");
        response = createResponse(200, JSON.stringify(params));
    }
    callback(null, response);
    });
};
```

With the code in place, we can now go ahead and start up the plugins. However, before we start directly with the `serverless-offline` plugin, we need to first install the DynamoDB server locally. To do that, run the following command:

```
# sls dynamodb install
```

With the installation of our DynamoDB on the local system completed, we can now start the `serverless-offline` plugin, which will listen on the local port 3000, whereas our local DynamoDB will run on port 3000 (*as we had configured this earlier*):

```
# serverless offline start
```

```
[ec2-user@ip-172-31-70-9 serverless-plugins-2]$
[ec2-user@ip-172-31-70-9 serverless-plugins-2]$ serverless offline start
Dynamodb Local Started, Visit: http://localhost:8000/shell
Serverless: DynamoDB - created table foodTable-serverless-plugins
Serverless: Starting Offline: dev/us-east-1.

Serverless: Routes for create:
Serverless: POST /food/{name}/{description}

Serverless: Offline listening on http://localhost:3000
```

As you can see, the plugin automatically creates the DynamoDB table locally and even starts it on port 3000.

To test the application locally, duplicate your terminal session and issue a POST command using the following URL:

```
# curl -d POST http://localhost:3000/food/taco/ymmmy/
```

You should see serverless load your function and execute just as Lambda would if the function were deployed to it. You can even verify the data written to your local DynamoDB by querying it using the DynamoDB Shell UI by running the following URL in your browser: `http://localhost:8000/shell`.

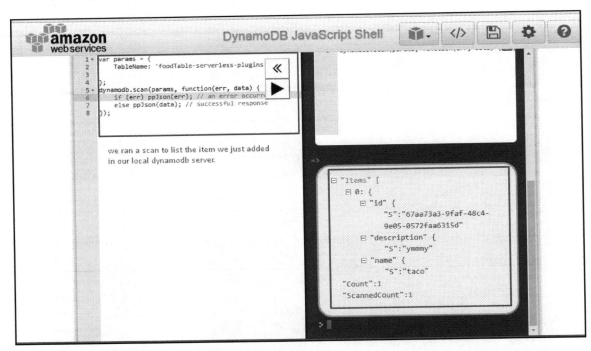

With the function working as expected, you can now go ahead and deploy it over to your AWS environment using the following command:

```
# serverless deploy --verbose
```

With this, we come toward the end of our exploration and understanding of the Serverless Framework, but before we move on to the next chapter, here are a few handy recommendations and tips that you ought to have a look at.

Recommendations and best practices

To start off, here are a few simple recommendations when it comes to working with the Serverless Framework:

- Use `sls deploy <functioname>`: Although seemingly straight forward, `sls deploy` and `sls deploy <function_name>` have a lot of difference between them and knowing what command to use when can significantly improve the time it takes to deploy your applications. For starters, running the `sls deploy` command redeploys the entire CloudFormation stack from the ground up, so each time you run this command, CloudFormation will tend to go through the entire resource list for your application. This can be time-consuming if you have a complex application using a lot of AWS resources. On the other hand, `sls deploy <function-name>` simply packages and uploads your code to a new Lambda function without changing any of the other AWS resources.

- Test your functions: Although repeated in quite a few chapters, testing your functions before deploying them is a must. You can leverage the vast array of plugins provided by the Serverless Framework to simulate and run tests on your functions locally before packaging and deploying them over to the cloud. Here's a good read on testing your functions provided by the Serverless documentation: `https://serverless.com/framework/docs/providers/aws/guide/testing/`.

- Log everything: With testing, it's equally important to log your functions as well as your serverless execution by running the following command in a separate terminal window:

```
# Serverless logs -f <function-name> -t
```

  The `-t` parameter is used to tail the logs.

- Implement CICD pipelines: A continuous integration and continuous deployment strategy can significantly improve the quality of your applications while minimizing the time and effort it takes to build and deploy them. You can leverage a set of AWS services, such as CodeBuild and CodePipeline, to create a customized set of **continuous integration and continuous deployment (CICD)** pipelines that roll out your Lambda functions while your developers build, package, and test the applications locally using the Serverless Framework. Here is an excellent example of how CICD can be integrated with the likes of the Serverless Framework for faster code build and deploy: `https://serverless.com/blog/cicd-for-serverless-part-1/`.

Summary

With this, we come toward the end of yet another chapter. With just two more chapters left now, I'm sure you will have obtained a really good grasp of Lambda and its associated services, tools, and frameworks. But, before we leave this chapter, here's a quick summary of what you learned so far!

This chapter has been all about the Serverless Framework and how you as a developer can leverage it to build, package, and deploy serverless applications on multiple cloud platforms with special emphasis on AWS Lambda. You learned about a few important concepts of the Serverless Framework and along the way, explored its functionality by deep diving into three use cases that covered the basics of deployment, all the way up to leveraging third-party plugins for developing and testing your applications locally. Toward the end, we topped it all off with some handy recommendations and tips as well!

In the next chapter, we will be exploring some really interesting real-world Lambda use cases with their deployment code, so stick around; there's plenty more to do!

9
AWS Lambda - Use Cases

In the previous chapter, we took a quick dive into the Serverless Framework and how you as an end user or developer can leverage it to build, package, and deploy your serverless applications to Lambda.

In this chapter, we will be looking at some of the most commonly used Lambda use cases and how you can leverage them to manage your AWS environments. The use cases are broadly classified into the following categories:

- Infrastructure management--this section will demonstrate how to leverage Lambda functions
- Managing the costs of your AWS account by shutting down large instance types during off hours
- Tagging untagged instances for better governance and cost control
- Taking scheduled snapshots of your volumes for data backups
- Data transformation--how to use Lambda functions to transform either streaming or static data before it gets uploaded to a database

Sounds interesting, right? Then what are you waiting for! Let's get started right away!

Infrastructure management

One of the core and most frequently used use cases for Lambda has been effective management of the AWS infrastructure, mainly around EC2 instances, as this is where a majority of the costs are incurred unnecessarily. Before the advent of Lambda functions, a lot of organizations had to rely on third-party automation tools and services to run simple and straightforward tasks on their instances, such as taking periodic backups of an EBS volume, checking whether an instance is tagged or not, or shutting down large instances if they are not required to run 24/7, just to name a few. The worst issue in this case was also the management of the automation tool itself! In most cases, you would have to run it off an EC2 instance, and this just created an unnecessary overhead for administrators. But not anymore! With Lambda, administrators can now create simple functions that are capable of performing a lot of these tasks without the need for complex third-party tools that were required to perform earlier. Let's take a look at each of these use cases in a bit more depth and see how you can use them for your environments as well.

Scheduled startup and shutdown of instances

First up, we have a simple function that shuts down your instances and powers them back on, based on CloudWatch scheduled events.

To begin, we first create a simple function that will start up a particular instance or set of instances using the following code. You will need to replace the <YOUR_INSTANCE_ID_GOES_HERE> field with the actual IDs of your instances; the rest of the code remains the same:

```
'use strict';
console.log('Loading function');
exports.handler = (event, context, callback) => {
  var AWS = require('aws-sdk');
  AWS.config.region = 'ap-southeast-1';
  var ec2 = new AWS.EC2();
  var params = {
    InstanceIds: [ /* required */
      '<YOUR_INSTANCE_ID_GOES_HERE>'
      /* more items */
    ]
    //AdditionalInfo: 'STRING_VALUE',
    //DryRun: true || false
  };
  ec2.startInstances(params, function(err, data) {
    if (err) console.log(err, err.stack); // an error occurred
    else      console.log(JSON.stringify(data));
```

```
        });
    }
```

For the functions to start and stop instances on our behalf, we will also need to provide a custom IAM role for them. Remember to provide your function's ARN in the IAM role's resource section, as shown in this example:

```json
{
    "Version": "2012-10-17",
    "Statement": [
    {
      "Sid": "Stmt1483458245000",
      "Effect": "Allow",
      "Action": [
        "ec2:StartInstances",
        "ec2:StopInstances"
      ],
      "Resource": [
        "*"
      ]
    },
    {
      "Sid": "Stmt1483458787000",
      "Effect": "Allow",
      "Action": [
        "logs:CreateLogGroup",
        "logs:CreateLogStream",
        "logs:PutLogEvents"
      ],
      "Resource": [
        "*"
      ]
    },
    {
      "Sid": "Stmt148345878700",
      "Effect": "Allow",
      "Action": [
        "lambda:InvokeFunction"
      ],
      "Resource": [
        "arn:aws:lambda:ap-southeast-1:01234567890:function:Instance_Stop",
        "arn:aws:lambda:ap-southeast-1:01234567890:function:Instance_Start"
      ]
    }
    ]
}
```

So far, so good; we have just one small bit to take care of for the last--the trigger for our function that will be created using CloudWatch Event Rule. Now, you can create and configure the Event Rule using the CloudWatch dashboard as well as by leveraging the **Configure triggers** configuration page on the function's dashboard, which is what we are going to be using for this use case. The triggers' configuration page on the function's dashboard, is what we are going to be using for this use case.

Select the **CloudWatch Events** option from the **Add trigger** page, as shown here. This will pop up some simple fields that you will need to fill out for your *instance start* rule. Provide a suitable **Rule name** and **Rule description**, as shown in the following screenshot:

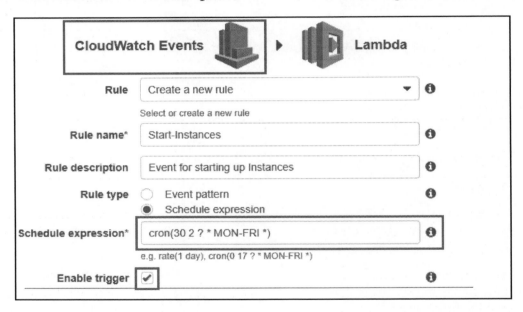

Next, select **Schedule expression** from the **Rule type** choice and provide a valid Cron expression based on your requirements. In my case, the Cron expression looks a bit like this: `cron(30 2 ? * MON-FRI *)`.

 You can get more examples of the Cron expression at `https://docs.aws.amazon.com/AmazonCloudWatch/latest/events/ScheduledEvents.html`.

Remember to select the **Enable trigger** option before saving the trigger. With this, we have created a simple event-driven function that will start up a set of EC2 instances at a particular time. Similarly, you can create a second function that will stop the EC2 instances based on another CloudWatch Event. You can actually reuse the previous code and simply change the `ec2.startInstances` method to `ec2.startInstances`, as shown in the following snippet, and that's it! You are good to go!

```
ec2.stopInstances(params, function(err, data) {
  if (err) console.log(err, err.stack); // an error occurred
  else      console.log(JSON.stringify(data));
});
```

You can additionally modify these functions to accept the instance IDs as environment variables or even pass them as event parameters at runtime, but that is something I leave completely up to you.

Let's look at a similar use case, where we leverage a Lambda function to take periodic snapshots of your EBS volumes.

Periodic snapshots of EBS volumes using Lambda

This use case follows along the same lines as the earlier one, where we take backup of our instances in the form of an AMI as well as conduct a snapshot of that instance's EBS volume if the instances have a tag named `backup`.

To get started, your Lambda function needs to have permissions to be able to create snapshots, create an AMI, as well as change some snapshot attributes, and so on. Here is a snippet of the function's IAM role that we have created for this exercise:

```
{
  "Version": "2012-10-17",
  "Statement": [
  {
    "Sid": "myEC2Permissions",
    "Effect": "Allow",
    "Action": [
      "ec2:Describe*"
    ],
    "Resource": [
      "*"
    ]
  },
```

```
        {
          "Sid": "myEC2AMIPermissions",
          "Effect": "Allow",
          "Action": [
            "ec2:CreateImage",
            "ec2:Describe*",
            "ec2:ModifyImageAttribute",
            "ec2:ResetImageAttribute"
          ],
          "Resource": [
            "*"
          ]
        },
        {
          "Sid": "myEC2SnapshotPermissions",
          "Effect": "Allow",
          "Action": [
            "ec2:CreateSnapshot",
            "ec2:ModifySnapshotAttribute",
            "ec2:ResetSnapshotAttribute"
          ],
          "Resource": [
            "*"
          ]
        },
        {
          "Sid": "myLogsPermissions",
          "Effect": "Allow",
          "Action": [
            "logs:CreateLogGroup",
            "logs:CreateLogStream",
            "logs:PutLogEvents"
          ],
          "Resource": [
            "*"
          ]
        }
      ]
    }
```

With the IAM role setup, let's quickly understand how the function code actually works out. The code maintains two arrays--one for instance IDs and the other comprising their corresponding EBS volume IDs:

- The code first filters instances with the `backup` tag and adds all the instance IDs returned in the response to the `instanceIDs` array.
- It then uses the `describeVolume` call to get all the EBS volumes IDs of those particular instances and adds them to the corresponding `volumeIDs` array.
- Once done, the code will call the `createImage` function and provide each instance ID in the `instanceIDs` array to create an AMI out of them.
- It will also invoke `createSnapshot` along with the `createImage` function and provide each volume ID in the `volumesIDs` array to create snapshots out of it--simple, isn't it?

Let's take a look at the function code itself now:

```
'use strict';
console.log('Loading function');
const aws = require('aws-sdk');
const async = require('async');
const ec2 = new aws.EC2({apiVersion: '2016-11-15'});
let instanceIDs =[];
let volumeIDs = [];
function createImage(instanceID, createImageCB){
  let date =
  new Date().toISOString().replace(/:/g, '-').replace(/\..+/, '');
  //console.log("AMI name: "+instanceID+'-'+date);
  let createImageParams = {
    InstanceId: instanceID, /* required */
    Name: 'AMI-'+instanceID+'-'+date /* required */
  };
  ec2.createImage(createImageParams,
  function(createImageErr, createImageData) {
    if (createImageErr){
      console.log(createImageErr, createImageErr.stack);
      // an error occurred
      createImageCB(createImageErr);
    }
    else{
      console.log("createImageData: ",createImageData);
      // successful response
      createImageCB(null, "AMI created!!");
    }
  });
}
```

```
function createSnapShot(volumeID, createSnapShotCB){
  let createSnapShotParams = {
    VolumeId: volumeID, /* required */
    Description: 'Snapshot of volume: '+volumeID
  };
  ec2.createSnapshot(createSnapShotParams,
  function(createSnapShotErr, createSnapShotData) {
    if (createSnapShotErr){
      console.log(createSnapShotErr, createSnapShotErr.stack);
      // an error occurred
      createSnapShotCB(createSnapShotErr);
    }
    else{
      console.log("createSnapShotData: ", createSnapShotData);
      // successful response
      createSnapShotCB(null , "SnapShot created!!");
    }
  });
}
exports.handler = (event, context, callback) => {
  instanceIDs = [];
  volumeIDs =[];
  let describeTagParams = {
    Filters: [
    {
      Name: "key",
      Values: [
        "backup"
      ]
    }
    ]
  };
  let describeVolParams = {
    Filters: [
    {
      Name: "attachment.instance-id",
      Values: []
    }
    ]
  };
  ec2.describeTags(describeTagParams,
  function(describeTagsErr, describeTagsData)
  {
    if (describeTagsErr){
      console.log(describeTagsErr, describeTagsErr.stack);
      // an error occurred
      callback(describeTagsErr);
    }
```

```
else{
  console.log("describe tags data: ",
  JSON.stringify(describeTagsData));
  // successful response
  for(let i in describeTagsData.Tags){
    instanceIDs.push(describeTagsData.Tags[i].ResourceId);
    describeVolParams.Filters[0].Values.push(
      describeTagsData.Tags[i].ResourceId);
  }
  console.log("final instanceIDs array: "+instanceIDs);
  console.log("final describeVolParams: ",describeVolParams);
  ec2.describeVolumes(describeVolParams,
  function(describeVolErr, describeVolData) {
    if (describeVolErr){
      console.log(describeVolErr, describeVolErr.stack);
      // an error occurred
      callback(describeVolErr);
    }
    else{
      console.log("describeVolData:",describeVolData);
      // successful response
      for(let j in describeVolData.Volumes){
        volumeIDs.push(describeVolData.Volumes[j].VolumeId);
      }
      console.log("final volumeIDs array: "+volumeIDs);
      async.parallel({
        one: function(oneCB) {
          async.forEachOf(instanceIDs,function (instanceID,
          key, imageCB)
          {
            createImage(instanceID, function(createImageErr,
            createImageResult){
              if(createImageErr){
                imageCB(createImageErr);
              }
              else{
                imageCB(null, createImageResult);
              }
            });
          }, function (imageErr) {
              if (imageErr){
              return oneCB(imageErr);
              }
              oneCB(null, "Done with creating AMIs!");
          });
        },
        two: function(twoCB) {
          async.forEachOf(volumeIDs,
```

```
          function (volumeID, key, volumeCB)
          {
            //console.log("volumeID in volumeIDs: "+volumeID);
            createSnapShot(volumeID, function(createSnapShotErr,
            createSnapShotResult){
              if(createSnapShotErr){
                volumeCB(createSnapShotErr);
              }
              else{
                volumeCB(null, createSnapShotResult);
              }
            });
          }, function (volumeErr) {
              if (volumeErr){
                 return twoCB(volumeErr);
              }
              twoCB(null, "Done with creating Snapshots!");
          });
      }
    }, function(finalErr, finalResults) {
        if(finalErr){
          callback(finalErr);
        }
        callback(null, "Done!!");
    });
  }
});
}
});
};
```

With the code and IAM roles created, you can now go ahead to create the trigger. We are going to trigger this function using a CloudWatch scheduled event. You can alternatively even use a cron job or rate expression, as per your requirements. For this exercise, we have gone ahead and created rate expression for simplicity, as shown here:

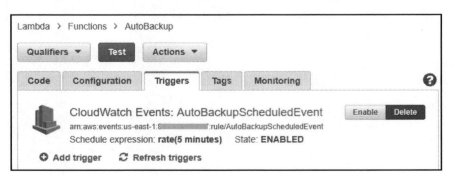

Make sure your trigger is set to **ENABLED** before testing the function out. To test the function, simply create a new instance with a tag of `backup` or create a new tag with the same `backup` name to an existing set of instances as well.

Once the function is triggered based on the rate expression or cron job execution, you should see new AMIs and EBS volume snapshots created, as shown in the following screenshot:

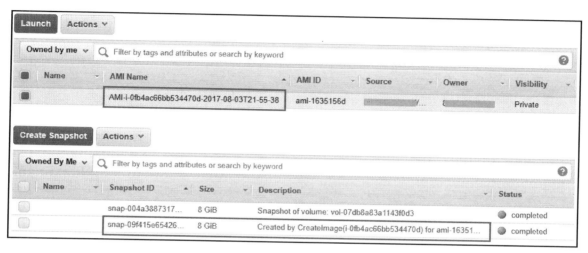

Here's a handy tip! Although we have created a really useful instance backup utility here, it's equally important to have an automatic backup deletion system in place as well; otherwise, your account will be soon flooded with too many copies of AMIs and EBS volumes, which will pile up on your overall costs.

With this use case completed, let's look at yet another simple yet useful infrastructure management use case that can potentially enable you to govern your AWS accounts much better, as well as cut some costs in the process.

Enabling governance using EC2 tags and Lambda

Governance has always been of one of the key issues faced by cloud administrators, especially when it comes to tracking EC2 instances for cost and compliance purposes. In this use case, we are going to automate the tagging of EC2 instances and its corresponding resources using a simple Lambda function used in conjuncture with AWS CloudTrail and CloudWatch. The function will ensure that users can work only on those resources that they have created based on resource tags.

How it all works is as follows. We start off by creating a *trail* in CloudTrail to track all the API calls and events taking place within the AWS account. Next, we create a dummy user in IAM, which will not only have permissions of creating tags, but also the permission to create and use their own resource. This is essential as if the user has the permission to create tags; then, they can manipulate the tags themselves, which is something we don't want. After this, we create a function that will tag the resources automatically with the following tag key values:

- `Owner`: The current user's name value or the resource creator's name value
- `PrincipalId`: The current user's `aws:userid` value

The code will also get triggered for the following events:

- EBS volume creation
- Snapshot creation
- AMI creation
- Run instances

Let's get started by creating a simple trail in CloudTrail. You can refer to the steps mentioned in this guide to get started with CloudTrail: `http://docs.aws.amazon.com/aws cloudtrail/latest/userguide/cloudtrail-create-and-update-a-trail-by-using-th e-console.html`.

In our case, we have provided the following values for the trail's parameters:

- **Trail name**: Provide a suitable name for your trail. In this case, we have provided it with the name `taggerTrail`.
- **Apply trail to all regions**: You can select **Yes** for this option.

- **Read/Write events**: These events are correspondents to operations that occur in your AWS account. For this use case, we have selected **All** as the option.
- **Storage location**: Here, you can either select an S3 bucket to store your trial logs or, alternatively, go ahead and create one:

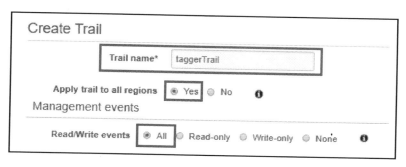

With the trail created, we now move on toward creating a policy for our IAM users. The policy basically states that if you are the owner of that particular EC2 resource, then you can stop, start, reboot, and terminate your machine; otherwise, you won't be permitted to perform it. Running and describing instance operations is, however, allowed to all users.

Create a new policy using IAM and attach this policy to your users or user groups:

```
{
  "Version": "2012-10-17",
  "Statement": [
  {
    "Sid": "LaunchEC2InstancesPermissions",
    "Effect": "Allow",
    "Action": [
      "ec2:Describe*",
      "ec2:RunInstances"
    ],
    "Resource": [
      "*"
    ]
  },
  {
    "Sid": "AllowActionsIfYouAreTheOwnerPermissions",
    "Effect": "Allow",
    "Action": [
      "ec2:StopInstances",
      "ec2:StartInstances",
      "ec2:RebootInstances",
      "ec2:TerminateInstances"
    ],
```

```
      "Condition": {
        "StringEquals": {
          "ec2:ResourceTag/PrincipalId": "${aws:userid}"
        }
      },
      "Resource": [
        "*"
      ]
    }
  ]
}
```

With the IAM policy created and the trail enabled, let's us go ahead and set up the Lambda function and its triggers. To start with, you will first need to create the function's IAM role, as described in the following snippet:

```
{
  "Version": "2012-10-17",
  "Statement": [
    {
      "Sid": "Stmt1501655705000",
      "Effect": "Allow",
      "Action": [
        "cloudtrail:LookupEvents"
      ],
      "Resource": [
        "*"
      ]
    },
    {
      "Sid": "Stmt1501655728000",
      "Effect": "Allow",
      "Action": [
        "ec2:CreateTags",
        "ec2:Describe*"
      ],
      "Resource": [
        "*"
      ]
    },
    {
      "Sid": "Stmt1501655809000",
      "Effect": "Allow",
      "Action": [
        "logs:CreateLogGroup",
        "logs:CreateLogStream",
        "logs:PutLogEvents"
      ],
```

```
    "Resource": [
      "*"
    ]
  }
 ]
}
```

Next, we move on to creating the Lambda function for this use case. The function's code has been broken down here for simplicity and ease of understanding. You can always get the complete code using this link as well: `https://github.com/masteringAWSLambda/Mastering-AWS-Lambda`.

Here's a look at what the code does snippet by snippet.

First up, the code uses an ID array to store all the resource IDs it needs to create tags for. The code will get all parameters, such as `region`, `eventname` (the API call the user makes: for example, `RunInstances`), `PrincipalId`, and so on from the event it receives:

```
Id = [];
region = event.region;
detail = event.detail;
eventname = detail.eventName;
arn = detail.userIdentity.arn;
principal = detail.userIdentity.principalId;
userType = detail.userIdentity.type;
if(userType === 'IAMUser'){
  user = detail.userIdentity.userName;
}
else{
  user = principal.split(':')[1];
}
```

After this, the code looks for the resource IDs in the CloudWatch Event. For each API call (for example, `RunInstances`, `CreateVolume`, and so on) the resource IDs can be found in different sections of the received event response:

```
To process this, we have implemented a switch case that checks for the
event name and then appropriately gathers all the resource IDs and adds
them to the id array.
switch(eventname){
  case "CreateVolume":
    id.push(detail.responseElements.volumeId);
    console.log("id array: "+id);
    createTag(function(err, result){
      if(err){
        callback(err);
      }
```

```
      else{
        callback(null, "Done tagging!!");
      }
    });
    break;
  case "RunInstances":
    runInstances(function(err, result){
      if(err){
        callback(err);
      }
      else{
        createTag(function(createTagErr, createTagResult){
          if(createTagErr){
            callback(err);
          }
          else{
            callback(null, "Done tagging!!");
          }
        });
      }
    });
    break;
  case "CreateImage":
    id.push(detail.responseElements.imageId);
    console.log("id array: "+id);
    createTag(function(err, result){
      if(err){
        callback(err);
      }
      else{
        callback(null, "Done tagging!!");
      }
    });
    break;
  case "CreateSnapshot":
    id.push(detail.responseElements.snapshotId);
    console.log("id array: "+id);
    createTag(function(err, result){
      if(err){
        callback(err);
      }
      else{
        callback(null, "Done tagging!!");
      }
    });
    break;
  default:
    console.log("None of the options matched!!!");
```

```
      callback(null, "None of the options matched!!!");
  }
```

Since the `runInstances` and `createTag` functions were a little more complicated, we decided to take them out, create them as functions, and call them from our handler.

Here are the functions:

```
function createTag(tagCB){
  async.forEachOf(id, function (resourceID, key, cb) {
    var tagParams = {
      Resources: [
        resourceID
      ],
      Tags: [
        {
          Key: "Owner",
          Value: user
        },
        {
          Key: "PrincipalId",
          Value: principal
        }
      ]
    };
    ec2.createTags(tagParams, function(tagErr, tagData) {
      if (tagErr){
        console.log("Couldn't tag the resource "+tagParams.Resources+"
         due to: "+tagErr); // an error occurred
        cb(tagErr);
      }
      else{
        console.log("Tagged successfully");
        // successful response
        cb(null, "tagged!");
      }
    });
  }, function (err) {
      if (err){
        console.log(err);
        tagCB(err);
      }
      else{
        console.log("Done tagging!");
        tagCB(null, "Done!!");
      }
  });
}
```

```
function runInstances(runCB){
  let items = detail.responseElements.instancesSet.items;
  async.series({
    one: function(oneCB) {
      async.forEachOf(items, function (item, key, cb) {
        id.push(item.instanceId);
        cb(null, "added");
      }, function (err) {
          if (err){
            console.log(err);
            oneCB(err);
          }
          else{
            console.log("id array: "+id);
            oneCB(null, "Done!!");
          }
      });
    },
    two: function(twoCB){
      describeParams = {
        InstanceIds: [
        ]
      };
      async.forEachOf(id, function (instanceID, key, cb) {
        describeParams.InstanceIds.push(instanceID);
        cb(null, "added");
      }, function (err) {
          if (err){
            console.log(err);
            twoCB(err);
          }
          else{
            //console.log("describeParams: ", describeParams);
            twoCB(null, "Done!!");
          }
      });
    },
    three: function(threeCB){
      ec2.describeInstances(describeParams, function(err, data) {
        if (err){
          console.log(err, err.stack); // an error occurred
          threeCB(err);
        }
        else{
          console.log("data: ",JSON.stringify(data));
          // successful response
          let reservations = data.Reservations;
          async.forEachOf(reservations, function (reservation,
```

```
key, resrvCB)
{
  console.log("******** inside reservations foreachof
  async loop! *************");
  let instances = reservation.Instances[0];
  //console.log("Instances: ",instances);
  // get all volume ids
  let blockdevicemappings = instances.BlockDeviceMappings;
  //console.log("blockdevicemappings: ",blockdevicemappings);
  // get all ENI ids
  let networkinterfaces = instances.NetworkInterfaces;
  console.log("networkinterfaces: ",networkinterfaces);

  async.each(blockdevicemappings,
  function (blockdevicemapping, blockCB) {
    console.log("************* inside blockdevicemappings
    asyn each loop! ***********");
    id.push(blockdevicemapping.Ebs.VolumeId);
    console.log("id array from blockdevicemapping: "+id);
    blockCB(null, "added");
  }, function (err) {
      if (err){
        console.log(err);
        resrvCB(err);
      }
      else{
        async.each(networkinterfaces,
        function (networkinterface, netCB) {
         console.log("******** inside networkinterfaces each
          async loop! *******");
         id.push(networkinterface.NetworkInterfaceId);
         console.log("id array from networkinterface: "+id);
         netCB(null, "added");
        }, function (err) {
            if (err){
              console.log(err);
              resrvCB(err);
            }
            else{
              resrvCB(null, "Done!!");
            }
        });
      }
});
}, function (err) {
    if (err){
      console.log(err);
      threeCB(err);
```

```
                   }
                   else{
                    threeCB(null, "Done!!");
                   }
              });
          }
       });
    }
 }, function(runErr, results) {
      if(runErr){
        console.log(runErr);
        runCB(runErr);
      }
      else{
        //console.log("id array from final runInstances: "+id);
        runCB(null, "got all ids");
      }
   });
}
```

Phew! That's some code! But, if you have gotten this far, then we are just a few more steps away from testing our setup. But before that, we need to create and configure a CloudWatch Event rule that will trigger the Lambda function each time it receives a log from the CloudTrail trail we created earlier.

To do that, simply select the **Create rule** option from the **Rules** section in your CloudWatch dashboard. This brings up the **Create rule** wizard, using which we will configure our trigger.

First up, from the **Event Source** section, ensure that the **Event pattern** option is selected, as shown in the following screenshot. Select **EC2** from the **Service Name** drop-down list and **AWS API Call via CloudTrail** as its corresponding **Event Type**.

Next, specify the operations for which you wish to trigger the function. In this case, we have opted for the EC2 instance's **CreateImage**, **CreateSnapshot**, **CreateVolume**, and **RunInstances**, as shown in the following screenshot:

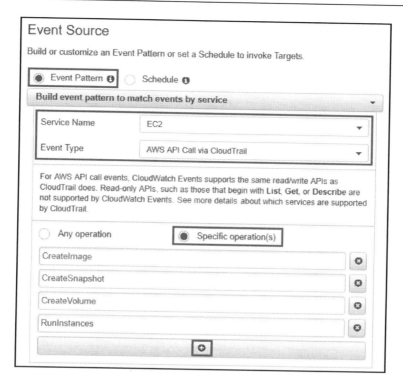

You can even copy and paste the following in the **Event Pattern Preview** dialog box:

```
{
  "source": [
    "aws.ec2"
  ],
  "detail-type": [
    "AWS API Call via CloudTrail"
  ],
  "detail": {
    "eventSource": [
      "ec2.amazonaws.com"
    ],
    "eventName": [
      "CreateImage",
      "CreateSnapshot",
      "CreateVolume",
      "RunInstances"
    ]
  }
}
```

Next, select your newly created **Function** from the **Targets** section, as shown here:

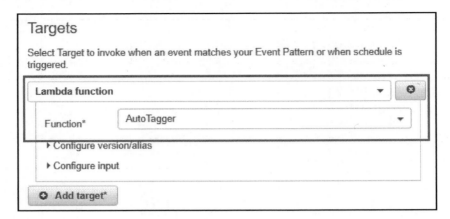

Now let's look at this in action--to test the setup, simply launch a new EC2 instance in your account. Once the instance is up and running, it will obtain two tags--Owner and PrincipalId values. The associated EBS volume of the instance as well as the **Elastic Network Interface (ENI)**, *if attached* should also get tagged with these two tags!

Here is a screen grab of the instance showing the two tags, as described earlier:

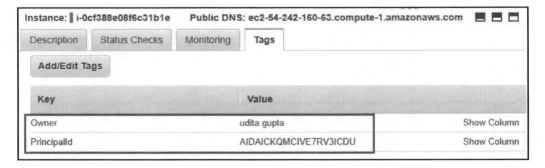

With this, we come toward the end of the infrastructure management use cases for Lambda. In the next section, we will be looking at a simple example of leveraging Lambda functions for conduction data transformation.

Data transformation

Yet another key use case for Lambda has been its ability to transform data on the fly. Say you have a stream of data coming into an S3 bucket in the form of one or more CSV files, each CSV file being different in size. For your application to process this data, it first needs to be transformed into a JSON file and then uploaded to a DynamoDB table. So, how do you get this done effectively? One way is to leverage an EC2 instance that will periodically poll or pull the CSV files from S3, transform it, and upload it to DynamoDB. However, this can have potential issues, for example: what happens when there are no files coming into S3 for a long time? Do you keep the EC2 instance up and running all this time? Also, polling or pulling the files from S3 will require its own set of logic that you will have to maintain, which can be an additional burden. So, what's the easy way out? You guessed it: Lambda functions!

For this particular use case, we will be creating a simple S3 bucket that will host our CSV files. A corresponding Lambda function will be used to convert the CSVs into JSON files and push the transformed data to a DynamoDB table.

For this to work, we will additionally need to configure a trigger on our S3 bucket so that it triggers the Lambda function whenever a new CSV file is uploaded to it. This will be achieved by leveraging the *S3 object created event* as the trigger for our Lambda function, which we will explain in the upcoming steps.

Go ahead and create a new bucket in S3. For this use case, you can name the bucket anything you want; however, the CSV files are all going to be placed within a folder in the bucket with the name csv. With the bucket created, configure a simple DynamoDB table in the same region with the following structure:

ID	Name	Age
1	John	23
2	Sarah	45

Next, create a Lambda function in the same region as the bucket. Copy and paste the following code in an index.js file:

```
'use strict';
console.log('Loading function');
const aws = require('aws-sdk');
const async = require('async');
const s3 = new aws.S3({ apiVersion: '2006-03-01' });
const csv = require("csvtojson");
const jsonfile = require('jsonfile');
const fs = require('fs');
```

```
const docClient = new aws.DynamoDB.DocumentClient();
exports.handler = (event, context, callback) => {
  async.auto({
    download: function(callback) {
      console.log('Received event:', JSON.stringify(event, null, 2));
      const bucket = event.Records[0].s3.bucket.name;
      let key =
       decodeURIComponent(event.Records[0].s3.object.key
       .replace(/\+/g, ' '));
      const downloadParams = {
        Bucket: bucket,
        Key: key
      };
      // removing the csv/ from the actual key-name
      key = key.replace('csv/', '');
      // files can be downloaded in the /tmp directory in lambda
      let csvFile = "/tmp/"+key;
      let file = fs.createWriteStream(csvFile);
      s3.getObject(downloadParams).createReadStream().on('error',
      function(err){
        console.log("Error while downloading the file from S3: ",err);
        callback(err);
      }).pipe(file);
      file.on('finish', function() {
        file.close();  // close() is async, call cb after close completes.
        console.log("Download complete! "+csvFile);
        callback(null, {'csvFile':csvFile, 'bucketName':bucket,
         'key':key});
      });
      file.on('error', function(err){
        console.log("Error while downloading the Id3 file from S3:
         ",err);
        callback(err);
      });
    },
    csvtojson: ['download', function(results, callback){
      console.log("Inside csvtojson function");
      let csvFile = results.download.csvFile;
      csv()
      .fromFile(csvFile)
      .on("end_parsed",function(jsonArrayObj){
        //when parse finished, result will be emitted here.
        console.log(jsonArrayObj);
        // Final file will have a .json extention
        let keyJson = results.download.key.replace(/.csv/i, ".json");
        console.log("Final file: "+keyJson);
        // we are writing the final json file in the /tmp directory itself
         in lambda
```

```
        let jsonFile = "/tmp/"+keyJson;
        jsonfile.writeFile(jsonFile, jsonArrayObj, function (err) {
          if(err){
            console.error(err);
            callback(err);
          }
        });
        callback(null, {'keyJson':keyJson, 'jsonFile':jsonFile});
      });
    }],
    sendToDynamo: ['download', 'csvtojson', function(results, callback)
{
        console.log("Inside sendToDynamo function");
        console.log("Importing data into DynamoDB. Please wait.");
        fs.readFile(results.csvtojson.jsonFile, function (err, data) {
          if (err){
            console.log(err);
            return callback(err);
          }
          let obj = JSON.parse(data);
          async.forEachOf(obj, function (obj, key, cb) {
            let params = {
              TableName: process.env.TABLE_NAME,
              Item: {
                "ID":   obj.ID,
                "Name": obj.Name,
                "Age":   obj.Age
              }
            };
            docClient.put(params, function(err, data) {
              if (err) {
                console.error("Unable to add ", data.Name,
                  ". Error JSON:", JSON.stringify(err, null, 2));
                cb(err);
              } else {
                  console.log("PutItem succeeded");
                  cb(null, "PutItem succeeded");
              }
            });
          }, function (err) {
              if (err){
                console.log(err);
                callback(err);
              }
              else{
                callback(null, "Done!!");
              }
          });
```

```
        });
      }]
    },
    function(err, results) {
      if(err){
        console.log("Finished with error!");
      }
      else{
        console.log(results);
      }
    });
  };
```

The code is pretty self-explanatory. We first download the `.csv` file from the `/csv` folder present in your S3 bucket locally into Lambda. The file gets downloaded into the function's `/tmp` directory as this is the only available local filesystem you can write to in a function. Once the function downloads the file to `/tmp`, it is converted into a new JSON file. The JSON file is written into the `/tmp` directory as well. Now that the file is converted, the `sendToDynamo` function gets invoked, which reads the JSON file and writes its contents to our previously created DynamoDB table.

Make sure you have provided the function the necessary permissions before saving the function. In this case, the function will require permissions to retrieve the CSV file from the S3 bucket, write logs to CloudWatch, as well as write the data into your DynamoDB table. You can use the following snippet to configure your IAM role; just remember to substitute the <YOUR_BUCKET_NAME> and <YOUR_TABLE_NAME> fields with the values from your setup:

```
{
  "Version": "2012-10-17",
  "Statement": [
  {
    "Sid": "myS3Permissions",
    "Effect": "Allow",
    "Action": [
      "s3:GetObject"
    ],
    "Resource": [
      "arn:aws:s3:::<YOUR_BUCKET_NAME>/*"
    ]
  },
  {
    "Sid": "myLogsPermissions",
    "Effect": "Allow",
    "Action": [
      "logs:CreateLogGroup",
```

```
        "logs:CreateLogStream",
        "logs:PutLogEvents"
      ],
      "Resource": [
        "*"
      ]
    },
    {
      "Sid": "myDynamodbPermissions",
      "Effect": "Allow",
      "Action": [
        "dynamodb:PutItem"
      ],
      "Resource": [
        "arn:aws:dynamodb:us-east-1:01234567890:table/<YOUR_TABLE_NAME>"
      ]
    }
  ]
}
```

With the function created and all set, the final step is to configure the trigger for the function. Make sure you provide the **Prefix** in the trigger's configuration, as shown here:

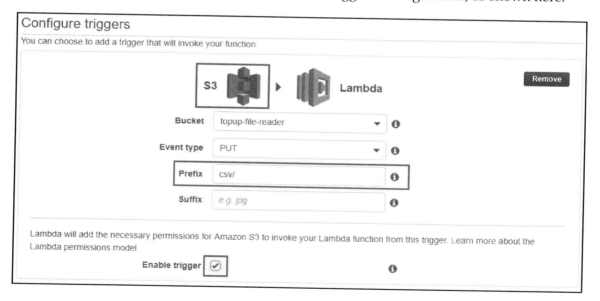

With this step completed, test the entire setup by uploading a sample CSV file to the /csv directory. Remember the CSV file will have to be of the same tabular format as we discussed earlier at the beginning of this use case. Once the file is uploaded, check whether the contents are populated successfully in the DynamoDB table or not. You can even verify this by looking at the function's logs in CloudWatch, as shown in the following screenshot:

With this, we come toward the end of our use cases, but before we move on to the next and final chapter, here's a quick summary of what you have learned so far!

Summary

With yet another chapter done, we are just one step away from the completion of this book. But before we go any further, let's summarize what we covered in this chapter!

First up, we started off by looking at a few commonly employed Lambda use cases to manage your AWS infrastructure. This comprised a use case where we leveraged simple Lambda functions to start and stop our EC2 instances during off hours, thus saving unnecessary running costs. We also explored two other infrastructure management use cases where a Lambda function is used to periodically take backups of an instance's EBS volumes as well as tag EC2 instances with some useful metadata for chargeback and governance. Lastly, we explored a use case where we leveraged a Lambda function to perform simple data transformation over a CSV file and stream that data to a DynamoDB table.

I hope this has been really useful and insightful for you! As we come toward the end of this book, let's take a quick look at what to expect from AWS Lambda in the upcoming chapter.

10
Next Steps with AWS Lambda

It's been quite a long journey so far, and yet here we are--the last chapter of this book! If you made it until here, then you definitely need to take a moment and give yourself a well-deserved pat on the back!

So far in this book, we have seen how to write, test, deploy, monitor, and manage your serverless applications using AWS Lambda and a bunch of other interesting tools and services. In this last and final chapter, I wanted to provide you with just a small glimpse into what you can expect from Lambda over the next few years and how is it going to change the way we view and do computing in the cloud!

In this chapter, we will be glancing through some new and recent product releases that are based on or work with AWS Lambda, namely the following:

- **Lambda@Edge**: Trigger Lambda to run functions in CloudFront edge locations based on CloudFront events
- **AWS Snowball Edge**: Store terabytes of data in a Snowball device and leverage Lambda to analyze and process data streams locally
- **Lambda bot and Amazon Lex**: Use Lambda functions to fulfill requests generated by the Lex chatbot framework
- **AWS Greengrass**: Execute Lambda functions locally on your IoT devices for near real-time responses and processing

Sounds interesting! Then what are you waiting for? Let's get started right away!

Processing content at the edge with Lambda@Edge

Lambda@Edge was launched by AWS during the 2016 *AWS re:Invent* summit; however, it had been in the preview mode until right now. The service basically allows you to execute Lambda functions in edge locations in response to CloudFront events. With this service, you now don't need to install, configure, or scale servers globally in order to customize your content. With Lambda@Edge, all this work is handled by the Lambda service itself. All you need to do is write the function and deploy it, and that's it!

At the time of writing, Lambda@Edge supports writing functions for the following CloudFront events:

- **Viewer request**: When CloudFront receives a request from a viewer
- **Viewer response**: Before CloudFront returns the response to the viewer
- **Origin request**: Before CloudFront forwards a request to the origin
- **Origin response**: When CloudFront receives a response from the origin

Where can I use Lambda@Edge? Well, the service has a few very specific use cases, some of which are explained here:

- You can use a Lambda function to generate custom HTTP responses when a CloudFront viewer request or origin request event occurs. A Lambda function can additionally be used to inspect headers or authorization tokens and insert the applicable header to control access to your content before CloudFront forwards a request back to the origin.
- A Lambda function can be used to add, drop, or modify headers, and can rewrite URL paths so that CloudFront returns different objects.
- You can even write Lambda functions that inspect cookies and rewrite URLs so that users see different versions of a site for A/B testing.
- CloudFront can return different objects to viewers based on the User-Agent header, which includes information about the devices that users are using in order to view your content. For example, CloudFront can return different images based on the screen size of devices. Similarly, the Lambda function could consider the value of the Referer header and cause CloudFront to return the images that have the lowest available resolution to bots.

How does it all work together? Well, it is a very simple and straightforward process! You first author a function using either the AWS Lambda management dashboard or the set of tools that we discussed earlier in this book, such as APEX, serverless, and so on. Once the function is created, you can configure its trigger by selecting a CloudFront distribution that you want to propagate the function over, along with a cache behavior in the distribution. Once these values are filled in, you can configure the trigger that will essentially execute your function over the edge location. These triggers can be any one of the four (viewer request/response, origin request/response) that we discussed a while back. With the trigger created, Lambda replicates the function to all the AWS regions and CloudFront edge locations around the globe.

 Note that once the replica functions are created and distributed across the globe, you will not be permitted to perform any changes on them, not even deleting them.

Let's examine Lambda@Edge with a simple use case walkthrough. For this section, we will be looking at how to leverage Lambda@Edge to generate a custom **404 Not Found** HTTP redirect for one of our static hosted websites on S3.

First up is creating the function. For this, log in to your AWS Management Console and select the **AWS Lambda** service from the main dashboard.

Next, from the Lambda management dashboard, select the **Create a Lambda function** option to get things started.

On the **Select blueprint** page, you can choose to use an existing Lambda@Edge boiler template for this use case as well. Simply type **Edge** in the filter and select the **cloudfront-response-generation** template, as shown in the following screenshot:

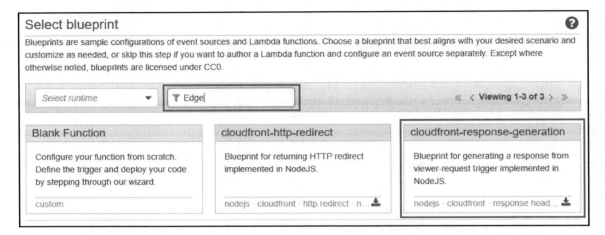

Alternatively, you can also select the **Blank Function** template and copy and paste the following code snippet:

```
'use strict';
let content = `
<\!DOCTYPE html>
<html lang="en">
  <head>
    <meta charset="utf-8">
    <title>404 - Not Found</title>
  </head>
  <body>
    <p>Looks like the page you are looking for is not available for
    the moment... try again after a while.</p>
  </body>
</html>
`;
exports.handler = (event, context, callback) => {
  const response = {
    status: '404',
      statusDescription: 'Not Found',
        headers: {
          'cache-control': [{
            key: 'Cache-Control',
            value: 'max-age=100'
          }],
          'content-type': [{
```

```
          key: 'Content-Type',
          value: 'text/html'
        }],
        'content-encoding': [{
          key: 'Content-Encoding',
          value: 'UTF-8'
        }],
      },
      body: content,
    };
  callback(null, response);
};
```

Next, from the **Configure triggers** section, select the particular CloudFront **Distribution ID** for which you need to enable Lambda@Edge. Note that the static website in my case is hosted on S3, and its content is distributed globally using a specific CloudFront **Distribution ID**.

Next, from the **CloudFront Event** drop-down list, select the appropriate event for which you wish to enable this function. In my case, I've selected the **Viewer Request** option, as shown in the following screenshot:

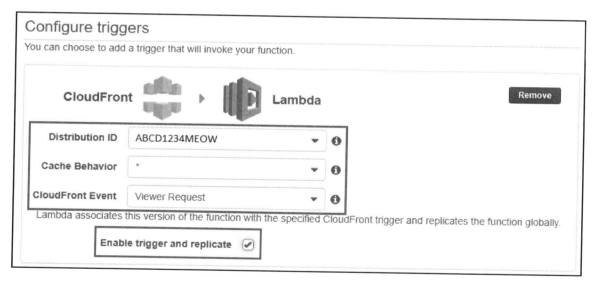

Remember to check the **Enable trigger and replicate** option as well before you select the **Next** option.

On the **Configure function** page, start off by providing a suitable **Name** for your function. Before you go ahead and paste the function code, you will be provided with a list of restrictions that currently apply to Lambda@Edge functions:

- **Memory (MB)** is limited to 128 MB.
- The uncompressed size of the code and associated libraries that upload for a function is limited to 1 MB. Deployment packages must be compressed in the `.zip` or `.jar` format.
- The **Timeout** for CloudFront origin request and origin response events is three seconds. For these events, the function can make network calls.
- The **Timeout** for the CloudFront viewer request and viewer response events is one second. For these events, the function cannot make network calls.
- The `/tmp` space is not available.
- Environment variables, the **Dead Letter Queues (DLQ)**, and Amazon VPCs cannot be used.

Next, paste the preceding code in the code editor window. Provide a suitable name for your Lambda@Edge IAM role and select the **Basic Edge Lambda permissions** option from the list of existing **Policy templates**, as shown here:

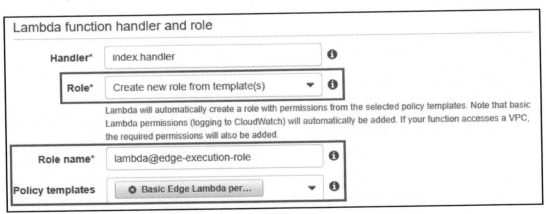

Leave the rest of the fields at their default values and go ahead and complete the function's creation process. Once your function is deployed, it will take a good few minutes for the function to replicate and propagate to the CloudFront edge locations. You can verify the state of the propagation from the CloudFront dashboard as your **Distribution Status** would now be in a **InProgress** state. Once the state changes to **Deployed**, open your favorite web browser and type in your static website's URL. Pass an incorrect page at the URL, and you should get the customized error response page that we had configured earlier! You can use similar techniques to generate custom HTTP responses when a CloudFront viewer request or origin request events occurs. There's still a lot more that you can do and achieve using Lambda@Edge, such as optimizing latencies, compressions, added security, and so on. To learn more about how to leverage Lambda@Edge for your use cases, visit `http://docs.aws` `.amazon.com/AmazonCloudFront/latest/DeveloperGuide/lambda-at-the-edge.html`.

Building next generation chatbots with Lambda and Lex

Chatbots are all the craze right now, with practically each cloud provider dishing out its chatbot framework for end users and developers to build conversational interfaces with voice- and text-based applications, which brings us to the introduction of Amazon Lex--a powerful and scalable chatbot framework built using Amazon's intelligent personal assistant named *Alexa*.

Lex essentially provides you with a readymade framework complete with all the necessary integration capabilities to kick start your bot creation process without having to learn or have expertise in with Lex! All you need to do is specify the basic conversational flow using the Lex management console and let Lex take care of the rest by provisioning the required infrastructure and services as well as adjusting responses to your conversations. This enables you to build, test, and publish chatbots at lighting pace on various mobile, web applications, and even other chat platforms.

Amazon Lex also provides prebuilt integrations with AWS Lambda, using which you can trigger off custom actions based on your chat conversations! This proves extremely effective as both Lex and Lambda are completely serverless, which means you don't have to bother about the underlying infrastructure at all! Just create the framework, integrate it with the right set of Lambda functions, and you have a complete chatbot all ready for use!

To summarize, here are some of the key features provided by Lex:

- **Fully managed service**: Lex is backed by the AWS infrastructure, which makes it that much easier to scale with no operational overheads whatsoever.
- **Simpler to learn and use**: Amazon Lex provides **automatic speech recognition (ASR)** and **natural language understanding (NLU)** technologies to create a **Speech Language Understanding (SLU)** system. Through SLU, Amazon Lex takes natural language speech and text input, understands the intent behind the input, and fulfills the user intent by invoking the appropriate business function.
- **Backed by Lambda**: The brains behind the chatbot's logic execution, Lambda essentially enables you to write code to fulfill the user's intent without having to worry about the scale or underlying infrastructure requirements.
- **Built-in integrations**: Lex also provides out-of-the-box integration capabilities with other messaging frameworks, such as Facebook Messenger, Twilio, and Slack.

With this in mind, let's understand some Lex concepts and terminologies:

- **Bots**: At a high-level, bots in Lex are the entities that perform some tasks. These tasks can be anything, from booking a restaurant table to ordering food, and so on. The bot is powered by ASR and NLU capabilities, the same technology that internally powers Amazon Alexa.
- **Intents**: As the name suggests, intents are actions that the user wishes the bot to perform. For example, a bot that books a restaurant table for you can have these three intents--check the availability of a table, book a table for two, and notify the chef's specials for that day. Each intent requires some special phrases or *utterances* that convey what sort of action you wish the bot to take. For example, "Can you book a table for me?" or "Can you let me know what's the chef's special tonight?" and so on. Once the utterances are created, you can choose one or more Lambda functions to fulfil your intent.
- **Slots**: Slots are nothing more than simple parameters that your intents can use as a part of the intent's configuration. For example, for the intent "Can you book a table for me at (restaurant)", Lex will prompt the user to provide the value for (restaurant) at the bot's runtime. Without this value, the bot will not be able to fulfil its intent. Lex also provides a few built-in slot types; for example, AMAZON.NUMBER is a built-in slot type that you can use for the number of pizzas ordered, and so on.

With these points in mind, let's quickly look at a simple example to get started with Lex and Lambda.

First up, log in to the AWS Management Console and select the **Lex** service from the main dashboard.

At the time of writing this, Lex is currently only provided out of the N. Virginia region. This means that your associated Lambda function will also need to be hosted out of the N. Virginia region.

On the main **Bots** page, choose **Create**.

Once selected, you will be provided with the following screen. Here, you can select any one of the three sample Lex examples to get started or alternatively select **Custom bot** to create your own chatbot. For this case, we will build a simple coffee ordering chatbot, so go ahead and select the **Custom bot** option:

Next, provide a suitable name for your bot in the **Bot name** field. You can select your bot to provide an optional **Output voice** for your conversations; however, for this exercise, I've chosen to keep this bot a strictly text-based application.

Next up, provide a value for the bot's **Session timeout**, as shown in the preceding screenshot. This field is used to configure the time for which your bot should retain context before dropping it. Fill out the rest of the details and select **Create** to get started.

With the bot created, we now need to create its subsequent **Slot types** and **Intents**. To do that, first, select the add sign + next to the **Slot types** option. This will pop up the **Add slot type** dialog, as shown here:

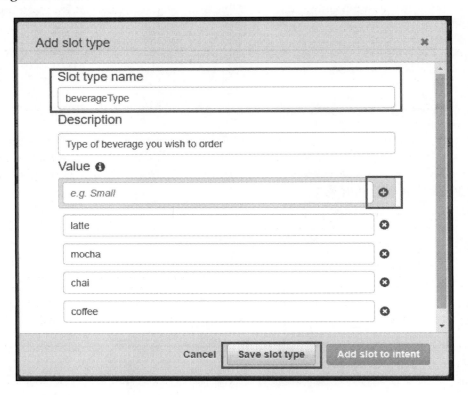

For this exercise, we have created three slot types, namely:

- beverageType: latte, coffee, mocha, chai
- beverageSize: small, medium, large, extra large
- beverageStrength: single, double, triple, quad, quadruple

Create the rest of the **Slot types** and click on **Save slot type** for each of the slots that you create. With the slots created, we now move on to the creation of the intent!

To create the intent, select the add sign + adjoining the **Intent types** option. This will pop up the **Add intent** dialog. Here, select the **Create new intent** option and provide a suitable name for it. Click on **Add** once done! Your intent should be created and displayed as shown here. Now you can go ahead and create a few utterances that will help the user order their coffee. In this case, I have created three utterances with different values in each case:

With the utterances populated, move on to the **Slots** section, where we can actually map the **Slot types** we created earlier with some meaningful **Name** and a user **Prompt**.

Remember, the **Slot types** were created during the earlier steps, whereas the names were simple placeholders for the slots:

Required	Name	Slot type	Prompt
Yes	beverageType	beverageType	What kind of beverage would you like? For example, mocha, chai, and so on.
Yes	beverageSize	beverageSize	What size? Small, medium, or large?
Yes	beverageStrength	beverageStrength	What kind of milk or creamer?

You can optionally even check the **Confirmation prompt** option and provide a suitable message for the user to confirm their order and even a custom message when the user cancels the order as shown in the following screenshot:

Finally, in the **Fulfilment** section, select **Return parameters to client** for now and test the chatbot first by saving the intent and selecting the **Build** option toward the top-right corner of the Lex dashboard. The build takes a few minutes to complete, and if no errors are present, it will pop up the **Test Bot**, using which you can test your intent by typing the **Sample utterances** you created a while back.

You should get an all success response similar to the one shown here:

ReadyForFulfillment beverageSize:small beverageStrength:single beverageType:coffee

This is a simple response generated by the Lex framework itself, and it indicates that our chatbot is now ready to be integrated with the Lambda function. So now let's create a simple Lambda function in the same N. Virginia region.

Create a new Lambda function with the following code in it:

```
'use strict';
function close(sessionAttributes, fulfillmentState, message) {
  return {
    sessionAttributes,
    dialogAction: {
      type: 'Close',
      fulfillmentState,
      message,
    },
  };
}
function dispatch(intentRequest, callback) {
  console.log('request received for userId=${intentRequest.userId},
  intentName=${intentRequest.currentIntent.intentName}');
  const sessionAttributes = intentRequest.sessionAttributes;
  const slots = intentRequest.currentIntent.slots;
  const type = slots.beverageType;
  const size = slots.beverageSize;
  const strenght = slots.beverageStrength;
  callback(close(sessionAttributes, 'Fulfilled',
```

```
    {'contentType': 'PlainText', 'content': `Okay, I have placed your ${size}
    ${type} order!`}));
  }
  exports.handler = (event, context, callback) => {
    try {
      dispatch(event,(response) => { callback(null, response); });
    } catch (err) {
      callback(err);
    }
  };
```

The code is very straightforward. It essentially comprises three sections: first up is the close() function that reports the state of the fulfillmentState object--whether it has failed or succeeded. The second is the dispatch() function that receives the data from the slots, processes it, and provides a callback() with the success message toward the end, and finally, the handler that routes the incoming request based on the specified intent.

Once you have pasted the function in the inline code editor, in the **Lambda function handler and role** section, select the **Choose a new role from template(s)** option and just provide a name for the role; that's it. The role will be created and assigned by Lex automatically when we attach this Lambda function to the chatbot. Go ahead and complete the creation of the function, and once it is all done, test it by selecting the **Configure test event** option from the **Actions** drop-down list and providing the following test sample data to it:

```
{
  "messageVersion": "1.0",
  "invocationSource": "FulfillmentCodeHook",
  "userId": "user-1",
  "sessionAttributes": {},
  "bot": {
    "name": "GetMyCoffeeChatBot",
    "alias": "$LATEST",
    "version": "$LATEST"
  },
  "outputDialogMode": "Text",
  "currentIntent": {
    "name": "GetMyCoffee",
    "slots": {
      "type": "Chai",
      "size": "small",
      "strength": "single"
    },
    "confirmationStatus": "None"
  }
}
```

You can modify the `type`, `size`, and `strength` parameters as per your requirements. Once done, click on the **Save and test** option and verify the results. You should see an output similar to the one shown here:

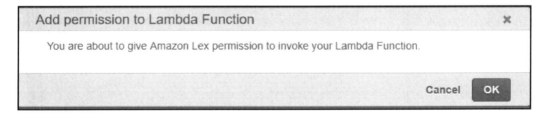

```
⊘ Execution result: succeeded (logs)

{
  "sessionAttributes": {},
  "dialogAction": {
    "type": "Close",
    "fulfillmentState": "Fulfilled",
    "message": {
      "contentType": "PlainText",
      "content": "Okay, I have placed your undefined undefined order!"
    }
  }
}
```

With this, you can now integrate your function to your chatbot. To do that, simply go back to your Lex dashboard and change the **Fulfilment** from **Return parameters to client** to **AWS Lambda function**. Next, select your newly created Lambda function from the drop-down list provided. On selecting your function, you will be provided with the following dialog, which will essentially provide your function with the necessary permissions to get invoked by Lex. Click on **OK**:

```
Add permission to Lambda Function                          ✕

    You are about to give Amazon Lex permission to invoke your Lambda Function.

                                              Cancel   OK
```

Finally, select the **Build** option to complete the chatbot's build. Test the chatbot once again using **Test Bot**. This time on your order's successful completion, you should see the success message that was passed using your Lambda function! This means that the function was able to obtain the parameters passed by the slots and successfully return an order fulfillment summary as well. You can create similar chatbots using Lex and Lambda and integrate them with other AWS services, such as AWS Mobile Hub, Cognito, and so on or even with other messaging platforms such as Twilio, Slack, and Facebook Messenger. To read more about how to leverage Lex with such messaging platforms, visit `http://docs.aw s.amazon.com/lex/latest/dg/example1.html`.

Processing data at the edge with Greengrass and Lambda

Greengrass is yet another recent offering in the space of IoT provided by AWS. In simpler terms, Greengrass is an extension of AWS's own IoT service, and it is specifically designed to extend AWS cloud capabilities to local IoT devices, thus making it possible for them to collect and analyze data closer to the source of information. This is made possible by enabling developers to write and execute serverless code. More specifically, developers who use AWS Greengrass can author serverless code using AWS Lambda either on the cloud or on the device itself and conveniently deploy it for the local execution of applications. Here is a representational architecture of Greengrass depicting the Greengrass Core SDK interconnecting various devices with the AWS Cloud:

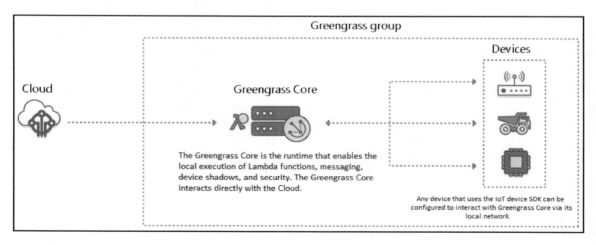

The AWS **Greengrass Core** software primarily consists of:

- A message manager that routes messages between devices, Lambda functions, and AWS IoT. The pub/sub message manager can intelligently buffer and resend messages if the connectivity to the cloud is disrupted or lost.
- A Lambda runtime that runs user-defined Lambda functions.
- An implementation of the *thing shadows* service that provides a local copy of thing shadows that represent your **Devices**. Thing shadows can be configured to sync with the **Cloud**.
- A deployment agent that is notified about new or updated AWS **Greengrass group** configuration. When a new or updated configuration is detected, the deployment agent downloads the configuration data and restarts the AWS **Greengrass Core**.

Besides the message manager and the local Lambda runtime, Greengrass also provides features such as Group management and Discovery services for your local IoT devices. Here's a quick look at a simple example of how you can connect your local devices (in this case, *a Raspberry Pi*) with Greengrass and run simple Lambda functions using it.

First up, we'll look at configuring and making the device ready for Greengrass! AWS has a really simple and straightforward tutorial for this, so I'll not be going too deep into this one. You can refer to the steps mentioned in this link to configure and prepare your device for AWS Greengrass: `http://docs.aws.amazon.com/greengrass/latest/developerguide/prepare-raspi.html`.

With the device prepped and ready, the next step involves the download of the Greengrass Core software from the AWS IoT dashboard and transferring it over to your device. To do that, log in to your AWS account and filter and select **AWS IoT** from the **Services**. You should have the IoT dashboard in front of you. Select the **Get started** option to view the various options for your IoT device management. Here, select **Software** from the options pane on the left-hand side to view a different version of the Greengrass Core software.

Follow the wizard and download the correct version of the Greengrass Core software, as shown here:

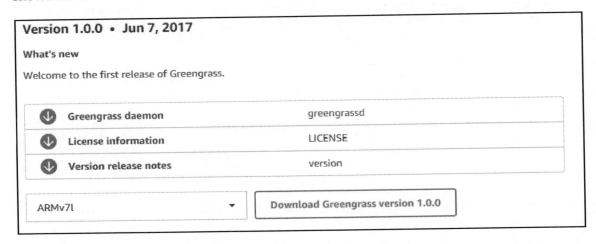

With the software downloaded, transfer it to your IoT device, in my case, the Raspberry Pi device. Extract the contents of your software using the following command:

```
# sudo tar -zxvf greengrass-<platform_version>.tar.gz -C /
```

With the extraction completed, we need to use the IoT dashboard and create something called a *Greengrass group*. A Greengrass group is a container that lists and describes your local device environment. The group contains an AWS Greengrass Core device with which all other devices in the group communicate, a list of devices that belong to the group, a list of Lambda functions, and a subscription table that defines how messages are passed between devices, the AWS Greengrass Core, and Lambda functions.

To create the group, from the AWS IoT dashboard, select **Greengrass** from the options pane. On the **Define a Greengrass group** tile, select the **Use easy creation** option and follow the wizard to create a certificate and key pair that your AWS Greengrass Core will use to authenticate with AWS IoT and AWS Greengrass:

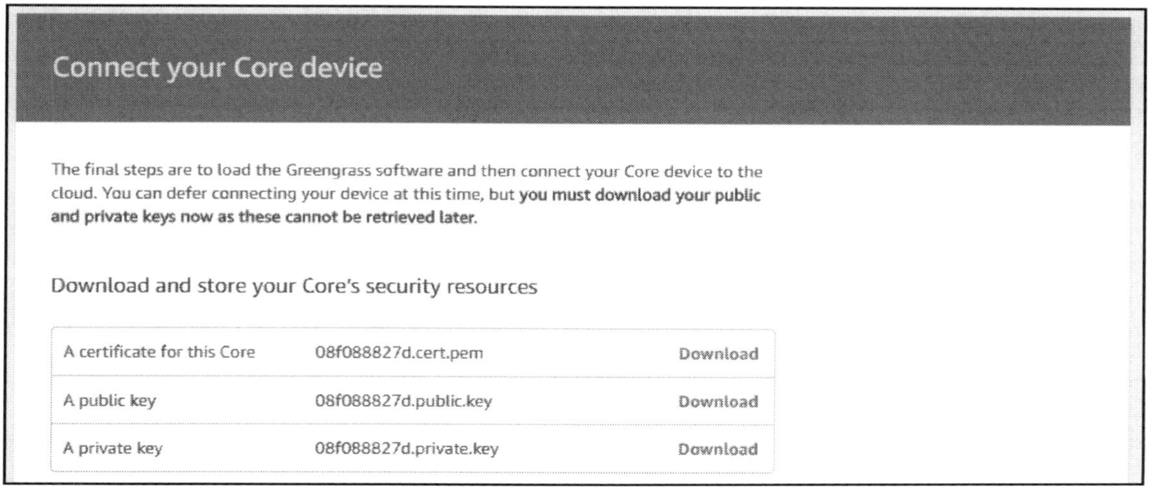

Connect your Core device

The final steps are to load the Greengrass software and then connect your Core device to the cloud. You can defer connecting your device at this time, but **you must download your public and private keys now as these cannot be retrieved later.**

Download and store your Core's security resources

A certificate for this Core	08f088827d.cert.pem	Download
A public key	08f088827d.public.key	Download
A private key	08f088827d.private.key	Download

Download and transfer the certificate and the private key over to your IoT device. Next, open the Greengrass code `config.json` file and substitute the filenames, as depicted here:

```
# sudo nano /greengrass/configuration/config.json
```

The preceding command opens the following code:

```
{
  "coreThing": {
    "caPath": "rootca.pem",
    "certPath": "<your_CRT_Filename>",
    "keyPath": "<your_Private_Key_Filename>",
    "thingArn": "<your_Device_ARN>",
    "iotHost": "<IoT_Host_Prefix>.iot.[AWS_REGION_HERE].amazonaws.com",
    "ggHost": "greengrass.iot.[AWS_REGION_HERE].amazonaws.com",
    "keepAlive": 600
  },
  "runtime": {
    "cgroup": {
      "useSystemd": "yes"
    }
  }
}
```

For a list of complete steps and how to obtain the root CA certificate, check out the complete link at http://docs.aws.amazon.com/greengrass/latest/developerguide/gg-setup.html.

With the certificates in place and all configs done, we are now ready to start the Greengrass Core daemon service. Use the following command to start the service. You should see output similar to what's shown here:

```
# sudo ./greengrassd start
```

```
pi@raspberrypi:/greengrass $
pi@raspberrypi:/greengrass $ sudo ./greengrassd start
Setting up greengrass daemon
Validating execution environment
Found cgroup subsystem: cpu
Found cgroup subsystem: cpuacct
Found cgroup subsystem: blkio
Found cgroup subsystem: memory
Found cgroup subsystem: devices
Found cgroup subsystem: freezer
Found cgroup subsystem: net_cls

Starting greengrass daemon.....
Greengrass daemon started with PID: 1815
pi@raspberrypi:/greengrass $
```

If you got this far, congratulations! You are that much closer to setting up the device with Greengrass. Next, we need to add our IoT device to the Greengrass group. To do that, from the Greengrass group, select the **Device** option, and from the **Add a device** dialog, select the **Use an existing IoT Thing as a Device** option. You can select your newly added device on the next page and click on **Finish** once done. The device takes a few minutes to sync with Greengrass. You can verify the status by viewing /greengrass/var/log/system/runtime.log from the device's Terminal. With this process completed, we will now create a Lambda function in the same region as the region for our Greengrass deployment.

From the Lambda dashboard, select **Create a Lambda function** and filter `greengrass` from the filter box, as shown here. You should see a `greengrass-hello-world` example template; select it to proceed with the function's configuration:

Now this example function doesn't require any triggers as such, so we will skip through the **Configure triggers** section. On the next page, provide a suitable **Name** for your function and select the `lambda_basic_execution` role for your function's execution. At the time of writing this, Greengrass supports only Python as the programming language, with more languages possibly getting added as the service matures.

Back to the IoT dashboard, select the **Lambda** option from **Greengrass groups**. Here, you will need to select the newly created function from our earlier step. If your function is not visible here, make sure the function and Greengrass are both present in the same region.

To test your Lambda function, you first need to deploy it. To do that, simply select the **Actions** button from the Greengrass group and opt for the **Deploy** option. Wait until the state of the deployment turns successful and then select the **Test** option from the IoT dashboard. Under **Subscription**, type `hello/world` and then choose **Publish to topic** to subscribe to the `hello/world` topic.

If your `hello-world` Lambda function is running on your AWS Greengrass Core device, it publishes messages to the `hello/world` topic and is displayed in the AWS IoT console, as shown here:

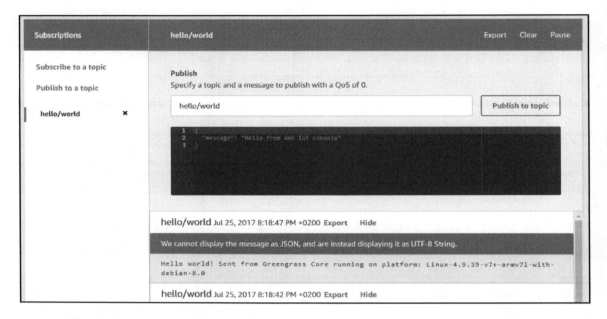

This was just a high-level view of what you can achieve with Greengrass and Lambda. You can leverage Lambda to perform all kinds of preprocessing on data at your IoT device itself. To know more about Greengrass service and how you can leverage it for your devices, visit `http://docs.aws.amazon.com/greengrass/latest/developerguide/gg-storyline.htm l`.

Introducing Snowball Edge

For those of you not familiar with the *Snowball* service in AWS, Snowball is essentially an external appliance that you can use to ship massive amounts of data from your on-premise site to AWS. This is achieved by first obtaining the Snowball device from AWS, transferring all your data to it, and then shipping it back out to AWS through a regional carrier. This service proves to be extremely useful when you have terabytes of data that has to be moved to AWS in a secure and fast manner, especially when your local network is limited by data bandwidth and geography.

Snowball Edge is an extension of this service that provides you with the same appliance features but with a few extra add-ons in terms of support for running Lambda functions locally, an interface that supports NFS, cluster support, and so on. You can actually cluster these appliances and integrate the entire set to your existing infrastructure and applications using standard storage interfaces.

Here's what the appliance actually looks like:

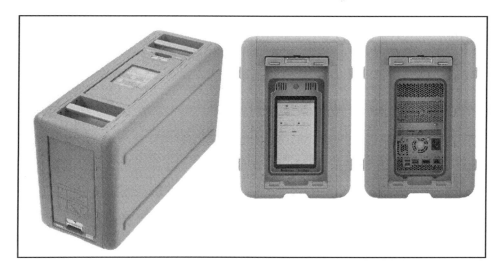

But that's not the part that we are interested in! The thing that makes sense for us is the appliance's support to run Amazon Lambda functions locally! This is extremely beneficial for IoT use cases, where you can analyze and process the data locally even before you can move it to the cloud! But what powers Lambda on the appliance? That's where AWS Greengrass comes into the picture. Snowball leverages Greengrass to execute Lambda functions remotely on your devices in order to process the data locally.

At the time of writing this, Snowball Edge supports only Python as the underlying programming language. To learn a bit more about Snowball Edge and how you can leverage it, visit `http://docs.aws.amazon.com/snowball/latest/developer-guide/using-appliance.html`.

Summary

As we move toward the end, I just wanted to take this time to say that it has really been a wonderful journey writing this book! Although the book may seem a lot to read and grasp, trust me; this is all just a drop in the ocean! The serverless paradigm is evolving really rapidly, and it's only going to be a matter of time before serverless computing replaces a majority of workloads that are running off of virtual machines!

To quickly summarize all that you learned so far--we started off with learning the basics of serverless computing and moved on to event-driven processing, followed by Lambda as a service, and slowly, but gradually, we covered so much--from writing functions to testing, deploying, managing, and monitoring them! Plus, a whole chapter on some really simple and easy to replicate use cases. I really hope this book serves as a means for you to go out there and experiment more with serverless and Lambda.

Until next time, cheers!

Index

A

aliases 49, 50, 51, 52, 53, 54, 55
Amazon CloudWatch Logs 13
Amazon DynamoDB 12
Amazon Lex 259
Amazon S3 12
Amazon Simple Notification Service (SNS) 13
APEX
  about 60, 61, 62
  reference 60
automatic speech recognition (ASR) 266
AWS CLI
  reference 158
  using 23, 24, 25, 26, 27, 28
AWS CodeCommit 13
AWS Greengrass 259
AWS Lambda
  about 11, 12
  GitHub, integrating with 127, 128, 130, 132,
    135, 136
  Slack, integrating with 136, 137, 138, 139, 141,
    142
  working 12
AWS Management Console
  using 14, 15, 16, 17, 18, 19, 20, 21
AWS Management
  Lambda functions, testing manually 69
AWS Serverless API 156
AWS Serverless Function 155
AWS Serverless SimpleTable 157
AWS services, supported as Lambda invoker
  reference 13
AWS services
  capabilities 32
AWS Snowball Edge 259
AWS step functions

about 166, 169, 170, 173
activities 168
choice state 168
parallel state 168
pass state 168
state machine 167
states 167
succeed/ fail state 168
task state 167
tasks 168
transitions 168
wait state 168
AWS X-Ray
  about 187
  example 189, 190, 192
  segments 188
  service graph 188
  subsegments 188
  trace 188

B

bots 266
Bunyan
  about 204
  reference 205

C

Chai
  about 70
  expressive assertion types 70
  Lambda function, testing with 70, 71, 74, 75, 76
  reference 70
chatbots
  about 265
  building, with Lambda 267, 268
  building, with Lex 267, 269
Claudia.js

about 63, 64
  reference 64
CLI supported commands
  reference 29
cloud providers, Serverless Framework
  Google Cloud Functions 212
  IBM Bluemix OpenWhisk 212
  Microsoft Azure Functions 212
CloudFront events
  origin request 260
  origin response 260
  viewer request 260
  viewer response 260
CloudWatch events
  Lambda, mapping with 112, 113, 115, 116, 117
CloudWatch
  used, for monitoring Lambda function 184, 185,
    186
concepts, Lex
  bots 266
  intents 266
  slots 266
concepts, Serverless Framework
  events 213
  functions 213
  plugins 213
  projects 212
  resources 213
  services 213
configuration and installation guide, AWS CLI
  reference 23
containers 8
continuous integration and continuous deployment
    (CICD) 229
create-function command
  options 25, 26
Cron expression
  reference 234

D

data transformation 253, 256, 258
Datadog
  reference 194
  used, for monitoring Lambda function 193, 194,
    195, 196, 197, 200

Dead Letter Queues (DLQ) 264
deployment 60
deployment tools
  APEX 60, 61, 62
  Claudia.js 63
distributed applications
  building, with step functions 174, 178, 179, 180,
    181
DynamoDB
  Lambda, mapping with 103, 106, 107

E

Elastic Network Interface (ENI) 252
end to end tests 68
environment variables 56, 58
Event Source Mapping 91
event sources, Lambda
  AWS services 91
  custom applications 91
event-driven architecture (EDA) 90, 91
events 213
external application
  used, for invoking Lambda 144, 148, 149

F

Free Tier usage, Amazon AWS
  reference 14
function 12
Function as a Service (FaaS) 9
functions
  about 35, 213
  logging, with Loggly 201, 202, 204, 205, 206,
    207, 208

G

GitHub
  integrating, with AWS Lambda 127, 128, 130,
    132, 135, 136
Google Cloud Functions 212
Greengrass
  about 274
  reference 280
  used, for processing data at edge 274, 275, 276

I

IBM Bluemix OpenWhisk 212
infrastructure management
  about 232
  governance, enabling with EC2 tags 242, 244,
    245, 250, 252
  governance, enabling with Lambda 242, 244,
    245, 250, 252
  periodic snapshots, of EBS volumes 235, 237,
    241
  scheduled shutdown, of instances 232, 234, 235
  scheduled startup, of instances 232, 234, 235
integration tests 68
intents 266
invoke command
  options 27

K

Key Management Service (KMS) 58
Kinesis Stream
  creating 118
Kinesis
  function, packaging 120
  function, uploading 120
  Lambda, mapping with 117
  log streaming, setting up 118, 119

L

Lambda architecture patterns
  backend services for mobile/IoT 94
  real-time stream processing 94
  serverless microservices 92
  serverless multi-tier applications 93
Lambda bot 259
Lambda function
  about 12
  best practices 64, 65, 85
  creating 14, 15, 16
  limitations 31
  monitoring, CloudWatch used 184, 185, 186
  monitoring, Datadog used 193, 194, 195, 196,
    197, 200
  pricing 29, 30
  testing 67, 68

testing, manually with AWS Management
  Console 69
testing, npm modules used 77, 79, 80
testing, with Chai 70, 71, 74, 75, 76
testing, with Mocha 70, 71, 74, 75, 76
testing, with simple serverless test harness 81,
  82, 84
Lambda programming model
  about 35
  context object 39, 40, 42
  error handling 46, 47, 49
  exceptions 46, 47, 49
  handler 36, 37, 38, 39
  logging 43, 44, 45, 46
Lambda
  chatbots, building with 267, 268
  invoking, external application used 144, 148,
    149
  mapping, with CloudWatch events 112, 113,
    115, 116, 117
  mapping, with DynamoDB 103, 106, 107
  mapping, with Kinesis 117
  mapping, with S3 95, 97, 99, 101, 102, 103
  mapping, with SNS 108, 112
  supported event sources 91
  used, for processing data at edge 279
Lambda@Edge
  about 259
  reference 16, 265
  used, for processing content at edge 260, 261
Lex
  about 265
  chatbots, building with 267, 268
  concepts 266
  key features 266
limits, on Lambda code deployments
  reference 31
logging
  best practices 208, 209
Loggly
  reference 201
  used, for logging functions 201, 202, 204, 205,
    206, 207, 208

M

Microsoft Azure Functions 212
Mocha
  about 70
  Lambda function, testing with 70, 71, 74, 75, 76
  reference 70
Morgan 204

N

natural language understanding (NLU) 266
Node-Loggly 204
non-supported scripting languages, Lambda
  reference 31
npm modules, Loggly's API
  Bunyan 204
  Morgan 204
  Node-Loggly 204
  Winston 204
npm modules
  used, for testing Lambda function 77, 79, 80

O

openweather API
  reference 144

P

packaging 59
plugins 213
Postman
  reference 161
programming model 36
programming pattern 36
projects 212

R

resources 213

S

S3
  Lambda, mapping with 95, 97, 99, 101, 102, 103
SAM templates
  writing 154

SAM
  about 153, 154
  serverless applications, building 157, 158, 159, 160, 161, 165, 166
scheduled events 13
segments 188
serverless applications
  building, with SAM 157, 158, 159, 160, 161, 165, 166
serverless computing
  about 8, 9
  cons 10
  pros 9, 10
Serverless Framework's Plugin Registry
  reference 213
Serverless Framework
  about 211
  best practices 229
  cloud providers 212
  concepts 212, 213
  reference 229
  working with 214, 215, 216, 217, 218, 219, 221, 223, 224, 226, 228
serverless microservices 92
serverless multi-tier applications 93
serverless-dynamodb-local module
  reference 223
serverless-offline plugin
  reference 224
service graph 188
services 213
Simple Notification Service (SNS) 213
Simple Workflow Service (SWF) 166
Slack
  integrating, with AWS Lambda 136, 137, 138, 139, 141, 142
slots 266
Snowball Edge
  about 281
  reference 281
SNS
  Lambda, mapping with 108, 112
Speech Language Understanding (SLU) 266
state machine 167
step functions

distributed applications, building with 174, 178, 179, 180, 181
stress 143
subsegments 188

T

Teamwork
  reference 127
test pyramid
  reference 68
trace 188
trail, in CloudTrail
  reference 242

U

unit 68
unit test 68

V

versioning 49, 50, 51, 52, 53
virtual machines 8

W

Webhooks
  about 125, 126
  best practices 151
Winston 204

Made in the USA
Las Vegas, NV
25 February 2022